D0982459

EUROPE TODAY AND YESTERDAY

EUROPE IN RETREAT
by Vera Micheles Dean

The truth about Europe's turbulent diplomatic history since 1919 by the Research Director of the Foreign Policy Association.

DEMOCRACY AND SOCIALISM
by Arthur Rosenberg

The origins and developments, changes in orientation, victories and defeats of democracy and socialism in Europe and America in the nineteenth and twentieth centuries.

EUROPE ON THE EVE
by Frederick L. Schuman

A brilliant authoritative analysis of the present situation in Europe and a detailed history of European diplomacy 1933–9. By the author of *The Nazi Dictatorship*.

THESE ARE *Borzoi Books*, PUBLISHED BY
ALFRED · A · KNOPF

LITHUANIA

Baltic Sea

POLAND
MARCH 1939

VILNA

⊙ VILNA

Gdynia
Danzig

EAST
PRUSSIA

(THE
CORRIDOR)

POMORZE

Niemen   River

Nowogródek
NOWOGRÓDEK

Thorn

BIAŁYSTOK
○ Białystok

WARSAW

POSNANIA

⊙ POZNAŃ

Vistula

Bug

River

POLESIE

Brest-Litovsk ○   ○ Pinsk

PRIPET MARSHES

WARSAW ⊙

ŁÓDŹ ⊙
ŁÓDŹ

River

LUBLIN

VOLHYNIA

Kielce
○
KIELCE

LUBLIN ⊙

Chelm
○

○ Luck

GERMANY

KATOWICE ⊙

CRACOW ⊙
CRACOW

Bogumin ○
Teschen

CENTRAL INDUSTRIAL DISTRICT

LWÓW
○
LWÓW ⊙

Tarnopol
○
TARNOPOL

Przemyśl
○

CARPATHIAN

Dniestr

Stanisławów
○
STANISŁAWÓW

MTS.

EAST PRUSSIA   LITHUANIA

DANZIG

SOVIET
RUSSIA

POLAND

GERMANY

Dnieper R.

FRANCE

HUNGARY

RUMANIA

0   20   40   60   80   100 MILES

POLAND, YEAR 1559

POLAND: KEY TO EUROPE

POLAND:

KEY TO EUROPE

by

RAYMOND LESLIE BUELL

SECOND EDITION, REVISED

[1939]

ALFRED · A · KNOPF

NEW YORK & LONDON

PREFACE

WHEN I visited Poland in the early summer of 1938, I intended to write only a report — to be published by the Foreign Policy Association — on the problems confronting that country. But these problems proved so complex, and so fascinating, that I decided to write a book. My decision was affected by the fact that, so far as I know, no other volume has yet appeared which endeavours to survey and analyse the problems of modern Poland in a sympathetic but scientific spirit.

As a country which in fifteen years will have as large a population as France, Poland is important in itself. Its rise as one of the great powers of Europe during the later Middle Ages, its partition and disappearance in the eighteenth century, and its resurrection at the end of the World War constitute one of the most romantic chapters of history. But this history is still unfinished. Germany's growing power in Europe has once more made Poland's future uncertain.

Although public opinion in the Western democracies is inclined to hold Poland responsible for its plight, this judgment is too severe. Poland is confronted by two fundamental problems, the solution of which depends not on Poland alone, but on the international situation as a whole. These problems are security against foreign aggression and security against internal want. Entering the world of commercial rivalry only at the close of the World War, Poland finds itself barred from many foreign markets. It has the most rapidly increasing population in Europe, yet lacks the resources to provide a decent living on the basis of self-

v

sufficiency. Today at least a quarter of its people are living close to starvation. If Poland could export enough of its agricultural and industrial products to industrialize the country, if it could borrow abroad, if it could continue to send out as many emigrants as before the World War, its economic problem might be solved. But because of economic nationalism, the world economy on which the solution of such problems depends has almost disappeared. Poland cannot adequately develop its export trade; it cannot find foreign loans; its emigrants are no longer welcome in foreign countries. As a result of causes largely beyond its own control, Poland can no longer rely on a collective peace system for defence against aggression; neither can it rely on a world economy to meet its fundamental economic needs. It is consequently forced more and more to live on a basis of autarchy, while internal maladjustments become intensified.

In other countries economic nationalism of this sort has led to fierce anti-Semitism, countless refugees, political dictatorship, and a terrifying imperialistic psychology. These symptoms have appeared from time to time in Poland, but in a far less acute form. It would be inaccurate to regard Poland as a Fascist state; it has not succumbed to the totalitarianism of either Germany or Italy. Although it has adopted a number of measures indirectly injuring the Jew, Poland so far has refrained from enactment of the Nuremberg laws, or the *numerus clausus* legislation of Hungary, despite the fact that it has the largest Jewish population in Europe. Through lack of wisdom the Western democracies contributed to the overthrow of the German Republic and the rise of Hitler. The analogy is not complete, yet today a false appraisal of the Polish situation on the part of the Western powers may have almost equally disastrous results. If the great democracies show a proper understanding of the serious problems confronting Poland and make some effort to co-operate in meeting them, Poland may remain outside the totalitarian camp, and thus help to maintain the equilibrium of forces in Europe, which is important if Western civilization is to be saved. To those interested in the profound social and political changes now sweeping the world, and to those seeking to appreciate the realities of international life, an understanding of Poland is important. This volume is, in short, a case study in present world distress.

My obligations in the preparation of this book are numerous. The Polish authorities extended to me every courtesy and assistance. The American Ambassador, the Honourable Anthony J. Drexel Biddle, and his colleagues were equally helpful. My wife, Frances Dwight Buell, who accompanied me on the trip, was of invaluable assistance in the collection of material and the preparation of notes.

Various chapters of the manuscript have been read by numerous critics, both Polish and non-Polish. I do not mention them here, not only because they are so numerous but because I do not wish to involve the responsibility of any of these readers, even indirectly, in the views advanced in this volume. I must, however, express a special debt of gratitude to Dr. Simon Segal, who for the past seven months has worked diligently in translating Polish material, checking facts, filling out chapters, and generally assisting in the preparation of the volume. I also wish to thank Vera Micheles Dean, Helen Terry, and Ona K. D. Ringwood of the Foreign Policy Association for editorial assistance.

RAYMOND LESLIE BUELL

Richmond, Massachusetts
March 1939

CONTENTS

POLAND: KEY TO EUROPE

•

CHAPTER I

THE IMPORTANCE OF POLAND

With the surrender of France and Britain to Hitler at Munich, many conclude that henceforth Germany will dominate Europe, at least east of the Rhine. France, with a population only half that of Germany, will be fortunate if it can cling to the periphery of Europe; while Britain will be equally fortunate if it can maintain intact its empire against the onslaught of the Berlin-Rome-Tokyo axis. Yet it may be too hasty to assume that, because of the weakened power of the democracies in Western Europe, Germany henceforth will reign supreme on the continent. This assumption overlooks the fact that, while the Germans today are twice as numerous as the French, they are greatly outnumbered by the Slavs.

Although in the Greater Germany there are now 80,000,000 Germans, the Slavic people, including the Russians, number 226,000,000.[1] Moreover, while Nazi Germany has increased its birth-rate from 14.7 per thousand in 1933 to

[1] Russia alone has 103,000,000 Slavs.

18.8 in 1937,[2] the Slavs are increasing more rapidly than any other people in Europe. It is estimated that between 1930 and 1960 the population of the continent will increase one hundred million, three quarters of which will be Slavs. At that time they will constitute more than half the population of the continent.[3]

Even if these calculations prove to be correct, Germany, while unifying the Germanic elements of Europe into a compact aggressive mass, may succeed in perpetuating Slavic disunity in accordance with the policy of " divide and rule." But there is some basis for the belief that the biological forces of history are working against the expanding influence of the German race, and that the new *Drang nach Osten* of the Nazis may prove little more than an effort to arrest a decline. The fulminations of Hitler against Communism are a new version of the traditional German antipathy to Pan-Slavism. And if the Slavs adopt Hitler's theories and reorganize their political existence on a basis of racial Slav unity, the Germans will be the first to suffer.

1. Germans versus Slavs

As we shall see in greater detail in another chapter, the struggle between German and Slav goes back at least to the tenth century. After the German Knights decimated the Slavic peoples of the Baltic, German settlers colonized the areas thus subjected by the sword. Through mediæval orders such as the Teutonic Knights, Germany planted its colonies in the heart of Europe long before Eu-

[2] Cf. an important article, "The German Birthrate," *The Times* (London), October 18, 1938.
[3] A. Reithinger: *Le Visage économique de l'Europe*, translated from the German by Claude Bourdet, preface by M. André Siegfried (Paris: Payot; 1937), p. 20.

rope thought of founding colonies overseas. As the German historian Treitschke states: " In the countries on the right of the Elbe, our nation once carried out the greatest and most fruitful schemes of colonization which Europe has seen since the days of the Roman Empire; for here it succeeded in obliterating the usual distinction between colony and motherland so completely that these colonized lands formed the nucleus of our new system of states, and since Luther's time were able to take part in the intellectual progress of the nation, as equal allies of the older stock. For more than two hundred years, Germany, solely by the power of its free citizens, held supremacy over the northern seas." [4]

Through the Baltic barons, Germans virtually governed Russian Baltic provinces until the end of the World War; while, in Russia proper, Germans occupied some of the most important industrial and government positions, German names being frequently found among influential counsellors of the Tsar.[5] In Mein Kampf Hitler went so far as to claim that the organization of the Russian state was " never the result of the political aptitudes of Slavism in Russia, but rather a remarkable example of the creative political action of the Germanic element in the midst of a race of lesser value. . . . For many centuries," Hitler insisted, " Russia lived at the expense of a directing superior class having a German nucleus." [6]

German colonies, moreover, existed in many Central Eu-

[4] Adolf Hausrath: *Treitschke, His Doctrine of German Destiny and of International Relations, together with a Study of His Life and Work* (New York: G. P. Putnam's Sons; 1914), p. 201; a translation of articles by Treitschke.

[5] For German influence at the Russian court at the beginning of the World War, cf. Leon Trotsky: *The History of the Russian Revolution* (London: Victor Gollancz, 1934), p. 88.

[6] Cf. *Mein Kampf* (Munich: Eher Verlag; 1936), Chapter XIV.

ropean countries — notably Rumania, Hungary, and Serbia; and German influence predominated in the Austro-Hungarian Empire. Triumphing over those who wished to give the Slavs a position of equality in the Empire, Pan-Germanism endeavoured to repress Slavic culture. Long before 1914, Germany supported a separatist movement among the Ukrainians in order to weaken the strength of Polish aspirations.[7]

When the World War broke out, Germany endeavoured to renew ambitions which go back at least to the thirteenth century. Making use of German colonies in the Baltic and in Eastern Europe, it endeavoured to build up a vast confederation, containing both Slavic and non-Slavic peoples, under German domination. For a period varying from one to three years the Baltic countries suffered the miseries of German military occupation. In co-operation with the Baltic barons, the German government planned to create a Duchy of Estonia and Livonia in personal union with the Crown of Prussia. The German general staff proposed the personal union of Lithuania with the Hohenzollerns.[8] Germany worked out vast plans for colonizing German settlers in these new states. Ludendorff, meanwhile, proposed the annexation of two million more Poles in order to increase the military security of East Prussia. Farther east the Ger-

[7] W. Alison Phillips: *Poland* (New York: Henry Holt & Company; 1915), pp. 218, 226. Before the World War Treitschke indicated his belief that Germanism was on the defensive. Referring to the alliance with Austria, he said: " It may have the useful effect of strengthening the German element in Austria, and finally checking the melancholy decay of our civilization in Bohemia, and Hungary . . . and the Tyrol." Hausrath, op. cit., p. 200.

[8] Henry Bidou: *Histoire de la Grande Guerre* (Paris: Gallimard; 1936), 6th ed., p. 546; C. R. M. F. Cruttwell: *A History of the Great War* (New York: Oxford University Press; 1934), p. 480; *The Baltic States* (London: Information Department of the Royal Institute of International Affairs; 1938), p. 22.

mans not only recognized the independent state of Ukraine but virtually imposed the Treaty of Brest-Litovsk, forcing the Soviet government to renounce its sovereignty over the Baltic, Congress Poland, the Ukraine, Georgia, Kars, and Batum. The treaty cost Russia 34 per cent of its population, 89 per cent of its coal, and a large proportion of other resources, cutting it off from the Black Sea.[9] For a time Germany towered above all the Slavic and other peoples who lived between the Baltic and the Black Sea. There is no doubt that, had Germany won the World War, it would have organized this vast area into a series of satellite states, permitted to enjoy a certain degree of autonomy, but narrowly bound, so far as foreign, military, and economic policy were concerned, to Berlin. It is also probable that Germany would have endeavoured to settle a new crop of German colonists on the land of these client states.

The Treaty of Versailles put an end to this grandiose dream. Germany lost a vast empire in southern Russia and Central Europe, containing probably as much natural wealth as the whole of equatorial Africa. Paradoxical as it may seem, the downfall of the Russian Empire was also a great blow at German influence in Europe. Following the Bolshevik Revolution, the Germans were driven from the central government of Russia. Hitler in *Mein Kampf* laments the fact that present-day Russia has been " despoiled of its Germanic directing class," which, according to him, has been replaced by Jews. Moreover, the formation of the independent Baltic states led to the decline of the Baltic barons. As a result of the World War, two Slavic countries obtained their independence — Poland and Czechoslovakia — while a third, Yugoslavia, was consider-

[9] Cf. J. W. Wheeler-Bennett: "The Meaning of Brest-Litovsk To-day," *Foreign Affairs*, October 1938.

ably enlarged. The creation of these states led to the diminution of German influence, particularly in the Danube and Baltic areas. German " islands " in Eastern and North-Eastern Europe were either completely wiped out or considerably weakened; the Austrian Tyrol passed to Italy. Generally speaking, the social changes in Central and Eastern Europe have worked against the influence of the Germans, who in many countries have been an aristocratic or bourgeois minority. Finally, the Slavic states were reinforced, until 1938 at least, by the French security system, which promised military aid to Poland, Czechoslovakia, Yugoslavia, and Russia (as well as Rumania) in the event of attack.

Even in post-war Czechoslovakia the German element until recently was on the defensive, fearing it would be overwhelmed by Czech migration from other parts of the country. One of the most important demands in Henlein's Karlsbad program was that Sudetenland be closed to Czech immigration, for fear that the German character of the territory be changed. Only to a limited extent was this slow penetration due to Czech government policy. Rather it seems to have been the natural result of the Czech's greater capacity to survive, as a result of a lower standard of living and a superior rate of increase. It is probable that, having annexed the Sudetenland, Germany will now strengthen the German element. But it does not follow by any means that, because France and Britain seem to have given Germany a free hand in Central Europe, the Reich will succeed in carrying out a far-reaching effort at colonization and settlement. Too many other peoples are crowding for room. Moreover, unless he lives in a compact colony, the German quickly loses his own distinctive nationality when

he intermingles with other peoples of the same social class.[10]
Only if Germany wields superior political and military
force over areas already marked by the commercial and
political awakening of the Slavic peoples can it succeed in
establishing new German settlements in Eastern Europe,
and even then it would have more to gain if it used its
power to exploit the economic resources of Central Europe so as to feed a population remaining at home.

2. Poland and Nazi Ambitions

There is abundant evidence, however, that Germany still
hopes to utilize its political power to advance its colonization in Europe. During the Paris Peace Conference, Foreign Minister Pichon of France expressed the fear that German colonization would take place in Russia unless a strong
government were established in that country. Speaking to
the Chamber of Deputies on June 11, 1919, he declared:
" It is necessary that a Russian power be reconstituted
under conditions which will guard against German colonization." [11] Before Hitler came to power, Dr. Schacht proposed German " colonization " of Russia at a Rome conference in 1932, and the question was revived in the famous
Hugenberg memorandum submitted to the World Economic Conference in London during the following year.[12]

[10] Cf. Henri Pirenne: *Histoire de l'Europe des Invasions au XVI
siècle* (Paris: Alcan; 1936), p. 248. Treitschke wrote: "Set in the midst
of a certainly less intellectual but commercially more energetic people,
the nationality of the German minority must inevitably be suppressed by
that of the majority, just as formerly the French refugees were absorbed
in Germany." Hausrath, op. cit., p. 208.

[11] Élie Borschak: *L'Ukraine à la Conférence de la Paix (1919–1923)*
(Paris: Le Monde Slave; 1938), p. 147.

[12] J. W. Wheeler-Bennett: *The Forgotten Peace* (New York: William Morrow & Co.; 1939), p. xvii.

The German Republic did not regard the settlement of its frontiers with Poland as anything more than provisional; and one clause in the commercial agreement which it offered Poland in 1925 went so far as to ask for " the recognition of a right of settlement in Poland for German immigrants." [13]

In 1934 Hitler made a ten-year truce with Poland which led some Poles optimistically to believe that Nazi Germany had abandoned the tradition established by the Teutonic Knights. Yet, only a few years before, a leading Nazi philosopher, Alfred Rosenberg, had written that Germany must apply a policy of " racial imperialism " by expanding in territory contiguous to the mother country, adding that the " disappearance of the Polish State is the chief necessity for Germany." [14]

In *Mein Kampf* Hitler declared that National Socialism must correct the discrepancy between the size of the German population and the area of German territory. According to Hitler, the two most outstanding facts in a thousand years of German history had been the colonization of the Eastern Marches and the conquest and penetration of the territory east of the Elbe.[15] These acts, he declares, " were the first effort, but unfortunately the only successful ones, of harmonizing the increasing number of our population and our territory." German historians, according to him,

[13] Casimir Smogorzewski: *Poland's Access to the Sea* (London: George Allen & Unwin; 1934), p. 269. Poland did not accept this agreement.

[14] Alfred Rosenberg: *Der Zukunftsweg einer deutschen Aussenpolitik*, pp. 20, 97; cited by I. F. D. Morrow: *The Peace Settlement in the German-Polish Borderlands* (London: Oxford University Press; 1936), p. 463. Elsewhere he wrote: "Poland is like a hysterical female who has to be hit hard over the head before she will let her rescuer pull her out of the water."

[15] He adds, as a third, the organization by the Hohenzollerns of the Brandenburg Prussian state.

had failed to appreciate the importance of this achievement. The only cause which justifies the shedding of blood is to obtain territory on which " the vigorous children of generations of German peasants " may one day multiply. The German people can gain such soil by no other means than the power of a victorious might. This land cannot be found in overseas colonies, but only in lands which will increase the area of the mother country. The new Germany must abandon the old colonial and commercial policy of before the war and inaugurate the territorial policy of the future. "Today we count only 80,000,000 Germans in Europe! One can consider our foreign policy a success only if, in less than a hundred years, 250,000,000 Germans may live on this continent, not packed together as serfs who work in the factories of the New World but as peasants and workers who assure each other's existence by labour." [16]

Thus Hitler's chief concern has been to find room for the German people, and to increase their numbers to 250,000,-000. He does not propose to do this by emigration of Germans, who will thereby lose their nationality. He proposes to add to the mother country for this purpose new land lying to the east. Whether he succeeds will depend largely on the opposition offered by Poland. This country — except for Russia — is the most important Slavic country in Europe. Coterminous with the German frontier, it contains territory which before the war formed a large part of Prussia and whose loss is regarded by Germany as a historic shame. From the point of view of colonization, however, Hitler's effort seems doomed to failure. Even if the Polish army cannot win battles against superior German forces, the Polish birth-rate is increasing more rapidly than that of Germany. Poland is already over-populated; and unless

[16] Hitler, op. cit.

Germany proposes to kill off the Poles, as the Teutonic Knights exterminated the Prussians seven centuries ago, the idea of settling a surplus German population in Poland in the future seems fantastic.

Even if the biological energy of Poland makes a German colonization venture unlikely, it does not necessarily follow that the German ambition to dominate Slavic Europe will not be realized. Hitler may give up his dream of colonizing Europe with German farmers and yet reduce Slavic Europe to the position of hewer of wood and drawer of water to an industrialized Germany, or he may give up the thought of colonizing Poland and still dream of peopling the Baltic and the Ukraine. Whether this ambition is realized again will depend on the resistance offered by the unified Slavic peoples, and particularly by the future policy of Poland.

Ever since the Bolshevik Revolution of 1917 the existence of Communism in Russia has been a barrier to Slavic unity so far as Poland is concerned. But even before the revolution, lasting differences separated the Pole from the Russian proper, although both are Slavs.[17] In 966 the first known Polish ruler, Mieszko, accepted Christianity from the Czechs mainly in order to deprive the Germans of the excuse that they were fighting the Slavs because they were pagan. Nevertheless, as a result of this acceptance, which subsequently made Poland a Catholic country, it has since been nurtured on Roman rather than Byzantine culture, which

[17] From the linguistic if not the anthropological point of view, the Slavs are divided as follows: the western group, including the Poles, Czechs, and Slovaks; the southern group, which anthropologically is the most heterogenous, comprising the Slovenes, Serbs, and Croats as well as the Bulgars; and the eastern group, divided into the White Russians who live in the upper basin of the Dvina, Vistula, and Dnieper, the Little Russians or Ukrainians, and the Great Russians. Cf. Eugene Pittard: *Les Races et l'histoire* (Paris: La Renaissance du Livre; 1924), p. 275.

has erected a lasting barrier against Russia. Except possibly for Ireland, there is no country in Europe today where the Roman Catholic Church has such influence. Poland thinks of itself as a bulwark protecting Europe from semi-Asiatic influence. The existence of a strong Poland before 1772 was an obstacle to Russian expansion. It was the partition of Poland which gave Russia an advanced post on the edge of Europe. While ideologically the differences between Poland and Russia are greater than ever because of Communism, Poland's national interests undoubtedly will now force it to think in terms of Slavic unity to a far greater extent than it has done in the past.

For if Hitler is to realize his ambition of dominating Europe, he must reduce Poland to a position of dependence or wipe it out altogether. Even if Hitler does not resume the historic Teutonic Knight policy of dominating the Vistula and the Baltic, Germany cannot be free to dominate Central Europe so long as a strong military power exists on its eastern border. Had a strong Poland existed in 1860–70, Bismarck would have hesitated a long time before embarking on wars with Austria and France. The partitions of Poland paved the way for the rise of the German Empire of the nineteenth century; so long as Poland manages to exist, the rise of a new Nazi Empire in twentieth-century Europe may be obstructed.

Hitler has frankly said that German ambitions can be satisfied only at the expense of Russia. This is not only because of Russia's wealth, particularly that of the Ukraine, which Germans believe can be colonized, but also because it is a cardinal principle of Nazi foreign policy not to tolerate the existence of any other continental power. Now that France has lost its position of supremacy, unable to obstruct Germany's eastward expansion, Soviet Russia is the chief obstacle to Nazi ambition. But the Nazis believe it can be quickly removed. They regard Soviet Russia as a corpse in a state of slow decomposition; and once they have consolidated their gains in Central Europe, they will undoubtedly be tempted to provoke dismemberment of the Soviet Union.

The fate of Poland is bound up in the future relations of Germany and Russia. Should its two great neighbours fight, they would inevitably do so on Polish soil. Whoever the victor might prove to be, Polish territory and independence would be imperilled, if not destroyed. There are some Poles who would join forces with Germany for the purpose of dismembering Russia; but, as Polish policy since Munich seems to indicate,[18] the chief result of any such plan would be that Poland would contribute still further to the strengthening of Germany and the weakening of its own independence.

On the other hand, the whole of Central Europe today fears that sooner or later Germany and Russia will not fight but rather reach an understanding. Between 1802 and 1879 Prussia and Russia were in alliance, with profit to both parties. The German Republic restored this policy in concluding the agreement of Rapallo.[19] The internal régimes of both Russia and Germany are becoming more and more similar. A strong element in each of the armies has favoured an understanding whereby Germany would have access to Russia's raw materials and provide Russia's industries with badly needed technicians. In *Mein Kampf* Hitler argued against the conclusion of such an alliance, not only because Russia had been despoiled of its traditional German governing class, but also because, in a war against Western Europe, Russia would have to conquer Poland before sending a

[18] Cf. p. 349.   [19] Cf. p. 324.

single soldier to the German front. Nevertheless, a situation may be created in the future under which Russia will be too strong to be dismembered, yet too weak to refuse a Nazi proffer of an exclusive agreement. Isolated from France and Britain and threatened by attack in the east by Japan, Russia may find it more profitable to come to terms with Germany than to fight. Such terms might involve the abolition of the Third International, the placing of Russian raw materials at German disposal, and the adoption of a policy of anti-Semitism. Any such agreement will prove difficult of achievement until after the death of Stalin. Nevertheless, the possibility either of a Russian-German war or, at the other extreme, of an exclusive understanding — with Germany as the senior partner — is one which cannot be excluded from the calculations of the future. Should either take place, the consequences for the future of international peace and Western civilization would be extremely grave.

Poland would be as vitally involved over the conclusion of an alliance between the two great totalitarian powers as in a Russian-German war. Indeed, it is not difficult to believe that an alliance would be followed by a new partition of Poland. Thus the existence of Poland is an obstacle to the ambitions of Nazi Germany both in the Baltic and in the Ukraine. Poland's independence during the next few years is consequently bound to be uncertain. Should it become involved in prolonged civil war, as nearly occurred in 1922 and again in 1926, the intervention of its two powerful neighbours would inevitably take place. Such intervention did not lead to a general war in Spain, because the leading protagonists — Germany, Italy, and Soviet Russia — were geographically separated. But should Germany and Russia intervene in Poland on behalf of conflicting factions, they would either clash or combine, in either case destroying the integrity of Poland.

Whether, during the next few years, Poland will be able to maintain its independence will depend in part on its inherent strength and wisdom. Wedged in between two great totalitarian powers, and lacking natural frontiers and industrial strength, it faces grave dangers from two sides. While its strength depends partly on qualities of national character, Poland's future depends largely on whether it can solve serious internal problems, renew its ties with allies abroad, and contribute to the unity of the Slavic peoples. Perhaps the greatest error of Polish foreign policy since the World War has been to desert the principle of Slavic unity — an error for which the Western democracies are in part responsible. But Poland now realizes that a change must come if its own interests are to be preserved. A wise domestic and foreign policy is an essential element of Polish independence and international peace. In more ways than one, Poland holds the key to Europe.

3. The Economic Struggle

So far as area and population are concerned, Poland is the sixth largest state in Europe. In territorial size it is exceeded only by Soviet Russia, France, Germany, Spain, and Sweden; in numbers, only by Russia, Germany, France, Britain, and Italy. Through some of its leading personalities Poland has well served the cause of world culture. Copernicus (1473–1543) was a Pole who studied at the University of Cracow in the Middle Ages.[20] Kościuszko played a role

[20] His monumental treatise, *De revolutionibus orbium cœlestium,* was published in 1543. An important book on the life of Copernicus was recently published by Wasiutyński: *Kopernik* (Warsaw, 1937).

in the American Revolution; during the following century the poems of Mickiewicz, the novels of Sienkiewicz, and the music of Chopin were known to an international audience. In contemporary times the names of Paderewski, Josef Hofmann, Rubinstein, Conrad, Reymont, and Madame Curie are world-famous. Poland was the first country in Europe to establish a department of education; it was one of the first continental governments to have a parliament and a bill of rights similar to *habeas corpus*.

The difficulties of Poland's existence arise largely out of geography. Generally speaking, it has no natural or well-defined frontiers, and it has never had a wholly secure access to the sea. Lying in the centre of Europe, Poland is part of a vast plain stretching from France across Germany to Russia as far as the Urals. Because of its location, Poland has been the meeting-place of conflicting cultures and armies; Germans, Scandinavians, Slavs, Tatars and Turks all have clashed with the Poles. During the Middle Ages Poland served as a crossroad for commercial and military movements between east and west, and even north and south. While the commercial value of this position today has declined, its military and diplomatic value remains.[21] The absence of natural frontiers not only has increased Poland's danger of invasion, but has tempted it to expand its frontiers at the expense of ethnic principles in order to obtain military vantage points. As a result, Poland has always embraced a large minority of non-Polish peoples, and today these minorities make up at least a third of the population. It still has 750,000 Germans and 1,500,000 White Russians. Its largest minority is about 5,000,000 Ukrainians,

[21] Cf. R. H. Lord: "The Resurrection of Poland," in *A History of the Peace Conference of Paris*, edited by H. W. V. Temperley (London: Oxford University Press; 1924), Vol. VI, p. 219.

who may some day create an international problem.[22] There is a difference, therefore, between the Polish state and the Polish nation, although the régime has not admitted this fact so far as its minority policy is concerned.

Poland is confronted not only with a problem of security but with an economic struggle more serious than that of any other great power. This struggle arises out of population pressure against an agricultural economy. Since the World War the population of Poland increased from 26,-664,000 (1920) to about 34,500,000 (1938) — an increase of eight million, or about 444,000 a year. The rate of increase is larger than that in any other important European country, and almost as large as that in Japan. In 1936 the natural rate of increase was 12 per thousand for Poland, in comparison with 14.8 for Japan and a decline of 0.3 for France.[23] As a result of the rapidity of population increase, Poland by 1950 should have 40,000,000 people. Today the Poles of military age — between twenty and forty — already equal the same class in France, the number having increased from 3,500,000 in 1920 to about 5,500,000 at the present time. In a world of *Realpolitik*, man-power still is of importance despite the growth of mechanized armies. No doubt partly because of these considerations, a recent German writer has stated: "The ascension of the young power of the East should be considered one of the most important facts of post-war history."[24] Poland may find some consolation in the fact that this rate of increase is lessening — before the war it reached 16.5 per thousand. Nevertheless, this upsurge of population creates serious so-

[22] For the Jewish population of 3,250,000, cf. p. 288.
[23] *Petit Annuaire*, p. 48. The Japanese figure is for 1935.
[24] Reithinger, op. cit., p. 161.

cial and economic problems and is another cause of the Polish demand for expansion.[25]

If the resources of the country were adequately developed, the present population could be supported. The population density of the country — 89 per square kilometre — is only 13 more than that of France, less than half that of Britain, and less than a third that of Belgium. Superficially Poland still can expand its population a good deal before it reaches the density of the latter two countries. But the difference is that Britain and Belgium are heavily industrialized, while Poland is supported by an agricultural economy which is extensive rather than intensive in character. After Russia, France, and Germany, Poland has the largest agricultural area in Europe. The average population density in the countryside is double that of Central and Western Europe; in parts of east and south Poland it is even triple.[26] Of the 34,500,000 people in Poland, 61 per cent are in farming and kindred occupations. The proportion was even greater in 1921 — namely, about 70 per cent.[27] While Poland has made progress in industrialization since the war, the fundamental character of the agricultural economy remains largely unchanged, partly because of the huge task of reconstruction, the absence of a strong middle class, and the difficulty of developing international trade.

Poland is still predominantly a country of peasants. For the most part, these peasants live grouped together in hundreds of tiny, primitive villages, going out to their fields daily during the planting and harvesting seasons. The Polish peasant family, in the larger sense of the word, embraces

[25] Cf. p. 231.
[26] Reithinger, op. cit., p. 163.
[27] *Petit Annuaire*, p. 32.

all relatives up to the fourth degree; in the more limited sense, it includes the married pair and the children. Marriage is a social and group institution; both bride and groom receive a dowry from their families. But the dowry remains part of the general family property. Landed property has been regarded as essentially " familial," the individual being the temporary manager.[28] " No land communism is acceptable to the Polish peasant. . . . Communism would destroy the very essence of the social value represented by the land. . . ." Until recently the most important personal influence on the peasants' life has been the parish priest. But as a result of modern life many of the traits of the Polish peasant, such as a traditional passivity, are being undermined; individualism and a sense of grievance — a desire to challenge adverse political and economic conditions — are coming to the fore.

The low level of peasant existence is indicated by the diet, the chief articles of which are rye and potatoes. The great increase in potato production during the depression is an illustration of advancing poverty. A peasant on a small holding can grow enough potatoes to keep him alive, but this is not possible in the case of wheat or rye. As a result of such meagre rations, the Polish peasant is virtually self-sufficient in food, but has extremely low purchasing power. The poverty of these people is proverbial. It is said that during the depression the peasant would split a match four or five times, and would boil potatoes over and over again in the same water to save the salt. A peasant village at night is usually without any form of light except at the Jewish shop

[28] For a standard work on the Polish peasant, cf. W. I. Thomas and F. Znaniecki: *The Polish Peasant in Europe and America*, 2 volumes (New York: Alfred A. Knopf; 1927), Vol. I, pp. 158, 161. For pre-war conditions, cf. Ladislas Reymont: *The Peasants* (New York: Alfred A. Knopf; 1924–5).

or the police office, because the people are so poor. Even
at this low level, it is estimated that there is a surplus peasant
population of between six and nine million. A writer describes the conditions in the north-east, the poorest part
of the country, as follows: " At the end of each winter
cattle are reduced to moving skeletons. Horses, having
exhausted their winter supply of fodder, are propped up
in their stalls in the hope that spring may arrive in time
for them to be carried to the pastures before death releases
them from their sufferings. The peasants themselves are
often in little better plight; mere skeletons racked with
fever and malaria, their clothes skins and rags, and their
foot-coverings of bark cut from trees." [29] Even if, as some
Poles insist, this is an exaggeration, the depressed level of
the peasants in many parts of Poland is difficult for West-
erners to imagine. While the existence of the urban worker
is somewhat better, and while wages increased toward the
end of the boom period, workers in 1929 were " still comparatively close to the subsistence level." [30]

The meagre level of existence is indicated by the height
of government expenditure. Poland has succeeded in maintaining its ordinary government budget at a lower figure
than nearly any other Central European country. If the ex-
traordinary budget is included, about half of Poland's expenditures are for military purposes. As a result of the low
level of national income as well as the comparatively large
sums spent for military purposes, Poland must neglect public education and even public works. According to the re-
porter of the educational budget before the Sejm, there

[29] H. Hessell Tiltman: *Peasant Europe* (London: Jarrolds; 1934),
p. 184.
[30] Charles S. Dewey, *Combined Reprint of the Quarterly Reports of
the Financial Adviser to the Polish Government* (Warsaw: Printing Office of the Bank of Poland; 1930), p. 217.

are three million children from six to twenty, mostly in the country, who lack educational facilities, and at least 25,000 more teachers are needed.[31] Although official statistics indicate that about 23 per cent of the entire population is illiterate, some observers believe that more than half the peasant population is unable to read or write.

The per capita national income of Poland in 1929 was far lower than the per capita income in the United Kingdom, Denmark, or France, and only higher than that of such low-standard countries as Bulgaria, Greece, and Japan.[32] In 1928 the Polish national income was estimated to be about 26,-000,000,000 zlotys (about 5,000,000,000 dollars). Between 1929 and 1933 the real income of Poland fell by 25 per cent, in comparison with a similar decline in Britain of 4 per cent.[33] Although the national income by 1937 was probably 20 per cent higher than in 1933, Poland suffered terribly from the depression.[34] If the estimates of a Polish writer are correct, wealth in Poland is also concentrated. He declares that 2,300,000 people consume an income of 3,600,000 zlotys while 31,300,000 consume 9,300,000 zlotys. At this rate, 7 per cent of the population in 1933 had an average monthly income of 135 zlotys (27 dollars), while 93 per cent had only 25 zlotys (4.50 dollars).[35] While production is at about the 1929 level, population has grown at least 10 per cent. During the past nine years population has increased more rapidly than either agricultural or in-

[31] Cf. Jacob Rappaport: "Chronique Polonaise," *Le Monde Slave*, May 1938, p. 265. For under-industrialization, cf. p. 145.
[32] *Concise Statistical Yearbook of Poland, 1937* (Warsaw: Chief Bureau of Statistics), p. 55.
[33] "The National Income of Poland," *Birmingham Information Service on Slavonic Studies*, July 1937, p. 6. For slightly different figures cf. p. 168.
[34] Cf. p. 144.
[35] Jan Mosdorf: *Wczoraj i jutro (The Past and the Future)*, 2 volumes (Warsaw, 1938).

dustrial production, which means a constantly reduced standard of living.

Poland's fundamental problem is to increase the production of wealth — both agricultural and industrial — so as to take care of its large population increases and raise general living-standards.[36]

4. Problems to be Solved

The divisive social structure, which was one factor in bringing about the overthrow of the old Poland, continues to exist in the country today. With the rise of the landed gentry at the beginning of the sixteenth century, the Polish middle class declined; and even now Poland does not have the substantial bourgeois class found in France or elsewhere. It is estimated that about five per cent of the population consists of descendants of the old gentry who ruled the country before the partitions. Even "noble" peasant families may be found in certain parts of the country. Although the 1921 constitution did not recognize titles of nobility (Article 96), the aristocratic tradition is stronger in Poland than in any other continental country except Hungary. Today the most important leaders, in government and elsewhere, are to a large extent descendants of the old gentry, and the general tone of the country is set by this class. This situation is likely to remain, no matter what party is in power. A comparatively large aristocratic class may bring certain assets to the country, such as qualities of leadership and standards of *noblesse oblige*, often lacking in

[36] Birth-control is known in both Polish and Jewish circles; but in view of the attitude of the Catholic Church and of the vast mass of uneducated peasants, this solution cannot be envisaged in the immediate future, particularly since any slowing-up of population increase will affect Poland's military strength.

new countries. The non-capitalist outlook of this class may
explain why Poland has accorded to its intellectuals a position not found in the United States. Nevertheless, the existence of this aristocracy explains why Poland, in matters
of economic and social policy, is comparatively conservative, why it is sometimes threatened by national vanity, and
why factional disputes, somewhat similar to those which
destroyed the old Poland at the end of the eighteenth century, remain an ever-present danger. Moreover, the visitor
to the provinces is impressed by the gulf separating the
lowly peasant from the government official or large estate-
owner — a difference almost as great as that which exists in
many tropical colonies.

The visitor to Warsaw may find criticism of the policies
and composition of the present government; but present-day
Poland gives the impression of stability. Except for Vilna,
which seems to be in a state of decay,[37] the cities have a
flourishing appearance. There is a deep poverty in the ghet-
tos and the countryside, but in the cafés and on the streets
throngs of bright, well-dressed people will be found day
and night.

The Polish civil service, although underpaid, impresses
one as being equal in ability and character to the services
of older countries. The charges of graft hurled before 1926
are no longer widely made. Politics seem less corrupt in
Poland than in other Central European countries. Despite
emphasis on the intellectual, Poland is creating a middle
class, and has produced outstanding engineers. The Poles,
moreover, have lived down their reputation for inefficiency.
Lloyd George once said that one might as well give a clock
to a monkey as Upper Silesia to the Poles — a picturesque

[37] Largely because of the closed frontier now being opened with
Lithuania.

reformulation of the German phrase: *Polnische Wirtschaft*. The unfairness of such remarks is evident to anyone who witnesses the imposing achievements at the port of Gdynia, or who sees the success with which Polish enterprise has taken over and developed its share of Upper Silesia.[38] Although Poland faces an uncertain future, it is undeniable that great progress has been made during the past twenty years. Poland undoubtedly has the capacity of becoming a great power. As one writer has said: " In all Europe there is no other people, with the possible exception of the French, which is naturally so gifted." [39]

Poland, however, is confronted with extremely difficult problems — population, industrial development, international markets, agrarian reform, minorities, and the Jewish question. It is confronted with the problem of establishing a government commanding the confidence of the majority of the people. It has two great totalitarian imperialisms for neighbours. Less courageous peoples might shrink from contemplating a future bound up with these issues. But Poland's confidence in itself, its patriotism, its attachment to its past, and its intense sense of mission may carry it through.

If not disciplined, however, these very virtues may prove Poland's undoing. Undoubtedly Poland suffers from the diseases common to all new states. For a country which prides itself on realism, it is extraordinarily romantic and must continually repress the extreme forms of individualism which led to its downfall a century and a half ago. It has a desire to be accepted by the world as a great power, with-

[38] Cf. W. J. Rose: *The Drama of Upper Silesia* (Brattleboro, Vt.: Stephen Daye Press; 1936), Chapter 21.
[39] Ralph Butler: *The New Eastern Europe*, as quoted in C. H. Haskins and R. H. Lord: *Some Problems of the Peace Conference* (Cambridge, Mass.: Harvard University Press; 1920), p. 197.

out as yet having developed the industrial or military strength to defend an independent policy. In domestic politics the Poles need to develop further the virtues of tolerance and compromise, and generally they would profit by a greater capacity for self-analysis and a healthy intellectual scepticism. In particular Poland needs to pay greater attention to the welfare of the peasants and minorities, who together form such a large part of the population. Meanwhile an intense patriotism will enable this people, if need be, to suffer adversity when other states having higher material standards might falter and even collapse.

CHAPTER II

LESSONS FROM THE PAST

POLAND's strength and patience, when confronted by problems which would frighten other people, is due to historical qualities. One of the motivating forces in Polish life today is the memory of a glorious past. In the tenth century Poland succeeded in building a kingdom, founded on the Piast dynasty, which extended from the Baltic to the Carpathians. But the Polish state experienced a long series of vicissitudes before it achieved its great position in middle Europe. During the twelfth and thirteenth centuries the country was disrupted by civil war, and was divided into a number of principalities and tormented by Tatar invasions. Poland's weakness made it an object also of German aggression.

The country regained unity and strength under Casimir the Great, who ruled from 1333 to 1370. His reign, marked by the acquisition of Galicia, was a period of peace and internal reforms. According to a folk-saying, " he found a Poland of wood, but left it of stone." On his death the throne of Poland passed by inheritance to his nephew, Louis of Hungary, who ruled half of Europe. Confronted by a common German and Russian danger, Lithuania and Poland formed a personal union in 1386 by the marriage of the Queen Jadwiga to Jagiello, Grand Duke of Lithuania, who was crowned King of Poland, at the same time that Lithuania accepted Christianity. For the next two centuries Poland and Lithuania were ruled by the Jagellon monarchy, a union which was consolidated in the Act of Lublin of 1569.

1. Grandeur of the Past

Poland now entered a period during which its civilization reached the height of its splendour, particularly under Sigismund I, Sigismund II (1548–72) and Stephen Batory (1576–86). During the fourteenth century the Polish towns enjoyed a flourishing existence, and in the fifteenth century the University of Cracow attracted scholars from the whole of Europe. Following the marriage of Sigismund I to a Sforza from Milan, the royal court at Cracow, which remained the capital until the Act of Lublin, became the home of Italian Renaissance art. Polish poetry and prose, influenced by Italian culture and the Reformation, flourished. A prominent American admirer of Polish institutions has written:

" In the sixteenth and seventeenth centuries this republic was the freest state in Europe, the state in which the greatest degree of constitutional, civil and intellectual liberty prevailed. In an age of religious persecution and chronic religious wars, Poland knew no such troubles; it offered almost complete toleration and an asylum to those fleeing from persecution in all western lands. Like the United States today, Poland was at that time the melting pot of Europe, the haven for the poor and oppressed of all the neighbouring countries — Germans, Jews, Czechs, Magyars, Armenians, Tartars, Russians and others. The complications of the nationality problem in Poland today are due in no small measure to the great number of aliens who here found a refuge from political and religious persecution. . . . A great enthusiasm for freedom in almost every branch of life; the principle of the sovereignty of the nation, calling the citizens to participate in the responsibilities of government; the conception of the well-being of society; aversion to absolute monarchy, standing armies and militarism; disinclination to undertake aggressive wars, but a remarkable tendency to form voluntary unions with neighboring peoples — such are some of the hallmarks of the old Polish state, which make it stand out as a unique exception among the rapacious and militaristic monarchies of that age."[1]

This picture may be regarded by some historians as romantic. But the criticism is beside the point, because it is the romanticism of Poland's past that is a very real inspiration to Poland today. Contemporary Poland dwells on the past, not only because of the strength of Polish culture, but because of the extent of the Polish domain, which stretched from the Baltic to the Crimea. Poland acquired a large part of this area as a result of the conquests of Lithuania; but its foothold on the Baltic was won only after years of hard fighting against the Germans. At the time of the great migrations during the fifth century, the Germanic tribes had abandoned the territory between the Elbe and the Oder, which was gradually occupied by Slavs, the Poles settling the basin of the Vistula. But beginning in

[1] Robert H. Lord, in C. H. Haskins and Lord: *Some Problems of the Peace Conference*, p. 167.

the tenth century the Germans began to reconquer these lands, setting up Marks along the frontier. This German advance threatened the newly formed Polish Kingdom, then involved in recurrent civil war.

The Order of Teutonic Knights, founded in the Holy Land at the beginning of the thirteenth century, consisted of Germans who dedicated themselves to the monastic life and the knightly vocation of fighting the infidel. In 1226 the Order was invited by a Polish duke, Conrad of Masovia, to assist in protecting his duchy against the aggressions of the natives of Prussia, who were a group of Baltic pagan tribes. In return for this help, Conrad gave the Knights grants of land.[2] The Teutonic Knights, assisted by some Crusaders and Polish princes, conquered Prussia after about fifty years. Lacking whatever idealism had originally inspired the Crusades, the Knights resorted to great brutality, regarding their campaign against the pagan Slavs as man-hunts.[3] After reading the history of this Order, one understands the fanaticism and sadism of the German Nazis. Having conquered Prussia by force, the Knights now undertook to settle the area with German colonists. The German nobility and middle class were followed by a large number of peasant farmers. Meanwhile the original Prussian population declined, finally dying out altogether in the seventeenth century.[4] Under a Grand Master located in the Holy Land, the "brothers" of the Order developed a unified and disciplined state in Prussia; for a time the Order was one of Europe's strongest military powers.

[2] Polish and German historians disagree as to whether these grants included those of sovereignty. A Polish historian charges that the Knights forged a document by Conrad purporting to give them sovereign rights. Stanisław Zajączkowski: *Rise and Fall of the Teutonic Order in Prussia* (Toruń, Poland: Baltic Pocket Library; 1935), p. 22.

[3] Cf. Pirenne: *Histoire de l'Europe des Invasions au XVI Siècle*, p. 373.

[4] Zajączkowski, op. cit., p. 35.

Not content with occupying Prussia, the Knights soon attacked the pagan Lithuanians in 1309, massacred the population of Danzig, which then formed part of Poland, and eventually conquered Baltic territory stretching to the Bay of Finland. By treachery and violence they succeeded in seizing East Pomerania, also inhabited by Poles. The headquarters of the Order was then moved to Prussia. Confronted by a common danger, Poland and Lithuania concluded the union of 1386; and in the " Great War " they succeeded in defeating the Order in the great battles of Tannenberg and Grünewald (1410). Owing to the failure of the Lithuanian-Polish forces to follow up their victory, the Knights succeeded in securing fairly favourable peace terms in the Treaty of Thorn of 1411. Meanwhile the towns of Prussia, which had prospered during the fourteenth century, as well as the Bishops, turned against the Knights, who had suffered moral deterioration and had little contact with the people. Thus encouraged, King Casimir IV incorporated into Poland nearly all of the possessions of the Order in 1454; as a result of this and other disputes the Thirteen Years' War was fought, ending in the second Treaty of Thorn of 1466. In this treaty the Order restored Pomerania and Danzig to Poland; West Prussia became the equivalent of a third state within the Polish-Lithuanian Union; East Prussia, which continued to be occupied by the Knights, became a feudal fief of the Polish Crown.[5] The second peace of Thorn deprived the Order of half its possessions on the lower Vistula and severed its connection with the Holy Roman Empire. Henceforth the Grand Master, having the title of Prince-Senator of the Kingdom of Poland, had to pay homage to the Polish king.

[5] Ibid., p. 78; Morrow: *The Peace Settlement in the German-Polish Borderlands*, pp. 5, 244; Smogorzewski: *Poland's Access to the Sea*, p. 46.

Once more Poland had a frontier on the Baltic. It had dealt a blow against German expansion equally with Bohemia and Hungary, which had been similarly threatened.[6] Subsequently the Order united itself with a princely German family for the purpose of gaining new resources; and in 1511 Albrecht, Margrave of Brandenburg, of the Hohenzollern-Anspach family, was elected Master. Following further difficulties, Albrecht decided to become a Protestant and secularize the Order. In a treaty of 1525 with King Sigismund I this was done and Albrecht swore allegiance to King Sigismund as the secular Duke of Prussia, and unconditionally accepted the Treaty of Thorn. The Teutonic Knights now disappeared from East Prussia. While Poland succeeded in colonizing part of this territory in the fifteenth and sixteenth centuries with peoples today known as "Mazurians," East Prussia continued to carry the stamp of Germanism. It was the first German colony.[7] Poland, however, continued to rule over West Prussia, restoring its Slavic character, until the Partitions at the end of the eighteenth century.[8]

Although Poland retreated in the west during the thir-

[6] Pirenne, op. cit., p. 379.

[7] In the Treaty of Wehlau of 1657 the Great Elector, who had inherited East Prussia, secured recognition by Poland of his independent status as "Duke of Prussia," subject to the provision that if he died without heirs, the reversion remained with the Polish Republic. Morrow, op. cit., p. 5.

[8] Danzig remained under the Teutonic Knights from 1308 to 1454, assuming more and more of a German character. To strengthen itself against the Order as well as Poland, Danzig joined the Hanseatic League in the fourteenth century. Following further disputes with the Order, Danzig extended its homage to King Casimir in 1454 and received a Great Charter in 1457, which gave it almost complete independence. This autonomous régime continued until 1793. Morrow, op. cit., p. 23. In the second Partition Danzig was given to Prussia. By the Treaty of Tilsit of 1807, Danzig became a Free City under the joint protection of France, Prussia, and Saxony. In 1814 it was again returned to Prussia, shorn of its former autonomy. This régime lasted until 1920. Ibid., pp. 23 ff.

teenth century, it advanced in the east, beginning with the conquest of what is Eastern Galicia in 1340. Its greatest gain came with the union with Lithuania, a kingdom which in the fifteenth century extended from the Baltic to the Black Sea, covering at one time almost half of modern Russia.[9] For several centuries Poland maintained a constant vigil in the east to resist the onslaughts of the Cossacks, Tatars, and then the Turks. In 1683 King John Sobieski rescued Vienna from the Turks — one of the high moments in Polish history. Poland served as a barrier resisting Russia's effort at expansion toward the west, and in 1610 actually occupied the Kremlin. In resisting the imperialism of Germany, Russia, Sweden, and Turkey, Poland believed it was fulfilling a mission of importance not only to itself but to the nationalities which it ruled.

At one time the kings seated on the Polish throne complained bitterly against the indifference of the gentry (*szlachta*) toward the aggressions of the Teutonic Knights. Even if Lithuania contributed a great part of the territory and military force to the new Kingdom, Polish culture succeeded in penetrating into Lithuania and other non-Polish areas. The upper classes of Lithuania and elsewhere accepted the Polish language and customs and came to regard themselves as Poles. The Lithuanian noblemen, in turn, were attracted by the privileges which the Polish gentry had exacted from their King. Moreover, an effort to increase the influence of Polish culture among the Galician masses at the expense of Russia was made with the formation of the Uniat church in 1596 — a church which accepts the supremacy of Rome, while retaining Slavic liturgy. "The old republic represented an effort to organ-

[9] K. S. Jusaitis: *The History of the Lithuanian Nation* (Lithuanian Catho-Truth Society, 1919), p. 26.

ize the vast open plain between the Baltic and the Black
Sea — a region containing so many weak and undeveloped
races and a region so much exposed to German ambitions
on the one side and to Turco-Tatar onslaughts on the other
side — into a compact and powerful realm, which was directed indeed by the strongest and most advanced within its
borders — the Poles — but which in its better period allowed
a genuine equality to the other races and extensive self-
government to some of them." [10]

It is not too much to say that in this mediæval period Poland thought in terms of unifying Central Europe. At the
beginning of the fourteenth century the King of Bohemia
reigned at Cracow; at the end of the same century the Ange-
vin dynasty ruled both in Poland and in Hungary. One
of the Jagellons had the idea of uniting the three kingdoms
of Poland, Bohemia, and Hungary under a common dynasty, in order to resist common enemies; and for half a
century (1471–1526) the Jagellons did rule over Bohemia
and Hungary. But with the death of Louis, the last Jagellon King, the Bohemian and Hungarian thrones passed
to the Habsburgs. Had this " grand design " triumphed,
the history of Europe might have been quite different.
Moreover, Sigismund III, who became King of Poland in
1587, as the first of the Vasa dynasty, was heir to the Swedish throne; and the desire of both Polish and Swedish parties to join Poland and Sweden in a personal union led
to a number of wars. Although the idea itself resulted in
bloodshed, Poland none the less during this early period
thought in federal rather than strictly nationalistic or imperialistic terms.

Poland lost some of its territories to Russia in the truce

[10] Haskins and Lord, op. cit., p. 167. For a critical view of a Ukrainian
historian of this period, cf. p. 259.

of Androszowo of 1667, being obliged to give up Smo-
lensk, Kiev, and the whole of the eastern bank of the
Dnieper. Notwithstanding this loss, it remained a multinational state until the Partitions at the end of the eighteenth
century, having a population of about 11,000,000, of whom
probably not more than half were Poles; about a third were
Little and White Russians, while the balance consisted of
Germans, Jews, Lithuanians, and others.

Today many Poles are inclined to believe that Polish culture can successfully assimilate non-Polish peoples as it did
before the Partitions. But this point of view overlooks the
fact that in the old Polish Republic only the gentry had the
slightest feeling of national consciousness — and this they
were prepared to sacrifice for class advantage.[11] The great
masses of people in those days were indifferent to questions of nationality. But during the nineteenth century
this sentiment took hold not only of the Polish but of the
non-Polish masses, each wishing to restore its ancient culture.
Had Poland retained its independence during the nineteenth
century, it probably would have had almost as serious difficulties with its "minorities" as the ill-fated Austro-Hungarian Empire. Nevertheless, Poland today is dominated by
the dream of its greatness during the Middle Ages — a great
culture and a vast domain which under one ruler sheltered
a large number of nationalities.

2. The Decay of the Polish Republic

While there is much in the early history of Poland which
serves as an inspiration today, there is also much to serve
as a warning. The grandeur of mediæval Poland decayed
during the seventeenth and eighteenth centuries, and this

[11] Cf. p. 64.

decay led to the loss of the country's independence. The fundamental reason for this decline was that, unlike France, which succeeded as early as the twelfth century in building up strong national unity by an alliance between the King and the bourgeoisie at the expense of the nobles,[12] Poland was not able to throw off its feudal institutions because of its lack of economic development. Moreover, with the extinction of the Jagellon dynasty in 1572, there was so much uncertainty as to the succession that the elective principle became accepted. In 1697, for example, there were eighteen candidates for the throne, many backed by foreign governments.

The strength of the Polish Crown was further impaired by the weak character of many of the monarchs after the Jagellons, and by the exacting military and financial needs of the Kingdom, arising out of the wars with the Teutonic Knights. All these factors worked to increase the influence of the *szlachta*, or military landowning gentry. During the fourteenth and fifteenth centuries the towns of Poland flourished and a middle class arose which to a certain extent offset the power of the *szlachta*. But as a result of the destruction of the Black Sea trade by the Turks and the shifting of the world's trade routes, the Polish towns subsequently declined. The gentry denied the townsmen participation in the Diet and the right to own land outside the city walls. The same period saw the transformation of the free peasants of Central Europe into serfs; as a result of a series of " constitutions " enacted largely between 1496 and 1573, the Polish peasant became bound to the land and was denied protection of the law. These developments made the *szlachta* supreme. At the height of its influence, this class consisted of only about ten per cent of

[12] Cf. Pirenne, op. cit., p. 371.

the population, numbering less than a million. In contrast, the people of the towns, both Jews and Christians, constituted 15 per cent, while the mass of the people were peasants, whose lot was probably as cruel as in any other part of Europe.[13] A contemporary writer declared: "These people differ little from cattle, having no property, live from hand to mouth, and rot in filth and poverty; half their offspring die from lack of sunlight and proper nourishment . . . and they themselves finally perish from hunger, if a year of bad harvest comes. It must be confessed that whatever fate should befall Poland, their condition could not become any worse." [14]

The gentry themselves were divided into numerous groups. Sixteen or seventeen great families, such as the Czartoryskis, the Radziwiłłs, and the Potockis, maintained luxurious courts and regarded themselves as sovereign princes; the rivalry among these families was one of the strongest forces working toward disintegration. Although in the next level were a number of fairly well-to-do and hard-working estate-owners, the great majority of the *szlachta* constituted what Professor Lord calls an " aristocratic proletariat," barely able to make a living, poverty-stricken, unkempt, and the object of derision of foreigners. Hundreds, if not thousands of these minor gentry " lived at the courts of the magnates, serving in their militia, in the administration of the estates or even in menial capacities. It was a point of honor and almost a matter of necessity for

[13] For the decline of the Polish state, I have relied largely on the admirable work by Robert H. Lord: *The Second Partition of Poland* (Cambridge, Mass.: Harvard University Press; 1915), pp. 27 ff. Cf. also Phillips: *Poland*, Chapters iv–vii.

[14] Cited in Von der Bruggen: *Polens Auflösung*, as in Lord: *The Second Partition of Poland*, p. 27. Cf. also W. J. Rose: *Stanislas Konarski* (London: Jonathan Cape; 1929), Chapter ii.

every great 'lord' in Poland to have hosts of such 'clients' at his disposal, and their services were extremely useful. For it was from this class that the magnates recruited those hordes of tattered and drunken 'citizens,' who swarmed into every Dietine, ready to acclaim 'whatever the Lord Hetman (or the Lord Palatine) wishes' and quick to use their swords in case of opposition. As almost everybody in old Poland, from the Diet down to the humblest law-courts, was subject to mob-rule, it was indispensable to have the mob on one's side. It was the magnates who ruined Poland and the 'barefoot *szlachta*,' who formed their constant and efficacious instrument. And it was a sad commentary upon 'golden liberty' that more than half of the class which boasted of its republican freedom and equality, had been reduced to pauperism and to lives of groveling servility."[15] Contemporary preachers called the gentry selfish, quarrelsome, brutish, corrupt and ignorant.[16] It was the members of this class, which owned the land and provided the military forces, that dominated Poland during two hundred years.

In order to win the support of the gentry for the succession of his daughter to the Polish throne, King Louis of Anjou granted the privilege of Kaschav (1374), exempting the *szlachta* from nearly all taxes and from all duties to the state except military service. In the Statute of Nieszawa of 1454, Casimir IV promised not to make new laws or call the nation to arms without their consent. To exercise this legislative power, the *szlachta* slowly developed a Diet, which was legally recognized in the Statute of Nihil Novi in 1505. Although the Jagellon dynasty did something to increase royal power, the extinction of this dynasty in 1572

[15] Lord: *The Second Partition of Poland*, p. 29.
[16] Cf. W. J. Rose: *Stanislas Konarski*, Chapter ii.

led the *szlachta* to claim that sovereign power lay in their hands. They now exercised complete freedom in naming a successor, in defining his duties, or in revoking his authority. The Senate even selected a wife for the King, who was merely a delegate of the Diet. Poland thus became a royal republic. The prerogative of the King was reduced to the appointment of countless officials; but once appointed, these officials were virtually a law unto themselves. Thus unlike other nations, which during this period succeeded in reducing the powers of the feudal class, Poland exalted these rights. Had the gentry exercised their powers in the Diet effectively and with a view to the national good, the situation might have developed differently. But the work of the Diet was doomed to impotence by virtue of two customs, the first of which was called the Imperative Mandate. Each delegate to the national Diet came with detailed instructions from his local Dietine. Under this system, the Diet became less a legislative body than a miniature League of Nations, composed of delegates from fifty to sixty sovereign "palatines." [17]

The second custom was the *liberum veto*, which developed in the seventeenth century. Under this custom any deputy could "explode" the Diet — that is, adjourn it — by imposing his veto. The effect of this veto was to nullify all decisions previously taken. Forty-five out of fifty-five diets between 1652 and 1772 were "exploded." [18] As a result Parliament, which was the only agency equipped to exercise central power, was doomed to inaction and the monarchy deprived both of military and financial support. It was possible in an emergency to escape from this impasse

[17] The Chamber of Nuncios was the lower house; and there was a Senate made up of high church and royal officers, palatines, and castellans.
[18] Lord: *The Second Partition of Poland*, p. 21.

by resorting to the "Confederation" — an armed group of deputies determined to force through the adoption of a desired project, regardless of opposition. But the use of the "Confederation" often resulted in civil war — a choice which at times became preferable to anarchy. Partly as a result of the unwillingness of the gentry to vote the necessary credits, the annual revenues of Poland in 1750 were only a thirteenth of those of Russia and one seventy-fifth of those of France. Because of fear of "despotism," the Polish Diet in 1717 authorized a standing army of only 24,000 men, hardly half of which in fact was kept on foot. Although between the fourteenth and the end of the sixteenth century Poland underwent development in various directions, in the seventeenth and eighteenth centuries it fell into economic stagnation and political anarchy, suffering intellectual and moral retrogression. While the country was being drained by a series of imperialistic wars, the gentry, devoid of patriotism and lacking constructive energy, led lives of reckless gaiety on their estates. Poland was "a republic, but the most anarchical and the least free at the same time; its laws had as their object the independence of each, but resulted in the oppression of all."[19] The Cracow school of historians had little difficulty in concluding that the Partitions of Poland were mainly due to defects in the internal régime of the state and the breakdown of national character. Poland at the end of the eighteenth century vied with Turkey for the questionable honour of being the sick man of Europe. Modern Poland is conscious of this aspect of its past, and determined that these internal causes of the downfall of the royal Republic shall not recur.

[19] Albert Sorel: *L'Europe et la Révolution Française* (Paris: Plon; 1907, 10th ed.), Vol. I, p. 507.

3. *The Partitions of Poland*

Surrounded by the three rapacious empires of Russia, Austria, and Prussia and menaced by the Swedish empire across the Baltic, the Polish Republic, even had it maintained perfect order, would have been confronted by a precarious existence. The temptation of foreign powers to intervene was infinitely increased by the defects of the Polish political system and character.

Between the Treaty of Westphalia of 1648 and the outbreak of the French Revolution in 1789, Europe was dominated by a diplomatic system based on the most unscrupulous balance-of-power principles. Reason of state was the rule of every sovereign, and aggrandizement or expansion the object of every foreign policy.[20] Sovereigns might pay lip service to the principles of international law and justice, but in fact each state followed what it called its " interests." If any immediate advantage was to be gained thereby, states did not hesitate to tear up treaties. To remove the danger of an enemy who might become powerful in the future, a state did not scruple to fight preventive wars. Every great power agreed that no single one should become stronger than the others — the system of equilibrium. This system implied a balance of power which could be achieved by restraining a stronger power by a counter-coalition or, more rarely, by strengthening a weak power so that it would serve as a buffer state; or again by partitioning a weaker country so as to maintain an " equality " in booty. Monarchs talked about the principle of legitimacy, but they had no compunction in destroying a brother sovereign, in the name of " dismemberment," if he ruled over a weak country. The great monarchs of the old Europe violated

[20] Ibid., Vol. I, pp. 19 ff.

the principle of legitimacy when it was to their "interest" to do so, and thus set an unconscious example for the French Revolution.

Turkey and Poland, internally weak but controlling vast territories of strategic importance, were the natural victims of the principle of dismemberment. During the hundred years preceding the French Revolution, both states were menaced by Russian expansion. Peter the Great, and later Catherine II, fought many wars to get a window on the Baltic, expand toward the Danube, and wrest the Crimea from the Turks. In the Treaty of Nystadt of 1721, Russia obtained from Sweden Estonia and Latvia, areas which Peter settled with Germans.[21] But Poland still obstructed Russia's communications with the West, while it governed many Orthodox Russians whom the Tsars wished to protect. Finally, Poland was the spearhead of a western invasion against Russia, and consequently the Tsars wished to dominate this country for reasons of self-defence.

A second rising power during this period, starting from much weaker foundations than Russia, was the newly founded house of Prussia. By virtue of its geographic position, Frederick the Great and his son believed that Prussia could become strong only by destroying Poland, completely dominating the Vistula, and linking Prussia with Silesia. A third imperial power, Austria, governed by the Habsburgs, was interested primarily in maintaining the *status quo*. The interests of Austria would be served best by the existence of an independent Poland, acting as a buffer state, separating Russia from the Danube and holding back the rising power of upstart Prussia.

For its part, France, already declining from the zenith

---

[21] Bernard Pares: *A History of Russia* (New York: Alfred A. Knopf; 1926), pp. 197 ff.

reached under Louis XIV, was interested in maintaining
its existing position and holding in check the other imperialisms of Europe. In support of these ends France sought to
maintain alliances with Sweden, Poland, and Turkey. In
the sixteenth century it had made two alliances with Poland against the Habsburgs and had succeeded in installing
a Valois on the Polish throne. But this policy finally failed,
largely because of Polish anarchy and the intrigues of other
powers.

A hundred years before the Partitions finally took place,
the idea of dividing up Poland was discussed. Following
the Thirty Years' War, foreign armies for the first time
marched across Polish soil and the gentry deserted their
King in large numbers in favour of the invaders. During
the second half of the seventeenth century the gentry regu-
larly took bribes from foreign courts which competed
against each other to control the election of the Polish King.
One of the eighteen candidates to the throne, Augustus II
of Saxony, owed his election in 1697 to the bribes and violence of Russia and Austria; and he maintained his authority
only by relying on St. Petersburg. When Charles XII
of Sweden invaded Poland in the Second Northern War,
he had no difficulty in winning the support of a large
part of the gentry and, after forcing Augustus to flee to
Saxony, actually enthroned a rival King.[22] Russia, however, delivered a terrible blow to Sweden, and Russian troops
restored Augustus to his throne. Henceforth Russian influence was predominant. In 1716–17, Peter the Great intervened to restore peace between Augustus II and his re-
bellious gentry; and in 1719 Poland was obliged to accept
a treaty promising not to persecute its Orthodox subjects.

[22] Cf. Ragnar Svanstrom and Carl F. Palmstierna: *A Short History of
Sweden* (New York: Oxford University Press; 1934), p. 178.

The next year Russia and Prussia made an alliance binding themselves to watch over the " liberties " of Poland, which meant they would co-operate in perpetuating anarchy. In 1733 a Russian army, appearing before the Diet, forced the election to the throne of Augustus III of Saxony. During this same period Catherine II imposed her will on the Polish dependency of Courland.[23] Russia at that time was probably strong enough to have recovered the Orthodox population ruled by Poland; but it preferred to extend a shadowy authority over the Republic as a whole. For this reason it exercised its right to protect the " Dissident " population, as the non-Catholics were called; and it continued to interfere in the election of kings.

Meanwhile a reform movement had arisen in Poland and, as a result of French influence, popular interest in education was aroused, led by such authors as Stanislas Konarski.[24] The powerful Czartoryski family demanded political reforms, such as the abolition of the *liberum veto*. Although some progress was made, neither Russia nor Prussia was interested in seeing the regeneration of Poland. Both wanted the maintenance of anarchy until they could agree on a more drastic solution.

In 1764 Russia, by means of force and bribes, secured the election to the Polish throne of one of Catherine's cast-off lovers, Stanisłas Poniatowski. Poniatowski, Poland's last King, was a man of charm and intelligence, but lacking in character. His extravagant nature kept him hopelessly in debt, from which he was periodically extricated by never-ending subsidies from Russia. He was a tool used by Catherine eventually to partition the country.

Poland, under Jesuit influence, was undergoing a period

---

[23] Pares, op. cit., p. 258.
[24] Cf. W. J. Rose: *Stanislas Konarski*.

of sharp religious intolerance; the government would not allow new churches of the Orthodox confession to be erected, and denied political rights to non-Catholics.[25] These measures were in violation of the treaty of 1719 and gave Catherine an opportunity to demand the application of the principle of religious equality. Following a new occupation of Polish territory by Russian troops in 1767, and the seizure of some Polish reformers at the order of the Russian Ambassador, Repnin, who was the virtual ruler of the country, a Confederation at Radom was coerced into accepting the Empress's demands. In a treaty of February 1768 with the Empress, Poland accepted the principle of religious equality and placed its constitutional system, including all its notorious defects, under Russian guarantee.

Thereafter, Catherine experienced a number of setbacks. The Poles did not take kindly to a Russian protectorate and revolted, throwing the country into a four-year guerrilla war. At the same time Catherine became involved in a conflict with the Turks, instigated by the French, and was also threatened with an attack from Austria, allied with Turkey. Menaced by wars with Poland, Turkey, and Austria, Catherine concluded that her own interests could be best safeguarded by a Partition of Poland among the leading rivals.

Consequently, on August 5, 1772, the three eastern powers signed the first Partition treaty in St. Petersburg. The Partition was justified on the ground of continuing anarchy in Poland and the refusal of the Poles to co-operate with the efforts of its neighbours to restore order. To obtain a "legal title" and to satisfy the moral forms of the age, the powers now insisted that the Polish Diet formally approve the Partition. By dint of a bribery fund and the

[25] Pares, op. cit., p. 259.

presence of troops, the representatives of the three powers soon secured the Diet's approval — in an atmosphere marked by public avowals of patriotism, the secret acceptance of subsidies, and general gaiety. As a result of the first Partition, Poland lost about a third of its territory and population. While the territory ceded to Russia was poor, and inhabited largely by Orthodox Russians, the loss of fertile Galicia to Austria and of West Prussia to Prussia was serious. The latter cession cut off Poland from the sea and the control of the Vistula, although Danzig still remained in its hands. Despite this Partition, Poland still retained 7,000,000 people, being the sixth largest state in Europe. Preoccupied elsewhere, Catherine withdrew her troops in 1780 and exercised her influence merely through an ambassador.

In the twenty-one years between the first and second Partitions, Poland made a genuine if belated effort at reform. The towns shook off their decadence; revenue increased; administration improved; under Konarski, following the dissolution of the Jesuit Order in 1773, a national system of education was established for the first time. The ideas of enlightenment and later of the French Revolution came to penetrate intellectual circles; Poles became aroused at the Russian guarantee of an anarchical constitution and at the derision heaped on Poland by the outside world. The King himself hoped to win over the support of Russia to a program of reforms. But the opposition, calling themselves the Patriots, demanded the elimination of the Russian guarantee, and the conclusion of an alliance with Prussia, Britain, and similar powers — the proposed Federative System — as the only means of casting off the Russian incubus.[26]

In the fall of 1788 the Great Diet of Poland came together in a session which was to last four years. Carried away by

[26] Lord: *The Second Partition of Poland*, Chapter vi.

an offer of help from Prussia, the Polish deputies demanded the withdrawal of all Russian troops from Polish soil, and actually made an alliance with Prussia in March 1790. In addition to mutually guaranteeing the possessions of each party (not excluding a voluntary agreement about certain territorial questions — apparently a reference to Danzig and Thorn), the alliance pledged that if any foreign power should seek to assert the right to interfere in Poland, the King of Prussia should offer his good offices to secure a peaceful settlement of the dispute; but if this did not prevent hostilities, Prussia would extend military aid to Poland. The Prussian alliance was a blow at the Russian guarantee. Poland had swung from the Russian to the Prussian camp.

Although the preoccupation of Russia in the Eastern War gave Poland a unique opportunity to adopt reforms, it delayed more than a year before enacting a new constitution. On May 3, 1791 the Diet, by means of a bloodless coup, adopted a document which was inspired by British practice and the French Revolution. This constitution represented a sincere effort to convert the country into a constitutional monarchy. It abolished the *liberum veto*, the right of Confederation, the Mandate, and the elective monarchy; and established a hereditary King controlled by the principle of parliamentary responsibility. The constitution further elevated the Chamber of Deputies above the Senate, and each deputy was declared to be the representative of the whole country rather than of his immediate constituency. Certain steps were taken toward the emancipation of the townsmen and peasants. The latter were given the protection of the law; and the former were given representation in the Diet. The adoption of this model constitution came as a surprise to Europe, which regarded the Poles as fickle and vain, incapable of constructive action.

Poland, however, had acted too late. It had failed to seal its alliance with Prussia by ceding Danzig,[27] and found itself exposed to Russia's wrath following the termination of the Eastern War. Catherine II encouraged Austria and Prussia to form a coalition against revolutionary France for the purpose of maintaining the monarchy in Paris, but in reality to give her a free hand in Poland. The two allies agreed to march on France, but only in return for compensation and indemnities. Prussia made it quite clear that it must have compensation at the expense of Poland, notwithstanding the existence of the alliance of 1790, but Russia and Prussia hoped to satisfy Austria by giving it Bavaria in exchange for its Belgian province.

Meanwhile members of the Polish aristocracy, led by one of the Potockis, approached Catherine and asked her intervention to restore the privileges shorn by the 1791 constitution. Under Catherine's leadership they formed the Confederation of Targowica. In a proclamation they denounced the 1791 constitution because it had spread " the contagion of democratic ideas," and asked Russia to intervene for the purpose of restoring the old régime. Thus both France and Poland were exposed to foreign intervention to repress new social movements on behalf of the old régime. Although France was accused of overturning a monarchy in favour of a republic, and Poland of the opposite offence of destroying a republic in favour of a monarchy, intervention in each case took place in the name of counter-revolution.[28]

[27] Subsequently a great German historian wrote that the Polish constitution of 1791 was a declaration of war against Prussia. Poland now made the Saxon house hereditary in Poland, thus creating an " unnatural alliance " with Saxony. Prussia thus found itself surrounded by two unfriendly states in alliance, and the matter was made worse by the fact that Prussia was Protestant and Poland Catholic. Von Treitschke: *Deutsche Geschichte im Neunzehnten Jahrhundert* (Leipzig: G. Hirzel; 1927), Vol. I, p. 113 (first edition, 1879).   [28] Sorel, op. cit., Vol. II, p. 458.

Following the "request" from the Confederation of Targowica, the Russian representative at Warsaw declared to the Diet in May 1792 that Russia was obliged to intervene to enforce the old system, as guaranteed in 1768. At the same time Russian troops invaded the Ukraine and Lithuania. Inspired by the King's temporarily bold eloquence, the Diet determined to resist while turning to the Prussian alliance for aid. But Frederick William II flatly declined to honour his obligations, under the pretext that the adoption of the new constitution had so altered the situation that his engagements were no longer binding. In fact he was already secretly engaged in negotiations for the further dismemberment of the country. Despite this overwhelming rebuff, Polish patriots continued to resist the Russian troops; in this they were encouraged by the victory of the French revolutionists at Valmy and Jemappes. Patriotic fervour became so strong that the Confederation at Targowica told Catherine that the work of the counter-revolution would be undone unless she withdrew her troops.

Finally realizing the difficulties of controlling Poland through a rump government of unpatriotic gentry, Catherine concluded that the best way out was further to partition Poland, in agreement with Prussia, which was entitled to compensation for its war against France. They hoped, meanwhile, to satisfy Austria with the Bavarian exchange. In the agreement of January 23, 1793, Russia and Prussia referred to the "imminent and universal danger" that threatened Europe from the "fatal revolution in France," and declared that steps should be taken to arrest the progress of this evil in Poland. They recognized that "the same spirit of insurrection and dangerous innovations which now reigned in France was ready to break out in the Kingdom of Poland, in the immediate vicinity of their own possessions." In order to guarantee their own security and to indemnify themselves for the "exorbitant" expenses to which they had been subject as a result of the Polish danger, Russia and Prussia would proceed to a second Partition. Russia acquired the whole eastern half of Poland, including the Ukraine, while Prussia obtained the whole of Great Poland, including Danzig and Posen. Prussia thus received the "most important acquisition" yet of the House of Hohenzollern — an acquisition that made Prussia for the first time a "coherent kingdom." [29]

Although the frontier of Prussia was now only a few miles from Warsaw and Cracow, Russia received three times as many subjects as Prussia. The second Partition took from the Polish Republic about half of its remaining territory and people. It was now reduced to a long narrow corridor extending from Courland to Cracow.

The two powers assumed that it would be an easy matter to secure the approval of this second Partition by the Diet, now in control of the nobility of Targowica, who had raised the cry of "Jacobinism" (an early equivalent of Communism) to justify foreign intervention. But the second Partition was too much even for this Confederation, now sitting at Grodno. Despite the fact that more than half the members were under obligation to the partitioning powers and that during the course of the Diet the Polish King received 35,000 ducats from the Russian Ambassador, it took this body a month to approve the treaties. A small group of "Zealots" patriotically made a stand against them; and their opposition was overcome only by the arrest and re-

[29] Lord: *The Second Partition of Poland*, p. 387. The treaty authorized Austria to exchange the Low Countries for Bavaria. Treitschke writes: "The fight lasting five hundred years between Poles and Germans for the eastern Baltic was finally decided in favour of Germany," op. cit., Vol. I, p. 65.

moval of a number of leaders from the city by Russian
troops. In July 1793 a deputation representing the Diet
finally signed a treaty ceding to Russia the lands already
partitioned, and, in return, the Empress guaranteed the remaining possessions of the Republic. As an act of generos-
ity, the Empress condescended to agree not to oppose any
changes in the form of government which Poland might
choose to make and even offered to guarantee the new constitution! In September the Diet was induced, by the presence of Cossacks, to approve the cession to Prussia, despite
the great betrayal. Throughout the whole sorry proceed-
ings the deputies were " alternatively dined and imprisoned
by the Russian Ambassador. . . . They consider here,"
wrote a disgusted onlooker, " that no nation ever gave away
its land and people so merrily as the Poles! " [30] A further
act of the " Dumb Session " was to make a perpetual alliance with Russia, giving the latter power the right to send
troops into the country " in all cases of necessity." Poland
thus was dismembered, and the remains were converted into
a Russian protectorate. One of the last acts of the Diet was
to reduce the army to 18,000 men; annul the acts of the
Four Years' Diet; and approve a set of " cardinal laws "
restoring the *liberum veto*, the elective kingship, and serfdom.

Writing in 1915, Professor Lord called this Partition " the
classic example of the moral degeneracy and rottenness of
the old monarchical Europe." A post-war generation which
has witnessed the ambitions of the new Poland, together
with the partition of Czechoslovakia, is less shocked by
these events than was Professor Lord. Nevertheless, the
Partitions [31] did create a " Polish " problem that plagued the
nineteenth century and, in one sense, may have been a

[30] Ibid., p. 474.   [31] Ibid., p. 504.

cause of the World War. Poland succumbed to the intervention of the imperial powers, whereas France survived, because Poland had failed to develop a sentiment for national solidarity which in France extended to every element of the population except the aristocratic refugees. This seems to have been the first time in history when rival powers effected the partition of a third state without war or bloodshed.

Meanwhile, Poland was rescued from complete ignominy by a number of patriots who had gone to Leipzig. The chief of this group was Kościuszko, who had distinguished himself in the American Revolution. Going to Paris in January 1793, he endeavoured to induce the French revolutionists to organize a league of republics against the coalition of sovereigns, led by Catherine, who had successfully intervened in Poland and were endeavouring to intervene in France. Despite the ideology of the French revolutionists, who, in December 1792, publicly offered aid to all peoples "who should wish to recover their freedom," France did nothing to save Poland, even though it should have been in its interest to do so. Suspicious of the aristocratic reformers in Poland, the revolutionary authorities believed that the interests of France lay in making an alliance with Prussia who, therefore, should not be disturbed in its Polish spoils.[32] Although the French monarchy had aided the American Revolution, the French Republic would not defend Poland. Just as in 1938 a world league of the democracies to check Fascist aggression failed to materialize, so the effort before the outbreak of the French Revolution to build up a Federative System which might protect Poland, as well as Kościuszko's proposal of a League of Re-

[32] Sorel, op. cit., Vol. IV, p. 247.

publics, fell to the ground because of immediate national interests or apathy.

Exasperated by the severity of the Russian occupation, the Poles organized a revolt, regardless of foreign aid. Kościuszko surprised Europe by driving the Russians out of both Warsaw and Vilna in the spring of 1794. By fall, however, overwhelming reinforcements from Russia forced the Poles to surrender or flee. Despite this failure and the cruelties which followed, the revolt accomplished two results. It again diverted from France a blow which the partitioning powers had planned to deliver across the Rhine.[33] Second, it created a new Polish patriotism among the gentry, if not the peasants, which continued to burn during the next century. As a Polish historian states: " It is not too much to say that in those hours of failure and downfall the foundations of a new existence for Poland were laid. The happenings of those days are the first of a series of Poland's protests against the loss if its independence. . . . The Poland of today and tomorrow is essentially the Poland of Kościuszko and of the makers of the Constitution of the Third of May." [34] As a result of the Partitions, modern Poland was given its first national hero.

Relations with Prussia having become strained, Russia and Austria signed an agreement on January 3, 1795, under which Austria acceded to the Partition treaty signed by the two other powers in 1793. In a further instrument, Russia and Austria agreed to a new Partition, reserving a portion to Prussia. Finally they made a secret alliance against Prussia and agreed to a plan for the dismemberment of Turkey. To give Austria some compensation for the 1793 Partition,

[33] Ibid., Vol. IV, p. 47.
[34] Roman Dyboski: *Outlines of Polish History* (London: George Allen & Unwin; 1931), p. 149.

Russia agreed that Austria might acquire part of the territory of France or of the Republic of Venice, and also Bavaria.[35] Such were the methods of the old Europe — methods which many fear are on the way to resurrection in the new Europe of 1939.

4. The Present and the Past

Such is the history of the first Republic of Poland. And it has many lessons for the new Poland of today. The past makes Poland realize that it can survive only if it can suppress the social cleavages and excessive individualism which dominated the gentry a hundred and fifty years ago. The past is a vivid and ever-present reminder that the existence of internal anarchy, coupled with lack of military strength, constitutes an invitation to foreign interference. Seeing the consequences of the lack of patriotism under the old régime, Poland today is one of the most patriotic nations in Europe.

Poland does not need to have history remind it of the ever-present danger of German and Russian imperialism. Yet in view of this history — the Baltic ambitions of the Teutonic Knights and the betrayal of the 1790 alliance by Frederick William — few Poles are willing to entrust their fate to the promises of Adolf Hitler. On the other hand, Poland must be equally distrustful of Russia. It can have no confidence in " guarantee " pacts, such as the Eastern Locarno agreement sponsored by Soviet Russia, in view of the fateful consequences of Catherine II's " guarantees " in the agreement of 1768. Nor, in view of the equally fateful consequences arising out of the presence of foreign troops on its soil recurrently during the eighteenth century, can

[35] Sorel, op. cit., Vol. IV, p. 193.

Poland today contemplate giving a right of " free passage " to Russian troops under Article XVI of the Covenant.[36] Finally, Poland remembers that in 1793, at the critical moment of its existence, it was abandoned by both France and Britain — powers supposedly interested in maintaining liberal institutions and in preventing an upset in the balance of power. The lesson for modern Poland is ominous, but it helps to explain why Piłsudski decided in 1934 that Poland could not be tied to either Paris or London.

[36] Cf. p. 333.

CHAPTER III

THE RESURRECTION OF A STATE

DESPITE the fact that during the nineteenth century the people of Poland remained divided among the three empires of the Romanovs, the Habsburgs and the Hohenzollerns, the flame of Polish liberty continued to burn. During this Period of Captivity, as it was called, the spirit of Polish nationalism was stimulated by a number of great writers and other leaders, many of them living abroad.

1. Poland Partitioned

As a result of the Partitions, about three fifths of the old Poland remained under the Russian Tsar. The Final Act of the Congress of Vienna guaranteed, however, that so-called Congress Poland should have "the institutions which will insure the conservation of their Nationality." In furtherance of this Act, Alexander I granted a liberal constitution to Poland which assured to Poles liberties denied the Russians, established a Diet, and reserved all places of public employment to Poles. Following the revolution of 1830, in which the Poles showed both heroism and lack of discipline, the Tsar dissolved the constitution, and many Polish leaders took refuge in Paris. A new effort at co-operation was later inaugurated by Count Alexander Wielopolski, a Polish nobleman who was given high office by the Russian authorities. The insurrection of 1830 convinced him that Poland could not count on the Western powers for help and should consequently attempt to come to terms with Russia. Owing to his influence, the Tsar agreed to establish a Polish Council of State with certain deliberative powers, and to make the civil administration entirely Polish in language and personnel. A special Ministry of Education for Poland was also set up, while the high schools and the University of Warsaw were Polonized. Meanwhile Polish peasants benefited from the abolition of serfdom by Tsar Alexander II in 1861.[1]

These reforms did not prevent another insurrection in 1863. The Poles yielded to exaggerated hopes regarding possibility of immediate independence. The direct cause of this revolt was Russia's attempt to enroll, in various Russian regiments, Polish youths who were politically suspect. Unlike the revolution of 1830, which had a disciplined Polish army at its command, the new revolt developed into guerrilla warfare. In contrast to 1830, when the insurrection had been organized by the gentry, the 1863 movement was more democratic, being led by middle-class townspeople. But neither revolt affected the peasant. After countless summary hangings, the widespread confiscation of Polish properties, and the deportation of many families to Siberia, peace was finally restored in 1864. Although

[1] R. Dyboski: *Outlines of Polish History* (London: George Allen & Unwin; 1925), p. 189. Cf. also Phillips: *Poland*, Chapters viii, xii.

outside aid was not forthcoming, the French, British, and Austrian governments did protest to Russia against violation of the Act of 1815, and asked that a conference of the powers should be convened to discuss the problem. Russia resented interference such as "no great power would admit." And there the matter rested.

Russia, which had hitherto endeavoured to conciliate the gentry without success, now attempted to cultivate the Polish peasants, hoping to withdraw them from the influence of the Catholic Church, and to stimulate a sentiment of Russian patriotism among them by abolishing serfdom and creating peasant communities.[2] This effort, too, was doomed to failure. The virus of Polish nationalism had now taken hold of the peasant as strongly as it had earlier gripped the upper classes. Despite ruthless Russification of the administration, courts, and universities, Polish culture continued to exist, and Warsaw came to be known as the Paris of Eastern Europe. What is more, Congress Poland made industrial progress. Polish towns such as Łódź became textile centres which provided the larger part of the Russian market — a development which fostered the growth of a workers' movement based both on nationalist sentiment and on demand for social justice.

Of all the Poles divided by the Partitions, those in Prussia suffered the severest fate. Prussianization in the provinces of Posnania and Pomerania was especially vigorous in the spheres of religion, language and ownership of land. Bismarck's *Kulturkampf* was waged with particular determination in Posnania, where it was not only a religious and cultural struggle, as in the rest of the Reich, but a national fight as well. A Polish writer calls attention to the essential difference between the Russian and German oppression of

[2] Phillips, op. cit., p. 151.

the Poles during the Partition period. Russia, while trying to assimilate here and there a special district of the country, had, however, some sort of Pan-Slavic Union under Russian hegemony as its main creed. In this vague Pan-Slav empire the Poles were to have their place as one of the Slav peoples. Russia opposed Polish independence, and tried to introduce dissension among the Poles by supporting one Polish faction against another. Always, however, in one form or another, the existence of an ethnically Polish territory was recognized. Not so in Germany. There the fight against the Poles took the form of a systematic attempt to denationalize the provinces inhabited by the Poles and transform them into purely German provinces, so that no room was left for the existence of Poles within the German Reich.[3]

In brief, if the Russian policy toward the Poles can be defined as incorporation and domination, German policy tended toward domination and extermination, which even the more liberal Germans interpreted as a vital necessity for their nation and not as a desire to persecute the Poles. The German position was clearly defined by Dr. Sattler, leader of the National Liberal party, in the Reichstag on January 17, 1898. "The opposition between us Germans and you Poles," Dr. Sattler said, "is a natural necessity; it is not the result either of ill will or of the desire to harm any Polish national, but primarily the consequence of the geographical situation of the territories on which our two nations live. We Germans cannot permit that another nation be the ruler of a territory which is at a distance of only a few hours' ride from our capital. From this point of view you [Poles] must realize that we are compelled to eliminate

[3] Eugenjusz Kwiatkowski: *Dysproporcje* (*Disproportions*), (Warsaw: Bibljoteka T.S.L.; 1932), p. 98.

this other nation . . . that it is our natural obligation to seek not only to make loyal citizens of the Prussians of Polish nationality, but also to transform them into real Germans." [4]

With the passage of the school and language laws of 1872 and 1876, the Germanization of Pomerania and Posnania became one of the most important internal tasks of the Reich. By the law of April 26, 1886, an Act "concerning the furthering of German settlements in the province of West Prussia and Posen," a fund of a hundred million marks was put at the disposal of the Colonization Commission to buy land from Poles for the purpose of settling German peasants and workers. This fund was increased several times, and by 1914 it amounted to a billion marks. According to a German source, by 1911 this Commission had founded and equipped 450 German villages; in 300 villages the German element was greatly increased; and 450 German schools and 80 Protestant churches had been built. [5]

Not only were the actual results in striking disproportion to the cost, but the Germanization policy had exactly the opposite effects from those expected by the German government. The Poles organized a successful resistance, and their national consciousness increased considerably. The Poles of Germany became the most nationalistic faction of the Polish nation, and the most bitter enemies of Germany. Although before and during the World War pro-Russian and pro-Austrian parties existed among the Poles, there was no similar pro-German party. In the fifteen parliamentary elections in which the population of Pomerania and Posnania participated, no German deputy was

[4] J. Buzek: *Historja polityki narodowościowej rządu pruskiego wobec Polaków* (*History of the National Policies of the Prussian Government toward the Poles*), (Warsaw, 1909).
[5] F. von Both: *Das Ansiedlungswerk* (Ostmarkenverein), p. 423.

ever elected. The deputies were always Poles and always those protesting against German rule. There is little doubt that these provinces, throughout the period of German rule, maintained their Polish character, for even the German census of 1910 admitted that the territory later ceded to Poland was inhabited by a Polish majority.[6]

It was only in Austria that, during the nineteenth century, the Poles were granted a comparatively liberal political régime. As rulers of a multinational monarchy, the Habsburgs regarded the Poles finally allotted to them in 1815 as merely another one of the many nationalities under their rule.[7] In order to strengthen itself for the coming struggle with Prussia, the Austrian monarchy issued an Imperial Diploma in October 1860 recognizing the principle of autonomy for each territory in the Empire, to an extent consistent with Imperial unity. To forestall the efforts of Napoleon III on behalf of oppressed nationalities, and to use the Poles as a means of checking Pan-Slavism, the Emperor Francis Joseph in 1861 granted Galicia a constitution, which included a Diet and a measure of autonomy.[8]

In order to win Polish support for the establishment of the Dual Monarchy, Count Beust made new concessions in 1867, establishing in the new Austrian government a special Minister for Galicia, and creating a special board of education in Galicia, where Polish, instead of German, was to be the language of the administration. Following new demands from the Galician deputies, German officials in Galicia were replaced by Poles in 1869, while Poles alone were appointed to the faculties of the Universities of Cra-

[6] Temperley: *A History of the Peace Conference of Paris*, Vol. II, p. 214.
[7] In 1846 the Grand Duchy of Cracow, which had been left a Free City by the Congress of Vienna, was incorporated in Galicia.
[8] Phillips, op. cit., p. 210.

cow and Lemberg (Lwów). Galicia became Polonized and autonomous at the expense primarily of the Ruthenians. As a result, it was transformed into the Piedmont of the Polish nationality movement. Its schools and universities attracted Poles from everywhere. The "Polish Club" in the Austrian parliament — which at that time had fifty-seven votes — often held the balance of power, and a number of Poles held office in the Vienna Cabinet. While in Russian and Prussian Poland the best Polish intelligence had been driven into engineering, literature, and business, in Austrian Poland government service became the goal of Polish ambition. Immediately after the World War, Austrian Poles to a very large extent met the urgent need of the newly organized Republic for government administrators.

Yet the Poles in Galicia, favoured by Austria, were an aristocratic minority, who could realize their ambitions only at the expense of the Ruthenes, or Ukrainians.[9] This had unfortunate social consequences for Galicia, for this province did not experience the economic reforms or the economic progress witnessed during the nineteenth century by Russian and Prussian Poland. As Professor Alison Phillips says: "The peasants were kept, by the narrow policy of their landlords and of the Catholic clergy, in brutish ignorance; the interests of the towns were neglected, and the failure to create a Polish middle class left the chief influence in them to the Jewish plutocracy. Moreover, as so often happens, the ideals of one nationality could only be realized in Galicia at the expense of another. The Poles used the liberties won for themselves to attempt to impose their culture on the Ruthenes, the result being the devel-

[9] Cf. p. 265.

opment of a conflict which was destined to have a momen-
tous influence on the causes and issues of the present World
War." [10]

The failure of the 1863 revolt and Bismarck's ruthless
Germanization policy caused a majority of the Poles to
abandon the idea of seeking independence by revolutionary means. Supporters of this view, known as the Passivist
group, were represented in Congress Poland by the National
Democratic party led by Roman Dmowski. This party
elected thirty-four members to the first Russian Duma — in
an election boycotted by the Socialists. In the Duma,
Dmowski asked that Russia restore the autonomy guaranteed in the Congress of Vienna. Believing Germany to be
Poland's most deadly enemy, and realizing the importance
of the Russian market, he was willing to accept the idea
of a Pan-Slavic federation in which Poland would be an
equal partner. But Russia refused to consider such views
and effectively reduced Polish representation in the third
Duma. The National Democratic party then began to break
up, and in 1908 Dmowski himself failed to secure re-election to the Duma.[11] This refusal of the Tsar to heed the demands of the Passivists played into the hands of a second
group, called the Activists, who still believed that freedom
could be won by revolution. Consisting largely of workers
and Socialists, this party eventually came under the leadership of Piłsudski, who believed that Russia was Poland's
most deadly enemy. Upon the outbreak of the Russo-
Japanese War in 1904, Piłsudski went to Tokyo and asked
for arms in order to organize a revolt.[12]

[10] Phillips, op. cit., p. 216.
[11] Ibid., p. 175.
[12] In a memorandum given the Japanese authorities in Tokyo, he contended that of the 126,000,000 inhabitants in Russia, less than 60,000,000

While Japan did not accept this proposal, Piłsudski subsequently organized about two hundred rifle clubs in Austrian Poland, which became the basis of the Polish army. The Cracow conservatives, led by Jaworski, supported Piłsudski, although they wanted a union of Russian Poland with Austrian Poland under the Habsburg dynasty.

Unlike other leading nations of the world, Poland as a nation may be said to have skipped the nineteenth century. During this period Polish resources were exploited for the benefit less of the Poles than of their masters. Divided among three empires, the Poles, while clinging to their language, developed three divisive psychologies. Partly as a result of political exploitation and partly as a result of social and nationalist evolution, the influence of Polish culture declined in certain areas. The country gentry were weakened by expropriation. The Russian Tsar forcibly returned to the Orthodox Church several million White Russians and Ukrainians who had, as members of the Uniat faith, previously been under Polish cultural influence. Among the Lithuanians and the Ukrainians, who before 1772 had accepted Polish rule, strong nationalist movements developed. In other respects, however, the cause of Poland gained. The emancipation of the serfs and the beginnings of a middle class laid the basis for a more healthy economic development. Most important of all, the persistence of the Polish language, and the unifying factor of Roman Catholicism, brought about extension of the idea of Polish unity. Adversity and compulsion contributed to the rise of a national culture founded on the mother tongue. The glorious past of Poland, which originally appealed only to the gentry, fired the imagination of the peasantry during the Period of

were really Russian. W. Bączkowski: " J. Piłsudski and the Problems of Russia," *Wschód-Orient*, No. 2, 1938.

Captivity.[13] While the gentry and middle class became discouraged at the end of the revolutions of 1830 and 1863, the revolutionary movement was continued by the Polish workers.[14] By 1914 Poland was more fitted for independence than at the end of the eighteenth century.

2. The War and the Peace Conference

Long before 1914 poets and political leaders realized that a new world war would create an opportunity to achieve independence which might otherwise be denied. In his *Litany of the Polish Pilgrims*, Adam Mickiewicz prayed for that " universal war for the liberation of the peoples " which would bring deliverance to his country. After the outbreak of the World War, however, the situation was discouraging so far as revolt against Russia was concerned. If the Western democracies had any humanitarian interest in the Polish question, they carefully concealed it for the sake of maintaining their alliance with Russia, one of Poland's oppressors. On the other hand, a majority of the Poles in Congress Poland seemed to believe that they would be safe against the German menace only if they remained within the Russian fold. These Passivists were greatly encouraged by the proclamation of Grand Duke Nicholas, commander-in-chief of the Russian armies (August 14, 1914), who announced that, under the sceptre of the Tsar, " Poland will be born again, free in religion, in language, and in self-government." Subsequently the Russian authorities confidentially admitted that this proclamation applied only to Prussian and Austrian Poland; but the Poles, par-

[13] A. P. Coleman: " Language as a Factor in Polish Nationalism," *Slavonic Review*, Vol. XIII (1934), p. 135.

[14] Cf. the chapter on " The Resurrection of Poland," by R. H. Lord, in Temperley: *History of the Paris Peace Conference*, Vol. VI, p. 229.

ticularly the National Democrats, took it at its face value.

In Austria Piłsudski adopted an opposite course. He at once offered to place 4,000 men from his rifle clubs at the disposal of the Austrian army, in the hope that they would be recognized as a Polish legion. By the beginning of 1916 there were three Polish brigades co-operating with the Austrian army, one led by Piłsudski, another by Haller,[15] and still another by Grzesiński. By this time Germany and Austria had succeeded in driving the Russian forces out of Galicia, which they had previously invaded, and out of Congress Poland as well. By a convention of December 14, 1915, Germany and Austria divided up Russian Poland between themselves. The German occupation caused untold misery, a million Poles being evacuated to Russia, where many died of starvation.

By this time it had become evident to Piłsudski that Austria was more interested in Polish man-power than in Polish independence. When Vienna did not meet his demands, he resigned as chief of his brigade in July 1916. Possibly inspired by this action, the Central Powers, which needed more Poles for their armies, proclaimed the existence of the hereditary Kingdom of Poland on November 5, 1916. Following the Russian example of making concessions only at the expense of the enemy, the new Kingdom did not include any part of German or Austrian Poland, and the army and foreign policy of the Kingdom — which presumably was to have a German king — was to be placed under the control of Germany. The creation of the Kingdom, however, focused international attention on the Polish question. Germany now established a Council of State for the Kingdom, of which Piłsudski became a member. He resigned in

[15] Haller later joined the Allies and became commander of the Polish army in France.

July 1917, when he became convinced that neither Germany nor Austria was willing to organize an independent Polish army. Several weeks later Piłsudski was imprisoned by the Germans at Magdeburg, where he remained until the end of the war. When the entire Council subsequently resigned, Germany and Austria placed the government of the Kingdom in the hands of a Regency Council, which remained in power until the armistice of 1918.[16]

One of the early acts of the first Russian Revolution (March 1917) was to announce the creation of an independent Polish state, formed of territories having a Polish majority. This state was to be bound to Russia by an alliance, and serve as a rampart against German pressure. When the Bolsheviks came to power in November 1917, they proclaimed the principle of self-determination for the " peoples of Russia," embodied in the famous Declaration of the Rights of the Peoples of Russia. Apparently at the request of the Bolsheviks, Poland was not represented at the Brest-Litovsk conference of March 1918, nor would Germany accept the Bolshevik demand that a plebiscite be held in Poland, and elsewhere, to determine whether these peoples should remain under German control.[17] In the name of self-determination, Germany demanded that Russia give up all claim to Congress Poland, while fostering a free Ukrainian state and giving this state the district of Chełm, which the Poles regarded as their own. Poland registered a bitter protest against the Treaty of Brest-Litovsk.[18] To Bolshevik Russia the Poles could not and would not look for support. Toward Germany they could feel only a sense of

[16] Robert Machray: *Poland, 1914–1931* (London: George Allen & Unwin; 1932), Chapters i and ii.

[17] Louis Fischer: *The Soviets in World Affairs*, Vol. I, p. 44.

[18] M. W. Graham: *New Governments of Eastern Europe* (New York: Henry Holt & Company; 1927), p. 764.

betrayal, for the Polish Kingdom, deprived of Austrian and Prussian Poland, was merely a pawn. Meanwhile Polish leaders had transferred their sphere of activity to Allied countries. Dmowski in Europe and Paderewski in America carried on effective propaganda in favour of the Polish cause.

With the elimination of Russia, the Allies could now proceed to endorse the goal of Polish independence. President Wilson made Poland the subject of the next to the last of his Fourteen Points; [19] and in a declaration of June 3, 1918 Britain, France, and Italy stated that the creation of a united Poland with free access to the sea constituted a condition of a just peace. Subsequently they authorized the formation in France of an autonomous Polish army, under the control of the Polish National Committee headed by Dmowski. This Allied recognition of the National Committee made possible the participation of Poland in the Paris Peace Conference — a right not granted to any Baltic country.

When Piłsudski was released from prison after the armistice, he was given full powers by the Regency Council in Warsaw. He now energetically proceeded to establish order in the country, evacuate the German troops, and form a government. His object was to win the support of the Left, believing that " revolution from the Left was always more dangerous than from the Right," particularly in view of the Bolshevik example to the north. Poland thus was in the hands of a former Socialist with a Left government, which probably saved it from Bolshevism; but the Allies

[19] "An independent Polish State should be erected which should include the territories inhabited by indisputably Polish populations, which should be assured a free and secure access to the sea, and whose political and economic independence and territorial integrity should be guaranteed by international covenant."

had recognized the Polish National Committee, headed by a conservative, Dmowski.

This internal conflict threatened to undermine the position of Poland at the Paris Conference and to bring about civil strife at home. But through the mediation of Paderewski, both groups were brought together. Paderewski and Dmowski were recognized as the Polish delegates at the Peace Conference; the Polish Committee recognized Piłsudski as the head of the government and Paderewski as Prime Minister, and agreed to add ten Left members to its own list.

Apart from the arduous task of reconstruction and relief, Poland now was confronted with two major problems. The first was that of securing international recognition at Paris for adequate frontiers. The second was that of protecting its interests in the east.

At the Peace Conference the Polish delegation struggled to restore the historic boundaries of 1772 — first established, as far as Germany was concerned, by the Peace of Thorn. It demanded the return of territory inhabited by a majority of Poles; it also laid claim to other territories for economic, historic, or strategic reasons. The Allied powers were committed to the restoration of territory having an "indisputably Polish" population, and to the principle of giving Poland a "secure" access to the sea. But Britain, as well as the United States, did not believe that the territories of this new state should violate the principle of self-determination. Frontiers drawn at the expense of Poland's potentially powerful neighbours, it was argued, would sooner or later prove a cause of weakness. France, however, supported the Polish claims for greatness; it wanted a strong Poland which would serve as a rampart against Bolshevik Russia and a potential restraint on Germany.

Although the Polish Commission of the Peace Conference tended to accept the Franco-Polish reasoning, the Peace Conference itself, after hearing a strong protest from the German delegation, declined to grant all the Polish demands. Generally speaking, the Polish-German frontier conformed to the principles of ethnic justice.

Despite Poland's need for secure access to the sea, the Conference rejected Poland's claim for the annexation of Danzig.[20] While Danzig has historic ties with Poland, it is inhabited today by an overwhelmingly German population. In an effort to reconcile the principle of self-determination with Poland's need of access to the sea, the Conference decided that Danzig should become a Free City, governed by a local legislative body, subject to the control of the League of Nations, represented by a high commissioner. Poland, in return, was given the right to control the customs and use the port. Moreover, free trade between Danzig and Poland was guaranteed.

Partly in order to connect the interior of Poland with the Baltic, the peace treaty restored to Poland a narrow strip of territory called by the Poles " Pomorze " (Pomerania) and by the Germans " the Corridor." The Germans denounced the existence of the so-called Corridor as bitterly as any other feature of the Treaty of Versailles. This land, however, formed an integral part of Poland before its Partition; and despite German efforts at Prussification, the majority of inhabitants of Pomerania were Polish at the end of the war. Germany's resentment was particularly aroused by the fact that the so-called Corridor separated East Prussia, one of the strongholds of German patriotism, from Germany proper.

While the Conference rejected the Polish demand with

[20] Cf. p. 32.

respect to East Prussia, it did agree to have plebiscites held in parts of this area inhabited by Protestant Mazurians who spoke Polish — namely, in the Marienwerder and Allenstein. These plebiscites, held on July 11, 1920, went overwhelmingly in favour of Germany.[21] The separation of East Prussia from Germany by a strip of Polish territory remained a major grievance of Germany. This grievance was not removed by the fact that, in conformity with the Treaty of Versailles, Poland signed a treaty in April 1921 guaranteeing Germany the right of transit across the Corridor.[22]

The most serious controversy over the Polish frontier, however, arose over the question of Upper Silesia. The first draft of the Treaty of Versailles proposed to hand over nearly all of Upper Silesia to Poland, on the ground that the majority of the inhabitants were Polish-speaking. The German delegation made a strong fight on this proposal. It pointed out that, unlike Posnania, Upper Silesia had not formed part of Poland since 1335, but had been conquered from the Habsburgs by Frederick the Great in 1742. It also contended that retention of this province was essential to German economic life, and that the people, even if Polish-speaking, did not wish to go back to Poland.[23]

[21] Miss Wambaugh agrees with the Polish charge that the plebiscites were imperfectly organized, but declares that they roughly reflected the wishes of the inhabitants. Sarah Wambaugh: *Plebiscites since the World War* (Washington: Carnegie Endowment for International Peace; 1933), Vol. I, p. 141.

[22] For a thorough analysis of all problems connected with Danzig, the Corridor, and East Prussia, cf. Morrow: *The Peace Settlement in the German-Polish Borderlands.*

[23] The Upper Silesians are said to speak a dialect called *Wasserpolnisch.* These Polish-speaking people had been governed as a unit under Germany since 1742, and some observers believe that they did not wish to be divided but rather favoured a régime of autonomy. Cf. W. J. Rose: *The Drama of Upper Silesia,* p. 168.

Moved by these arguments, the Conference amended the treaty so as to authorize a plebiscite under an inter-Allied commission. The peace treaty provided that the votes in each commune should be counted separately, implying that the boundary should separate Polish from German villages wherever possible, and that Upper Silesia should be divided. When the plebiscite was held, on March 20, 1921, 707,605 voted for Germany and 479,359 for Poland. While 59.6 per cent of the votes were for Germany, only 54 per cent of the communes had a German majority. Following a long period of tension marked by a third Polish insurrection led by Korfanty, the League Council finally drew a boundary line on October 12, 1921 that gave to Germany about 75 per cent of the area and 57 per cent of the inhabitants. The area given Poland, however, contained 76 per cent of the coal mines, 90 per cent of the coal reserves, 97 per cent of the iron ore, all of the thirteen ironworks, five of the eight zinc factories, almost half the steelworks, and the power and nitrate works erected at Chorzow during the World War for munition purposes. All together, the line was about as fair, from the point of view of self-determination, as could possibly be drawn.[24] In order to safeguard the economic unity of Upper Silesia, Germany and Poland signed an elaborate convention on May 15, 1922, providing for virtual free trade between Polish and German Upper Silesia for fifteen years and for the mutual protection of minorities within these areas.[25]

Although Poland received much less German territory than it had asked, and although the German-Polish frontier conformed roughly to the principle of self-determination,

[24] Cf. the excellent discussion in Wambaugh, op. cit., pp. 259 ff.
[25] For the text, cf. Karl Strupp, *Documents pour servir à l'histoire du droit des gens* (Berlin: Sack; 1923), Vol. LV, p. 719.

Poland did acquire territory which inflicted a great loss on Germany. The loss was felt not merely because a million or so Germans passed under Polish rule, or because of the transfer of economic resources. It was primarily a loss of historic prestige and power. In 1886 Bismarck declared that " we will never consent to the restoration of Poland. Between Prussia and Poland there is a struggle for existence." [26] Yet the Treaty of Versailles restored Poland as an independent nation. The power and expansionist ambitions of Prussia had rested in the nineteenth century on Polish soil, and now much of that soil was lost.

In view of the fact that Russia was not represented at the Peace Conference, that body could not legally draw a frontier between Russia and Poland. All that the Supreme Council attempted to do was tentatively to fix the Curzon Line as a minimum boundary in December 1919. This line, largely following ethnic considerations and confining Poland to the river Bug, proposed to give Poland much less than the frontier of 1772 and did not include Vilna within Poland. Consequently, few Poles were prepared to accept it.

The Peace Conference did, however, have the legal power to impose a boundary between Poland and the successors of Austria-Hungary. By Article 91 of the Treaty of Saint-Germain, Austria was required to cede the whole of Galicia, among other territories, to the Principal Allied and Associated Powers. In the " Certain Frontiers " Treaty of August 1920, the Allies assigned western Galicia to Poland on the ground that it was indisputably Polish, but the Poles declined to accept the treaty since it did not give title to Eastern Galicia as well. The Paris Peace Conference was

[26] Address to Prussian Landtag, January 26, 1886. Aulneau: *Histoire de l'Europe Centrale*, p. 55.

unwilling to admit the Polish claim to either Vilna or Eastern Galicia — in the latter case because of the Ukraine question.[27] But the Conference of Ambassadors finally recognized that both territories belonged to the new Poland. Polish tenacity, together with the desire of France to create a strong Poland, won the day.

3. War with Russia

While Poland carried on a diplomatic struggle at the Paris Peace Conference, Piłsudski continued the military struggle in the field. Poland at this time faced a double danger — from Bolshevik Russia on the one hand, and from Germany on the other.

Although the armistice of November 1918 had wiped out the Treaty of Brest-Litovsk, it had provided that the German troops should evacuate all territories formerly part of Russia " as soon as the Allies consider this desirable." Taking into account the internal situation of the country, the Allies had wished the German forces to serve as a buffer against the Red army, but Germany withdrew its troops immediately, thus facilitating Bolshevik invasion in the Baltic area. In February 1919, however, General von der Goltz returned to Latvia for the purpose of driving out the Bolsheviks in co-operation with the White Russian armies, and restoring German control. But in May the Allies sent a military mission to Latvia which eventually succeeded in eliminating the Germans once more. Although during 1919 Bolshevik troops had occupied these Baltic states, the Moscow government in the following year decided to recognize their independence, and the Allied governments eventually followed suit. The withdrawal of both Germany and

[27] Cf. p. 269.

Russia from the Baltic relieved Poland from enormous pressure and increased its own prospects of survival.

In 1919 Poland might have taken advantage of the weakness of Soviet Russia, torn by internal war and counterrevolution, to press its claims at Russia's expense. But Piłsudski did not launch a general offensive against Russia, partly out of fear that it would merely overthrow the Soviets and restore a conservative Russian government that would insist on the return of its Polish territories.[28]

In the spring of 1919, however, Piłsudski marched on Vilna, his place of origin, and, after driving out the Bolsheviks, issued a proclamation on April 20 addressed to "the People of the Grand Duchy of Lithuania," in which he spoke of his desire to federate Lithuania in union with Poland, White Russia, and the Ukraine. Thus he pressed his idea of federalism — a voluntary grouping of states carved out of Russia and led by Poland. Thereafter, desultory fighting continued between Polish, Lithuanian and Bolshevik troops.

In the following month Piłsudski launched an offensive against Eastern Galicia, inhabited largely by the Ukrainians, and Volhynia, despite the remonstrance of the Peace Conference, which was unwilling to allot these territories to Poland.[29] He wished not only to restore the 1772 frontier but also to link up Poland with Rumania to ward off an eventual German and Russian attack. By July the Ukrainian army had been driven out of Galicia into the Russian Ukraine.[30]

Meanwhile France urged Poland to adopt a strong antiSoviet stand. For its part, the Bolshevik government, having defeated the counter-revolutionaries, warned the Polish

[28] Cf. Fischer, op. cit., Vol. I, pp. 238, 240.
[29] Cf. p. 271.   [30] Cf. p. 270.

government in January 1920 that the Allies were driving it into an "unwarranted, senseless, and criminal war with Soviet Russia." It reaffirmed its recognition of the independence of the Polish Republic and urged the opening of peace negotiations. Poland showed no disposition to make peace, and negotiations broke down over Warsaw's insistence that they be held in the inconvenient town of Borisov and that hostilities be interrupted only for twenty-four hours. Piłsudski preferred to fight, apparently in the belief that, since the danger of Tsarist restoration had been eliminated, he could apply his ideas of federalism and permanently weaken Russia. Consequently, despite immense misery through a country already devastated by the World War, despite starvation and typhus, Piłsudski decided to launch an offensive war against the Soviet Ukraine.[81]

Piłsudski had no difficulty in occupying Kiev in the Soviet Ukraine. But subsequent events demonstrated that the Ukrainian peasants had no liking for the Poles, and that the occupation had merely served to divert Polish troops from the northern sector, where the Russians planned to attack. The Bolsheviks were determined to hold the Ukraine at all costs, not only because of its vast natural resources, but because it assured Russia an outlet to the Black Sea.[82] Meanwhile France tried in vain to persuade Rumania to come to the aid of Poland; and, when this failed, negotiated with Hungary. If the latter agreed to send 100,000 men to Poland, France was ready to recover for it twelve cities seized by Rumania.[83] This was *Realpolitik* with a vengeance, but Hungary had its own troubles, and Poland had to fight the

[81] For Piłsudski's alliance with Petlura, head of the Ukrainian government, cf. p. 271.

[82] Joseph Blociszewski: "La Restauration de la Pologne et la Diplomatie Européenne," *Revue Générale de Droit International Public*, Vol. III (1926), p. 446.   [83] Fischer, op. cit., p. 258.

war alone, except for the largely nominal aid of Petlura. In July the Soviet General Tukhachevsky launched his offensive on the northern front, with a proclamation stating: "The destinies of the World Revolution will be settled in the West. Our way toward world-wide conflagration passes over the corpse of Poland." [34-5]

The Bolsheviks promptly took Vilna and swept aside all opposition as they marched into the heart of Poland. Poland frantically appealed to the Supreme Council at Spa for aid. The latter promised assistance only if Poland abandoned all ideas of further conquest. Poland agreed to this condition, and also undertook to accept the decision of the Supreme Council concerning the status of Lithuania, Eastern Galicia, and Teschen. In return, the Allies agreed to give Poland their military support if the Russians refused an armistice.[36] A French and British military mission, which included Lord d'Abernon of England and General Weygand of France, now proceeded to Poland. Poland grudgingly accepted these terms, which involved acquiescence in the Curzon Line, but Soviet Russia proved obdurate. It had visions of reducing the whole of Poland to Communism; and its demands for peace called for the establishment in Poland of a civilian militia of 200,000 workers, which would have served as the vanguard of Bolshevism. Meanwhile Poland's difficulties had increased, owing to the refusal of the Czech and German governments to allow the transit of munitions, and the unwillingness of dockers in Danzig, apparently because of sympathy with Communism, to unload munitions.[37]

[34-5] Machray, op. cit., p. 148.
[36] For the agreement of July 10, 1920 signed by M. Grabski, cf. Borschak: *L'Ukraine à la Conférence de La Paix,* p. 182.
[37] Cf. p. 337.

Poland's dark hour had come and hope was lost, except on the part of Piłsudski. The latter decided to stand his ground; and, in what Lord d'Abernon called the " Eighteenth Decisive Battle of the World," Piłsudski was able to turn the enemy's flank outside Warsaw on August 16, 1920. The Bolsheviks now broke ranks and retreated. As a result of the further battles of the Niemen and the Szczara, the Bolsheviks were driven further into Russia, and the ground was laid for the Treaty of Riga. In undertaking this new offensive, which the United States also opposed,[38] Piłsudski seems to have believed that the pledge made at Spa was not binding because of the failure of the Allies to negotiate an armistice. He was determined to end the Russian danger and apply his federal idea of imperialism. In October the Polish General Żeligowski occupied Vilna, ostensibly on his own authority but actually with Piłsudski's blessing. General Weygand declared that the battle of the Vistula was a " Polish victory," executed " by Polish generals in accordance with a Polish plan." Lord d'Abernon subsequently wrote that " had the battle been a Bolshevik victory, it would have been a turning point in European history, for there is no doubt at all that the whole of Central Europe would at that moment have been opened to the influence of Communist propaganda and to Soviet invasion." [39] Had the Communists conquered Poland, they might have been equally successful in neighbouring Germany, where Communist agitation was already strong. The service rendered non-Communist Europe by Poland was

[38] In a note of August 21, 1920 Secretary Colby declared that the United States " could not approve the adoption of an offensive war program against Russia by the Polish Government." *Foreign Relations of the United States, 1920* (Washington, 1936), Vol. III, p. 391.

[39] *Gazeta Polska*, August 17, 1930; Machray, op. cit., p. 165.

dimmed, however, by the fact that Piłsudski had declined to negotiate peace when originally proposed by the Bolsheviks and that, encouraged by Allied hostility against Soviet Russia, he had taken the initiative in fighting a preventive war.

Lenin was so anxious for peace that he would undoubtedly have given Poland the 1772 frontier. On the other hand, Piłsudski might have gone so far as to overthrow the Soviet régime. He did not do so, fearing that its successor would be far more nationalistic than the Bolsheviks. Showing considerable moderation, Poland, in the Treaty of Riga of March 18, 1921, asked and obtained only a little more than the 1793 frontier. Even so, less than fifteen per cent of the five million people transferred from Russian to Polish sovereignty were Poles.

In addition to ceding this territory, the Soviet Union recognized that the Vilna matter concerned only Poland and Lithuania. Both parties agreed not to interfere in each other's internal affairs, and agreed to respect minority rights. Russia promised to restore to Poland a large number of trophies, collections, and other property; to pay to Poland thirty million gold rubles in compensation for the " active participation of the Polish Republic in the economic life of the old Russian Empire "; and to return certain rolling stock. Poland was discharged from any obligation for the debts of the old Tsarist régime.[40]

Although the Riga Treaty recognized the independence of White Russia and the Ukraine on the Russian side of the frontier, it gave Poland a large White Russian and Ukrainian population who were not guaranteed any po-

[40] For a French text, cf. Strupp, op. cit., Vol. V, p. 213. The Ukraine was a party also to this treaty.

litical rights apart from individual minority guarantees.[41]

Thus ended Poland's Battle of Frontiers. Ethnic Poland had an area of about 90,000 square miles and a population of 20,000,000 people, but, as a result of Poland's arms and diplomacy, the boundaries of the new state, by 1923, reached 150,000 square miles and included 28,000,000 inhabitants. This striking increase in area — largely at Russia's expense — exceeded that achieved by any other state arising out of the war. Poland today has about three fifths the area of pre-Partition Poland at the height of its power. This achievement was the more remarkable because it was won against the opposition of the Peace Conference, the United States, and Soviet Russia.

As a result of these gains, Poland obtained a world-wide reputation for unbridled imperialism. Yet such a sweeping judgment overlooks, first, the fact that the anti-Bolshevik policy of the Allies was as much to blame as Polish ambitions. Had the Allies been willing to make peace with Russia and immediately recognize the Soviet régime, rather than attempt to overthrow it, Poland would undoubtedly have done so without wasting two years in war.

Second, critics do not sufficiently take into account the strong historic sense of Poland. Before the Partition of 1772, Slavic peoples lived side by side under Polish rule, and the upper classes gradually accepted Polish culture, less as a result of brutal conquest than of peaceful penetration. It is a striking fact, for example, that three outstanding Polish leaders, Kościuszko, Mickiewicz, and Piłsudski, were all born in Lithuania. Upon recovering their independence in 1918, the Poles also hoped to restore old relationships, par-

---

[41] Polish recognition of the independence of White Russia and the Ukraine was largely of verbal importance, as they were incorporated in the Soviet Union.

ticularly in view of the danger that Eastern Galicia, which despite its Ukrainian majority had a Polish upper class and a majority of Poles in the larger towns, might fall into the hands of Bolshevik Russia.[42]

At the end of the World War Piłsudski believed that the re-creation of some form of co-operation among the Slavs, under Polish leadership, would prove a distinct service to Europe. There was also something to be said for the strategic argument that Poland, located between Germany and Russia, must have a large territory in order to enjoy freedom of movement. For historical reasons it was easier to get this base at the expense of Russia than of Germany. What the Polish argument overlooked, however, is that to-day the masses of non-Poles have imitated the Polish peasant in developing a sense of their own national consciousness. It is possible that, under certain conditions, various branches of the Slav race would gladly live under the same political roof; but the weakness of Poland's position was that it assumed to know the wishes of these other Slavs without giving them either an opportunity for self-expression or an adequate share in the government imposed by Polish arms.

4. The Task of Reconstruction

Poland's campaigns to extend its frontiers took place at a time when the people of Poland were suffering untold misery. Except for Belgium, Poland suffered greater devastation than any other European nation — a devastation increased by the fact that Poland fought Russia for two years after the World War had come to an end. The economic loss suffered by the country has been described by a Polish writer as follows:

[42] Cf. p. 269.

"The statistics of war show a total loss by fire of over 1,800,000 buildings in cities, towns, and villages, valued at over 1,500,000 [*sic*] francs. Just before the evacuation of Poland by the occupying Powers, nearly 11 million acres of agricultural land were put out of use. The losses in livestock amounted to 2 million head of cattle, 1 million horses, and 1,500,000 sheep and goats. Within the area of war operations were included about 15 million acres of forests, of which nearly 6 million acres were totally destroyed and devastated by alien armies, who removed 4,661 million cubic feet of timber from the country. The industries of the former Congress Kingdom were in total collapse. The textile industry centred round Łódź and Białystok suffered most, because, apart from the destruction of factory buildings, it was denuded of machinery and plant, raw materials and stocks of manufactured goods. The foundry and mining industries, as well as the metallurgical industry, were completely immobilized; and great losses were suffered by the oil industry in South-Eastern Poland."

Invading belligerents carried away from Poland 4,259 electrical motors and engines, and 3,844 tooling machines, the total losses to Poland being placed at ten billion gold francs. Before leaving Poland at the end of the war, the Austro-German armies blew up 7,500 bridges, and destroyed 940 railway stations.[43]

The human loss beggars description in terms of homeless refugees, starving children, families ravaged by typhus and other diseases. Except for the remarkable staying power of the Polish people, and for relief extended by the United

[43] Dr. Roman Górecki: *Poland and Her Economic Development* (London: George Allen & Unwin; 1935), p. 21; Aulneau, op. cit., p. 559.

States,[44] Communism might easily have triumphed during this early period.

Although the food situation was soon remedied, the financial distress of the government continued — partly owing to the cost of the Russian war. The country suffered a series of inflations. So serious was the financial problem, and so difficult was it for the political parties to reach agreement, that many voices predicted that the new Polish Republic would disappear — as had happened once before.

The magnitude of the task of reconstruction was increased by the problem of unifying the economic and monetary systems which had arisen during the nineteenth century. Before the World War about eighty-five per cent of the trade of Poland had been with the three empires of continental Europe. As a result of independence, Poland lost a large part of this internal market and had to look elsewhere. The task of unifying and amalgamating three different systems of foreign law, and of reducing the legal codes to the Polish language, was formidable, as was the task of unifying several types of social insurance and methods of public administration.[45] During the post-war period Poland has created a unified system of administration manned by a civil service. It has also equipped the country with a single system of roads, railways, posts, and telegraphic communication. It has established a stable currency system, and built an imposing port at Gdynia. That Poland

[44] For a standard history, cf. H. H. Fisher: *America and the New Poland* (New York: The Macmillan Company; 1928), pp. 161 ff.

[45] Cf. *La Politique Sociale de Pologne, 1918–1936* (Warsaw: Ministère de l'Assistance Sociale; 1936), p. 81. Russia had no system of social service, in contrast to Germany, which had an advanced system. This task is not quite complete even today. Thus, there is no marriage code. Cf. *Poland's New Codes of Law* (Birmingham University Information Service on Slavonic Countries, Monograph No. 3, 1937).

has been able to surmount these formidable post-war difficulties, establish a solid basis of existence, fix many contro-
versial frontiers, and maintain its political independence is
an achievement of importance. The gradual elimination of
the divisive psychologies which arose among the three parts
of Poland during the Captivity is producing a new nation.
Great diversity still remains in both the intellectual and the
economic sphere. The comparatively prosperous peasant
of Poznań stands far above the illiterate and poverty-
stricken inhabitant of Volhynia; while the wages of Katowice are considerably higher than in Łódż. Most striking of
all is the persistence of wide social cleavage. Nevertheless,
as a result of a common economic policy, the school and university system, and military conscription, a new national
unity is being forged.

CHAPTER IV

✧

THE POLITICAL SYSTEM

1. Organizing a Government

WHILE Poland was busy fighting the Battle of the Frontiers, it also had to organize its internal political life. One of the first acts of the Moraczewski government appointed by Piłsudski was to proclaim, on November 28, 1918, an extremely liberal electoral law providing suffrage for both sexes on the basis of proportional representation. January 26, 1919 was the date fixed for holding elections to the Chamber of Deputies, or Sejm as the House is traditionally called in Poland. In Eastern Galicia an election was impossible because of the conflict with the Ukrainians, so the former deputies from that province to the Austrian Reichsrat were made members of the Constituent Sejm by appointment. The province of Poznań did not send representatives to Warsaw until after the conclusion of the Versailles Treaty.

The Sejm, which convened in the winter of 1919, had authority to frame a constitution. Opening its doors on

February 10, 1919, the first Polish Parliament since the end of the eighteenth century, and the first chamber in a thousand years of national history to be based on popular elections, was almost equally divided between Right and Left parties. A candidate of the Right, M. A. Trąpczyński, dominated by the National Democrats of Dmowski, was elected Marshal or Speaker of the Sejm by a majority of only six votes over the peasant leader, Witos, candidate of the Left. The National Democrats, traditional opponents of Piłsudski, had thus the greatest influence in the Sejm, but no group had a majority. As a result of proportional representation, past cleavages within Polish political life and traditional individualism, the Sejm consisted of a large number of passionate, disparate groups, each struggling for immediate advantages. Even among those who fought for Polish independence, a deep cleavage existed between the groups who fought under Piłsudski against Russia and those who fought under General Haller with France against the Central Powers. Thus, from the very beginning of independence, a paradoxical situation developed in Poland. The Right, convinced that Piłsudski would be the next President, sought to limit the powers of the executive as much as possible; the Left advocated a better balance between the legislative and the executive. On constitutional issues the Right was successful in imposing its views. The so-called "Little Constitution" of February 20, 1919 went out of its way to elevate the power of the Sejm at the expense of the executive.

Although the Sejm was called chiefly to formulate a constitution, the subject was not seriously considered until the war with the Soviet Union was over. The discussions then assumed a passionate tone. There was a general understanding among the parties that a Parliamentary democratic régime should be established, but harsh debates took place between Right and Left over the question whether Poland should have a Senate in addition to a lower Chamber, and whether the Chief of State should also be commander-in-chief of the army. A wide difference of opinion also existed on the methods to be employed in elections, and the powers to be granted the President of the Republic. Except for the question of the Senate, all these issues were regarded by the parties in terms of personalities, for or against Piłsudski, rather than as basic principles.

In March 1921 the Sejm finally adopted a constitution that, except for the role and the powers of the Senate, resembled that of the French Republic in severely limiting the executive. The Senate was given the right to revise the acts of the Sejm, but a majority of the Sejm could overrule the Senate. The Sejm could not be dissolved by the President without the consent of three fifths of the Senate. Then the Senate would also be automatically dissolved.[1] The President could command the army in time of peace, but not in time of war. The constitution was to be periodically revised every twenty-five years.[2]

Owing to these initial dissensions, the constitution was not accorded the veneration that the American constitution, for example, has enjoyed in the United States. An important element of symbolic unity was therefore lacking. At best, the workings of democracy are difficult under modern conditions, but Poland adopted the trappings of the most advanced democratic institutions without the experience of unity or discipline necessary for their success.

Piłsudski, irritated by these signs of lack of confidence at

[1] In the French constitution the President has the right to dissolve the Chamber of Deputies if the Senate, by a simple majority, gives its consent. The French Senate can never be dissolved.

[2] For the English text of the constitution, cf. *The Polish Handbook, 1925*, pp. 13 ff.

the very time when he was fighting the war with Russia, and by a protracted struggle with the Sejm over the right of nominating cabinets, announced after the general elections of 1922 that, while he was ready to remain head of the army, he would not be a candidate for the position of President of the Republic. The constitution, in his opinion, did not give the President adequate powers. The National Assembly, consisting of the Sejm and Senate sitting together, elected as his successor Gabriel Narutowicz. His election was due to a coalition of the Centre and Left parties with the minorities, which infuriated the Right. Almost immediately the new President was assassinated by a Right fanatic — the first crime of its sort in the history of Poland.[3] The assassination deeply shocked the country, which now realized the depths to which partisan strife had descended. Fierce controversies, however, continued, in which the Peasant party swayed from Left to Right. No agreement among the parties could be reached over financial and agrarian questions. Following the formation of a second government by Witos, which brought the Right-Centre to power, Piłsudski resigned as chief of staff of the army in May 1923 and returned to private life.

2. The 1926 Coup d'État

In May 1926, however, Witos returned to form a third Cabinet, in which an anti-Piłsudski general was appointed as Minister of War. At this Piłsudski revolted. Accusing Witos of corruption, he marched on Warsaw with three regiments, and was supported with reinforcements from Vilna, led by his close friend General Rydz-Śmigły. After three days of street fighting, Piłsudski forced President

[3] Cf. Machray: *Poland, 1914–1931*, p. 242.

Wojciechowski and Prime Minister Witos to resign. Troops from Poznań, who remained loyal to the government, failed to arrive in time to save it. The Polish Republic, as created under the 1921 constitution, virtually came to an end on May 14, 1926, when Rataj, Marshal of the Sejm, became Acting President. During this period eighty parties existed and fourteen cabinets struggled for power.

Piłsudski's *coup d'état* was inspired less by personal ambition than by a belief that Poland was drifting back to the anarchy that had preceded the Partitions. What made matters worse was that, during the nineteenth century, Poles had become hostile to all government, and carried over into the republic habits of conspiracy and intrigue they had developed in resisting their oppressors. The most severe critics of the republican régime were the Poles themselves. Thugutt, leader of the Radical Peasant party, declared: " In Poland everybody desires to be in the Opposition, but nobody is willing to take responsibility. Poland cannot prosper by criticism alone." Piłsudski declared: " Poland is the victim of her Parliamentary system. The Government loses nine tenths of its force from the pacts made with party groups who, however, support a Minister only so long as he fulfills the requests of the deputies." Later he called the Sejm " a sterile, jabbering, howling thing that engenders such boredom as makes the very flies die of sheer disgust," and declared it was like a " locomotive drawing a pin." [4]

It is possible that Piłsudski might have found a less drastic solution than the *coup d'état*. The fact remains that the disorders of Polish Parliamentary life gave him the opportunity of imposing his own solution. Both the Peasant and the Socialist parties were partly responsible for the chaos

[4] Ibid., pp. 280, 359, 321.

that had arisen. The Socialists openly supported the *coup d'état* of 1926 by proclaiming a general strike. The peasants, who were divided into three factions, had since the beginning of the republic oscillated between Left and Right, failing to perform the function of stabilization which should be the role of a Centre party; while its leader, Witos, intrigued with the anti-Piłsudski element within the army.[5]

Immediately after the *coup d'état* of May 1926 Piłsudski, while declining to become prime minister, agreed to serve as Minister of War in the newly appointed Bartel Cabinet. A few days later the National Assembly elected Piłsudski President, but, to the surprise of the country, he declined the honour. In a letter to the National Assembly he explained that he could not accept the Presidency because " the role in Poland of the President of the Republic, withdrawn by the constitution from all direct participation in the affairs of state, demands a character other than mine." It is interesting to note that this time Piłsudski did not, as in 1922, decline in advance to be a candidate. On the contrary, he let the National Assembly elect him President, while refusing the office, to demonstrate that the majority of the nation approved his *coup d'état* and considered his election as an act legalizing his " historic work."

[5] " From 1922 to 1926 the Sejm had alternated between non-parliamentary ministries and those founded upon an alliance of the Centre and the Right. Usually Witos had sold the support of his peasant (Piast) party for a price at the time of the formation of a new cabinet. Throughout, the Left had been ignored or poorly treated. The result was a continuous disintegration of the small groups on the moderate fringe and the increase of radically minded cliques." M. W. Graham: *New Governments of Eastern Europe* (New York: Henry Holt & Company; 1927), p. 522. It might also be pointed out that in May 1923 the Witos peasant group, who had supported the Sikorski government, which rested on a coalition of the Left parties with the National Minorities, overthrew it, and Witos became Prime Minister with support from the nationalists. Machray, op. cit., p. 253.

This tendency toward formal observance of the letter, if not the spirit, of the democratic constitution is one of the most amazing characteristics of the Piłsudski régime. The *coup d'état* having proved successful, Piłsudski sought legalization of his revolt by the very authorities against which it was directed. He maintained democratic machinery and did not commit any outright illegal act. In practice, he dominated the political life of the country but did not abolish Parliamentary bodies. As a result, a certain freedom of opinion remained, allowing the existence of opposition parties and an opposition press.

While Piłsudski refused to accept the Presidency for himself, at his suggestion the Assembly elected Ignacy Mościcki, a prominent scientist and industrialist who was a professor in the Engineering School of Lwów. In May 1933 Mościcki was elected for a second term, expiring in 1940. Piłsudski became Inspector-General of the army, in addition to being Minister of War, on the understanding that his authority over the army be made definitive.

Although the 1921 constitution continued in force on paper, a constitutional law of August 2, 1926 gave the President power to dissolve the Diet and Senate and, in certain cases, to issue decrees having the force of law. It also authorized the President to put the budget into effect if the Diet had not approved it by a certain date. A Presidential decree of August 7, 1926 removed anti-Piłsudski and " political " officers from the army, and provided that the Inspector-General would be commander-in-chief in time of war. In October 1926 Piłsudski became Prime Minister, while retaining the war portfolio.

Although the *coup d'état* at first restored business confidence, Piłsudski continued to have difficulties with the Sejm. The Socialists had expected the new Piłsudski régime would be followed by the establishment of a "government of workers and peasants." But Piłsudski took a strongly conservative stand on financial and economic matters, and the Left deserted him. Unable to count on the National Democrats or the peasants, the Marshal decided to organize a "non-party government bloc" composed of representatives of disparate groups, ranging from the Legionnaires — war-time followers of Piłsudski — to a part of the conservatives. This bloc was headed in the Sejm by Colonel Sławek. Partly as a result of administrative pressure, the government bloc won the elections of 1928, at the expense of the Right and Centre, but failed to receive an absolute majority. In June 1928, following refusal of the Sejm to accept his candidate for Marshal, Piłsudski resigned abruptly as Prime Minister. In an interview he brutally attacked the Sejm, saying he preferred to resign rather than co-operate with the President in "imposing" new institutions on the country. But he warned that, in case of "grave crisis," he would put himself at the disposal of the President and "boldly" take responsibility. The whole country feared a new *coup d'état*.

The next two years witnessed a constant fight between the government and Parliament. The Marshal of the Sejm, Daszyński, Socialist leader and old friend of Piłsudski, headed the Parliamentary opposition against the authoritarian régime. Four Cabinets were overthrown, the government press decree introducing strict censorship was repealed, and the draft of a constitution strengthening the executive, which had been introduced by Colonel Sławek in the name of the non-party bloc, seemed to have no chance of being approved by Parliament. The climax of the struggle between the executive and the legislative came when the Centrist and Leftist parties united in the *Centro-*

lew to fight the régime and to bring about a really democratic system of government. At the Cracow Congress of June 29, 1930, attended by over 30,000 people, Polish democratic forces, in a unanimous resolution, demanded the end of the existing dictatorship, attacked the Marshal, and called for the resignation of President Mościcki.

The régime promptly answered this challenge. Parliament was dissolved by the President and in August 1930 Piłsudski became Prime Minister while continuing to hold the office of Minister of War. This time a new figure, Colonel Beck — who was a close friend of Piłsudski — entered the Cabinet as Minister without Portfolio. Determined to establish his authority over Parliament, Piłsudski employed strong administrative pressure to obtain an unquestioned majority for the government bloc in the 1930 fall elections. The issue of these elections was simply " either with or against Piłsudski." Several months before the actual voting he imprisoned several prominent deputies, including Witos, in Brest-Litovsk, where it is alleged they were tortured. Subsequently a number were convicted of revolutionary activity, and Witos, among others, was sentenced to eighteen months in prison. He succeeded, however, in making his escape. Although the government subsequently amnestied most of these political prisoners, it pardoned Witos only in March 1939, after the annexation of Czechoslovakia by Hitler. The amnesty of Witos should facilitate an understanding between the peasants and the government.

As a result of the severe measures of 1930, the nonparty bloc received about twice as many votes as it had in the previous election, but still lacked the two-thirds majority necessary to adopt a new constitution. The government's victory was most complete in the eastern provinces — the national minorities losing forty seats; and the Centre-Left coalition, which had arisen to oppose Piłsudski, also lost votes.

Shortly after the 1930 elections Piłsudski resigned as Prime Minister. On leaving for a rest in Madeira, he re-iterated his belief that Poland needed a new constitution to overcome the original distrust shown toward the executive. Meanwhile Parliament was distracted by the trial of the arrested deputies, the "pacification" campaign in Galicia, and strained foreign relations. These developments, together with the lack of a two-thirds majority for the government, prevented the Sejm from taking action on the constitutional question. But with 247 of the 444 seats in the Sejm and 74 of the 111 seats in the Senate held by the non-party bloc, the government had a subservient Parliament ready to accept everything it proposed without any real opposition. The elections of 1930 really marked the end of the Parliamentary régime in Poland and the disappearance of an independent legislature. Piłsudski became absolute master of the country, and, while the opposition parties still had representatives in Parliament, these were powerless. The *Centrolew* and the National Democrats both strongly opposed the dictatorship and demanded restoration of the rights of Parliament — but all in vain.

In the evening of January 26, 1934 the government parties, taking advantage of the temporary absence of the opposition from the floor of the Sejm, hastily adopted the proposed constitution. Although the Senate adjourned without taking action, the constitution was finally approved by it in January 1935 and went into effect on April 23, 1935.

The constitution, which gave Poland what was called an "authoritarian" democracy, was designed to provide a legal framework for Piłsudski's rule, and generally to

strengthen the executive power. But on May 12, 1935 Piłsudski, who had been seriously ill for some time, died amid
universal mourning. Following four days of funeral cere-
monies, he was buried with great pomp in Cracow. Even
his opponents acknowledged that he had served Poland
well. His régime probably prevented the growth of anarchy, which might have invited foreign intervention, and
ended the "mania of conspiracy" which had plagued Poland in the past; it improved public administration and
finance; furthered the unification of the three divisions
of the country; greatly strengthened the army; and made
peace with Germany. In tolerating the existence of Parliament after the *coup d'état* of 1926 and in consenting to
long delays in the formulation of a new constitution, Piłsudski displayed a patience lacking in authoritarian chiefs
of other states. He unified various factions without under-
mining traditional Polish values and without completely
destroying liberty. Poland thereby avoided paying the
price exacted by the German and the Italian dictatorial
régimes.

Following Piłsudski's death, the disparate elements of his
" dictatorship " continued in Poland, without the unifying
personality who had cemented them together. Poland is
one country in post-war Europe which has completed its
Great Man cycle. It overthrew Parliamentary democracy
in favour of the Leader; but the Leader disappeared, and
there is no one to take his place. His régime was a personal
régime; it did not found a system. In this respect it again
differed from the totalitarianism in other European countries, but this very difference increases the difficulty of
perpetuating the Piłsudski tradition.

Following the Marshal's death, President Mościcki announced that, in conformity with Piłsudski's desire, Gen-

eral Rydz-Śmigły had been named Inspector-General of the army. The *Gazeta Polska* reported that, immediately after the death of Marshal Piłsudski, a circle of his friends and collaborators was formed and held conferences at the Warsaw Château.[6] This group consisted largely of Colonels who had fought with the Piłsudski Legionnaires, the most conspicuous of whom were Beck and Sławek. It decided that the régime should go on, but in an even more totalitarian form than Piłsudski had intended. Although the 1935 constitution greatly reduced the powers of the Sejm, it still provided that its members should be elected by universal suffrage. One of the first acts of the Colonels' group was to have the Sejm enact the electoral laws of July 1935 that reduced the size of the Sejm by half, deprived political parties of the right of nominating candidates, and gave it to special electoral colleges. Each college, presided over by a government commissioner, included delegates from the local and municipal councils, the chambers of commerce and industry, and other professional organizations — and was in fact controlled by the government. The rank and file of the population were excluded to an even greater degree from voting for the Senate by the electoral law of July 8, 1935, which gave the right to vote for two thirds of the members of this body to a list of distinguished citizens, such as those who had received certain decorations and held certain educational degrees, including some local officials.[7]

The ostensible purpose of these new electoral laws was to abolish parties, eliminate professional politicians, and give Poland a non-political Parliament. In November 1935

[6] V. Fiala: *La Pologne d'Aujourd'hui* (Paris: Paul Hartmann; 1936), p. 193.
[7] The other third is appointed by the President. This system might be compared with the Italian Senate.

Prime Minister Sławek went so far as to dissolve the non-party government bloc, explaining that, as a result of the new constitution, there was no longer any need of an " organization of a political character intervening between the Parliament and the country."

The general public did not view the matter in this light. To them it was clear that the non-party Parliament envisaged by the Colonels was simply composed of hand-picked deputies. For, in fact, the local government commissioners would control all nominations. Declaring that the electoral laws violated the provisions of the new constitution guaranteeing universal, secret, equal, and direct suffrage, the opposition boycotted the elections of the fall of 1935. Although nearly 75 per cent of the voters had participated in the 1930 elections, only 46.5 per cent did so in the " dead elections," according to official statistics,[8] while the opposition contended that less than 35 per cent actually voted.

If Sławek and the other Colonels had intended to establish a totalitarian state, the results of the 1935 elections showed they lacked the popular support to effect such a policy. Following the elections, the peasants and workers particularly denounced the totalitarian tendency of the régime. While the country venerated the memory of Piłsudski, it did not respect either his régime or his associates.

3. The Present Constitutional System

The Polish government today is based on the constitution of April 23, 1935.[9] According to the official commen-

---

[8] *Statistical Year-Book, 1937*, p. 313.
[9] Cf. *Constitution of the Republic of Poland* (April 23, 1935), preface by Stanisław Car, General Rapporteur, Sejm Commission on the Constitu-

tary, this constitution represents a return to the old Polish
"state and national traditions," readapted to meet modern
times. But the new constitution certainly has little in common with that of 1791.[10] Rejecting the individualist ideology of the French Revolution, the 1935 constitution declares that "the Polish state is the commonweal of all its
citizens. . . . Resurrected by the efforts and sacrifices of
its worthiest sons it is to be a bequest — an historic heritage
from generation to generation. It is the duty of each generation to increase the power and authority of the state by
its own efforts." While admitting that the 1935 constitution is not an expression of liberalism, commentators
deny that it represents the totalitarian philosophy, since
Article 5, for example, declares that the "creative action
of the individual is the lever of collective life." They insist that the constitution is based on the principle of the
"solidarity of the élite."[11]

The constitution recognizes the élite principle by elevat-
ing the power of the President, who is now called the
"superordinate factor which co-ordinates the activities of
the supreme organs of state," and by creating a Senate
elected by a distinguished but exclusive voting list. In practice, however, the Polish constitutional system does not appear to have brought into power an "élite" differing from
the ordinary type of politician who has dominated Polish
public life in the past. Indeed, as the late Premier, M.
Władysław Grabski, pointed out, the Colonels have merely

---

tion, together with an outline of legislation of Presidential and Parliamentary elections by Michael Potulicki (Warsaw: Polish Commission for
International Law Co-operation, 1935).

[10] Cf. p. 47.

[11] Cf. Antoine Peretiatkowicz: "La Déclaration Constitutionelle de
Pologne de 1935," *Archives de Philosophie du droit et de sociologie
juridique*, No. 304, 1937.

developed a spirit similar to that of the former gentry —
" We are Poland." [12]

Although the 1921 constitution provided that the President should be elected jointly by the Sejm and Senate,
sitting in the National Assembly, the new constitution re-
moves the election one step from this jurisdiction. It provides that the President shall be chosen by an electoral
college, composed of the highest officials, and seventy-five
electors, two thirds chosen by the Sejm and one third by
the Senate. While this Assembly makes its own nomina-
tion for the Presidency, the novel feature of the 1935 constitution is that it also gives the Presidential incumbent the
right to nominate a candidate. If the President and the
Assembly cannot agree on a successor, the decision as between the two candidates is to be settled by a referendum.
According to the law of July 8, 1935 concerning the election of the President, all citizens, regardless of sex, aged
twenty-four or over and possessed of the right of active
suffrage to the Sejm can participate in this referendum.
While these provisions have not been put to a test, it seems
clear that they increase the influence of the existing administration over the choice of its successor. This is particularly true as long as both houses of Parliament are under
administrative domination.

In addition, the President has a suspensive veto over
legislation and, when the Sejm is not in session, may issue
decrees having the force of law, with the exception of (a)
amendments to the constitution, (b) laws concerning the
elections of the Sejm and Senate, (c) the budget, (d) taxes,
(e) the monetary system, (f) the issue of state loans, (g) the
disposal and mortgaging of state real estate of more than

[12] Władysław Grabski: *Idea Polski* (*The Idea of Poland*), (Warsaw, 1936).

100,000 zlotys. He may issue decrees at any time concerning the organization of the government, the administration, and the supreme command of the armed forces.[13]

Moreover, if the Parliament has not passed the budget within ninety days, the government may promulgate its own draft; and in the event of any emergency the Council of Ministers may make an expenditure not authorized by law, provided it is submitted to the Sejm within seven days. During a state of war the President has virtually unlimited power, and in case of internal disturbance the Council of Ministers may declare a state of emergency, suspending civil liberties. Thus the Polish President has far greater powers than the President of the United States, and is not subject to the independent criticism of the opposition as in America.

Under the 1935 constitution the Polish Parliament continues in existence and has a certain number of powers. The Sejm votes the budget and imposes taxes, and may demand the resignation of the Cabinet or any Minister. If the President does not dismiss the Cabinet, the question shall be examined by the Senate at its nearest session; and if the Senate agrees with the Sejm, the President must dismiss the Cabinet or dissolve Parliament. The Sejm is elected for a term of five years by the method above described; in the Senate, also elected for five years, two thirds of the members are elected and one third are appointed by the President.

Although Parliament retains certain shadowy controls over the executive, the composition of Parliament under the electoral laws of July 1935 is largely determined by the

[13] Actually, the executive power of the President is shared with the "second citizen" of the Republic, Marshal Rydz-Śmigły, a duality which does not seem to exist in any other modern constitution.

administration. Whether Poland becomes a totalitarian state
or remains an "authoritarian democracy" depends less on
the safeguards erected in the constitution of April 1935
than on the personality of the governing group, who in
turn are influenced by underlying political conditions.

The people have had little more control over local and
provincial government than over Parliament. In July 1920
the Polish Parliament, no doubt wishing to influence the voting in the forthcoming plebiscite, approved a statute con-
ferring autonomy on whatever part of Upper Silesia was
finally given to Poland.[14] Wide powers of self-government
were conferred, and the use of both German and Polish
guaranteed. While a governor was to be appointed from
Warsaw, he was to administer the province subject to a
broad grant of legislative power to a provincial Diet.[15]
Again desiring to obtain Allied consent for the annexation of
Eastern Galicia, the Polish Parliament in 1922 passed a
law accepting the principle of autonomy for Poland's sixteen provinces (województwa), and a particularly wide
form of autonomy for the provinces of Lwów, Tarnopol,
and Stanislawów; but in practice the law was not applied,
and the precedent established for Upper Silesia was not
even extended to the Ukrainian portions of Eastern Galicia.[16]

Today each province is headed by a governor (wo-
jewoda) responsible to the Minister of Interior. These governors, as well as the prefects mentioned below, are political
appointees and have wide influence. The province lacks
any legislative body, although the governor must consult
an advisory board containing representatives elected by

[14] For text of the law of May 15, 1920, cf. B. Mirkine-Guetzevitch:
La Pologne (Paris: Delagrave; 1930), p. 65.
[15] Cf. W. J. Rose: *The Drama of Upper Silesia*, p. 205.
[16] Cf. p. 273.

local self-governing groups. While occasional provincial governors, such as M. Graziński in Upper Silesia, show considerable independence of Warsaw, the local inhabitants have very little to say about provincial government.

In the eighty counties into which Poland is divided, the administrative system is somewhat the same. The Minister of Interior appoints a prefect (*starosta*) as head of each county, who is responsible to the governor concerned. Each county has an advisory board, but there is no popularly elected legislative body. Each of the three thousand communes, however, has a legislative council of between twelve and thirty members, who are elected by direct and universal suffrage and in accordance with the principles of proportional representation.[17] These councils in turn select a mayor and vice-mayor, but the prefect has a veto over such choices, which is from time to time exercised, and he may dissolve the council at pleasure. In the city communes the councils are somewhat larger, and the cities are divided into electoral districts of three thousand inhabitants each. The capital of Warsaw is regarded as a province governed by the central government, while commissioners appointed from Warsaw have served as mayors in Łódź and Lwów. Thus, while the principle of election has been technically preserved for members of Parliament on the one hand, and city councils on the other, in fact these elected bodies enjoy no real independent existence, let alone controlling administrative authority.[18]

It would be hardly correct, however, to say that Poland

[17] For the 1938 change, cf. p. 115.
[18] That the actual work of these local bodies is not unimportant is shown by the fact that the total expenditures of the communes and provinces in 1937–8 amounted to 729,000,000 zlotys, or about a third of the national budget. Cf. *Petit Annuaire, 1938*, p. 379. In addition, the Silesia Treasury has its separate funds.

is a totalitarian state in law or in fact. While a Parliament
dominated by one party exists, opposition parties continue
to carry on propaganda and hold meetings. Opposition
newspapers continue to be published, and university professors enjoy considerable freedom.

On the other hand, the Communist party and allied organizations are illegal, and in an address of April 1937
General Składkowski said: "We are ready to declare war
to the death on Communism." Under a Presidential decree
of June 17, 1934,[19] administrative authorities may detain
without a court order any person who menaces peace and
public order. Thus the government may resort to "protective custody" — which is a feature of totalitarian régimes — and has used this power to place such offenders
in the concentration camp at Bereza. Civil liberties cannot
be said to exist when government has such sweeping powers. The government radio can be used only by supporters
of the régime. A further example of the lack of civil liberty
may be found in the case of an instructor (*docent*) in the
University of Vilna who was sent to jail for three years
(a sentence later reduced to a year and a half) for publishing an article calling Piłsudski a "strolling player."

Poland has no preventive censorship; but when an article displeasing to the authorities is published, they may
confiscate the issue concerned, inflicting severe financial
losses on the paper. Thus all mention in the Polish press
of the peasant strike of August 1937 was censored. It often
happens than an article not censored in one city is censored
when reprinted elsewhere. A newspaper can appeal to the
courts against illegal confiscations, but tribunals seldom
overrule the administrative authorities or, if they do, it
is too late to be of practical value. After having its issues

[19] *Journal of Laws,* No. 50, item 473.

periodically confiscated, *Słowo*, a leading conservative newspaper in Vilna, recently wrote: " In respect to the press, we have a system here which is the equivalent of that found only in the totalitarian states. But in the totalitarian Reich, a Hitler liquidates unemployment, constructs auto roads, and realizes economic autarchy. In Italy, a Mussolini conquers Abyssinia, enriches Libya, and infuses life in the peninsula. The totalitarianism applied to us is limited to the seizure of newspapers and nothing more." While this no doubt is an exaggerated statement, it seems clear that, as a result of recurrent censorship, Polish newspapers can hardly reflect frank public opinion.

4. *Political Parties Today*

While the 1935 electoral laws curbed political parties, the old groupings continue to exist. The government is making an effort to hold together the followers of Piłsudski in an organization called the Camp of National Unity. While numerically strong, the opposition to the government is as divided as ever. The multiplicity of political groups is due to historical development and the individualism of the Polish character. The division of Poland before the war into three diverse areas produced political groups, each with particular objectives and points of view, that continued to exist after the restoration. Factionalism within each party, even more than multiplicity of parties, was responsible for the destruction of the Parliamentary system in 1926. The very fact that the parties no longer had the immediate prospect of holding office after 1930 purged them of many opportunistic elements, and gave them a new chance of improving their cohesion on a basis of principles. Thus the various warring factions united in the Peasant party, and that group abandoned many of the opportunist tendencies which had characterized it before 1926.

The Peasant party today has taken a stand in favour of democracy and civil rights, which it seems to believe are more important than material improvement. The recognized leader of the party is Wincenty Witos. Although Witos is still in exile, he is ably represented in Poland by leaders such as the former Marshal of the Sejm, M. Rataj, and Professor Kot of the University of Cracow, who know how to organize the villages. Largely because of their efforts, the present government has been unable to make headway with the peasant masses, despite emphasis on agrarian reform.[20] The peasants constitute the majority of the country, and although no one can tell to what extent they follow the leadership of the Peasant party, it seems clear that this party is stronger than ever and is the largest in the country. The Peasant party has had a pro-French orientation, has supported collective security, and has advocated a common policy for all democratic countries, including an understanding with Czechoslovakia.

To the Left of the Peasant party is the Polish Socialist party (P.P.S.), which has great influence among city workers. The late Marshal Piłsudski belonged to this party before the war, as did many of the important leaders of the present régime. The Polish Socialist party was always more nationalist than Socialist parties in other countries and, before the war, emphasized the fight for Polish independence rather than Socialism. Socialists who believed that social revolution was more important than independence refused to join the P.P.S. and instead adhered to the Russian Social Democratic Federation, the Polish section of which was led by Rosa Luxemburg. From its beginning in

[20] Cf. p. 209.

1892, the Polish Socialist party was the most active and determined group working for Polish independence.

Although the Socialist party helped the Piłsudski *coup d'état* in 1926,[21] it soon joined the opposition when it became clear that Piłsudski had shifted his allegiance to the conservatives. Many members of the party, however, were so loyal to Piłsudski — notably the first Prime Minister, M. Moraczewski — that they broke with the party. The Socialists were weakened by these defections. Having helped in the *coup d'état*, they could not now effectively oppose the Piłsudski dictatorship. The creation of pro-government labour unions,[22] and the reorganization of the government health-insurance bureaus so as to eliminate an important source of patronage, again weakened the party. Nevertheless, between 1928 and 1930, when the struggle between the régime and Parliament was at its height, a great Socialist leader, Marshal Daszyński, became the symbol of the fight for democracy. Piłsudski won the fight and after the imprisonments at Brest the party remained quiescent as long as Piłsudski dominated the country. But with Piłsudski's death in May 1935, the Polish Socialist party displayed new activity. It collaborated closely with the Peasant party in the advocacy of political reforms. In view of the fact that the great majority of voters in Poland live in villages, the Polish Socialist party alone is not likely to obtain power; but it might become an important factor in a Parliament based on free elections.

In recent years several new groups have arisen which strengthen the trend toward democracy. The Democratic

[21] The appeal of the P.P.S. calling a general strike in support of Piłsudski on May 14, 1926; Graham, op. cit., p. 792.

[22] Union of Trade Unions (Z.Z.Z.), which, according to official statistics (*Annuaire*, p. 272), had in 1935 about half of the membership of the Socialist unions.

Club, under the leadership of Professor Michałowicz of Warsaw, is an organization of liberal and democratic intellectuals. While the club does not represent large masses, it unites in one group intellectuals who play an important role in the social and intellectual life of the country. In October 1937 a new political party, called the Polish Labour party, was formed under the leadership of Ignace Paderewski and General Joseph Haller. This group opposes totalitarian ideas and "government by an élite."[23] The Polish Labour party has many generals, but few followers. Not to be confused with labour groups in other countries, it is nationalistic, Catholic, and anti-Semitic. While co-operation between this group and the Socialists or Peasants seems unlikely, the Labour party contains personalities capable of leading mass movements. The opposition groups of the Centre and Left that favour the democratic system and oppose the élite régime can usually count on the support of most of the political parties into which the national minorities are organized.[24]

While these parties stand to the Left of the government, equally strong opposition elements are found on the Right, the most important of which are the National Democrats, or *Endeks*. Organized at the end of the nineteenth century by Roman Dmowski, the National Democratic party represents the Polish anti-Semitic middle class, particularly the urban white collar and professional groups, containing a large number of intellectuals. Socially conservative, the program of the party calls for a nationalistic type of state, and opposes all autonomy for the national minorities in favour of assimilation,[25] except for the Jews. During the

[23] Letter of Paderewski to the first congress of the party on October 10, 1937.
[24] Cf. pp. 275, 298.
[25] Alicja Bełcikowska: *Stonnictwa i związki polityczne (Political Par-*

108   POLAND: KEY TO EUROPE

World War the National Democrats followed a pro-Russian and pro-Entente policy in contrast to Piłsudski, who fought against Russia. Dmowski was Piłsudski's greatest foe, even before the World War, and there was a saying that he passed his time following Piłsudski in order to undo what he did. It was this cleavage between the Piłsudskists and the National Democrats that was largely responsible for the downfall of the Parliamentary régime in 1926. Despite Piłsudski's victory at that time, the National Democrats remained an important social and political group, having to a large extent the support of the Catholic Church and a considerable part of the middle class. Although the non-party bloc made minor inroads, the *Endeks* lost comparatively little ground before 1934.

The universities became a centre of *Endek* influence, and anti-Semitic student riots served as the party's major weapon against the Piłsudski régime. But as Dmowski [26] grew older and the party failed to develop vigorous leaders, dissensions arose. In 1934 the younger elements, partly inspired by Nazi Germany, broke away and formed a frankly Fascist group, which called itself the National Radicals or *Naras*. As a result of terrorist activities, this group was dissolved by the police and its newpapers suspended. After Piłsudski's death, *Nara* activities, now illegal, steadily increased. The Fascist elements in Poland, however, were split into several factions, largely because of personal reasons. On February 7, 1937, representatives of different *Nara* groups agreed to a common program, recognizing the leadership of M. Bolesław Piasecki. The program called

---

ties and Groups), (Warsaw, 1927); also Marjan Gregorczyk: *Stronnictwa w Sejmie i Senacie (Parties in the Sejm and Senate)* (Warsaw, 1928).

[26] He died in January 1939.

for a national revolution, a totalitarian régime on the Nazi model, a national state, and assimilation of the Slavic national minorities. The Jews were to be expelled from Poland. Until their expulsion they were to be refused all civil rights, and their fortunes were to be confiscated. Leading industries were to be nationalized, but peasant ownership and small independent businesses were to be encouraged.[27]

The strength of the *Naras* and other Fascist factions lies mainly in the city youth, especially the university students. As yet the Fascists have failed to develop an outstanding personality with a popular appeal. The Polish Fascists, lacking a private army, are also handicapped by the fact that the régime against which they fight is already undemocratic and is led by army men, rather than by " opportunistic politicians." Thus they are deprived of many of the issues which brought Fascists to power in other countries. Although the *Naras* can concentrate on the anti-Semitic issue, they are not likely to win the support of the peasants and city workers on this issue alone — a support they need if they are to achieve power.

5. *The Struggle to Maintain the Piłsudski System*

Following the failure of the government to obtain real support in the " dead elections " of 1935, President Mościcki actively intervened for the first time in his career and asked Sławek to resign. M. Kościałkowski, a liberal who was not a member of the Colonels' group, was invited in October 1935 to organize a Cabinet, popularly known as

[27] Cf. p. 187. Bolesław Piasecki: *Przełom Narodowy: Zasady programu Narodowo-Radykalnego* (*National Revolution: Principles of the National Radical Program*). For the efforts of the Camp of National Unity to come to terms with the *Naras*, cf. p. 114.

the "first Cabinet of the President of the Republic," and containing only one member of the Colonels' group, M. Beck. This Cabinet included a number of figures such as M. Kwiatkowski, Minister of Finance and Vice-Premier, who realized the necessity of effecting fundamental economic reforms. The new Prime Minister endeavoured to come to terms with the Left; but his efforts met with opposition from the Colonels' group, and came at a time when the economic crisis was at its worst. A number of serious riots and strikes in eastern Poland took place; and although the Kościałkowski government put through a number of stern economic measures,[28] it was not strong enough to overcome the opposition of the Colonels and win the support of the peasants. As a result, the Cabinet resigned on May 15, 1936. For the first time, Rydz-Śmigły took an active part in the political life of the country;[29] and General Składkowski, who as Minister of the Interior had repressed the Ukrainian movement in 1930, became Prime Minister. Included in the Cabinet were two generals (one of them being the Prime Minister) and three colonels. In July the Prime Minister decreed that General Rydz-Śmigły should be honoured "as the first person in Poland after the President of the Republic," although there was nothing in the constitution to justify this position. On November 11 General Rydz-Śmigły was made a Marshal. By bestowing the mantle of Piłsudski on Rydz-Śmigły, the Colonels increased the general confusion regarding the nature of the executive power. Meanwhile the policy of the new Cabinet had been stated by Rydz-Śmigły in an address of May 24 in which he said: "It is absolutely necessary that the entire eco-

[28] Cf. p. 130 ff.
[29] Simon Segal: *The New Poland and the Jews* (New York: Lee Furman; 1938), p. 64.

nomic body adjust itself to military needs; the Piłsudski traditions should be continued."

The Cabinet found difficulty in obtaining popular support. Strikes continued, while the Peasant party, which had succeeded in uniting three different groups, persisted in demanding a return to democracy and amnesty for Witos.

In an effort to " consolidate " the country and to give it an " organized and single directed will," [30] the Marshal encouraged the organization of a new government bloc, called the Camp of National Unity *(Ozon)* — a return to the party idea — but in the totalitarian rather than the democratic sense. Its principles were enunciated by its first head, Colonel Adam Koc, in a radio address of February 21, 1937. Emphasizing nationalism, Catholicism, and anti-Semitism, he declared that the army was the one centre around which every class could rally; attacked Communism, while remaining silent on Fascism; recognized the importance of improving the condition of the peasants; but urged industrialization and the migration of the peasants to the cities as the real remedy for the overpopulation problem. He declared the state should co-operate with the national minorities; and " arbitrary and brutal anti-Jewish acts " should be condemned as a blow to the honour and dignity of a " great nation." The " instinct of cultural self-defence " and the " tendency for economic self-sufficiency," however, were in his opinion natural. Koc's declaration was interpreted as a bid for support from the National Democrats, who have been traditionally anti-Semitic. It was expected that, as a result of the *Ozon*, the opposition parties would be absorbed or disappear.

An elaborate organization that endeavoured to enlist

[30] Address of Marshal Rydz-Śmigły, May 24, 1936.

every element in Poland was set up, and government employees in particular were urged to join it. In order to keep the Polish youth from drifting into the National Democratic youth organizations, Colonel Koc also established the Union of Young Poland, headed by a henchman of the *Führer* of the Polish Fascists, M. Piasecki. This effort to win the support of the nationalist youth ended in failure. A group called *Naprawa*, composed of some of the oldest and most faithful friends of Piłsudski, insisted that Fascist influence be removed from the Union of Young Poland, which was done. The peasants, moreover, would not be bribed by promises of agrarian reform. The Peasant party continued to demand a democratic constitution, free elections, and the return of Witos. When the government remained deaf to these demands, the party in August 1937 called a ten-day strike for the purpose of preventing supplies from reaching the cities. This is probably the first case in modern European history when such a strike has been attempted. The workers in the larger towns supported the peasants by also going on strike. When the police destroyed the barricades erected on the roads, fighting broke out. According to the official count, forty-one peasants were killed, but most observers believe there were many more victims. Although the government charged that Communists were responsible for the strike, a leading conservative paper, *Czas*, said that the peasants merely wished "political emancipation."

This strike served as a warning to the government; and following an attempt on his life, Colonel Koc resigned as head of the *Ozon*, ostensibly for reasons of ill health, at the end of 1937, being replaced by General Skwarczyński, an old colleague of Piłsudski, with liberal inclinations. Some observers believed that Koc had hoped to establish *Ozon*

as the Nazi party of Poland.[31] A few months previously —
in October 1937 — the President had indicated his hostility
toward any such move by openly receiving a delegation of
Socialist leaders, who presented a memorandum insisting
that the situation was grave and the country needed a
democratic régime and fair elections. Koc's resignation
ended his effort at establishing a totalitarian state.

The new régime changed the leadership in the Union of
Young Poland. While supporting industrialization, General Skwarczyński emphasized the importance of finding a
solution of the peasant problem. All that the reorganized
Ozon got for its pains was the denunciation of the conservative press, which insisted that it had become "radical."
On the other hand, the Socialists and peasants continued
to vent their hostility against the undemocratic nature of
the present régime. Nor is the government any more popular with the National Democrats.

Meanwhile a struggle was going on within the government. Marshal Rydz-Śmigły was reported to favour a totalitarian trend, in contrast to the President, who was sup-
posed to support liberalism. In March 1938 both men made
speeches expressing the hope that a totalitarian régime
would not be established, and on March 24 the Vice-Premier and Minister of Finance, Eugenjusz Kwiatkowski,
made a plea for national unity without resort to totalitarianism. Although he changed the emphasis of his address
in a subsequent interview, he was thought to reflect the
government's view that an attempt would now be made to
come to terms with the peasants, and even to establish a
national concentration government. Thus the pendulum
swung from Right to Centre.

[31] Cf. S. Rousellet: "La Démission du Colonel Koc," *L'Europe Nouvelle*, February 12, 1938.

Improvement of the political atmosphere was indicated by the fact that the Peasant party called off the demonstrations commemorating the peasant strike of 1937. One deputy, M. Budzyński, representing Fascist tendencies within the régime, was expelled from the *Ozon* because of "lack of discipline." A few of his followers resigned with him and formed a Nationalist Piłsudskist group called *Jutro Pracy*. These losses, while strengthening the liberal elements in the *Ozon*, served to weaken the organization as a whole. The greatest blow came in June 1938 when, after the death of M. Car, Colonel Sławek was elected Marshal of the Sejm despite the opposition of the government. Since his resignation after the 1935 election, Sławek had remained in the background, declining to join the *Ozon*. But he saw an opportunity to regain power. Many deputies supported him for Marshal of the Sejm since they owed their election to the 1935 electoral laws, of which Sławek had been the author. They believed, moreover, that Sławek would oppose a change in these laws, and thus perpetuate them in office. As soon as he was elected, Sławek undertook to revive the non-party bloc which he had disbanded in 1935, and to strengthen his position as a Presidential candidate in 1940. He even went so far as to indicate that he did not recognize the decree declaring Marshal Rydz-Śmigły to be "second citizen." [32] It thus became clear that, with Sławek as Marshal of the Sejm, no co-operation between Parliament and the leaders of the government was possible. Apparently to break this deadlock, the President of the Republic boldly dissolved Parliament on September 13, 1938 — an act which took not only the country and Parliament but even some members of the Cabinet completely by surprise. The Presidential decree of dissolution

[32] Cf. p. 100.

declared: " Since the last elections important changes have occurred in Poland's internal life. . . . Among the masses of the people the feeling has grown that it is necessary to bring about more active co-operation in work for the state. I have, therefore, recognized that the composition of the Parliament must be changed in order to give better expression to popular sentiment. I will expect the new House to take a definite attitude on the problem of revising the electoral laws."

Whatever the cause of the dissolution of Parliament might have been, practically the entire country received the decree with praise and relief. The opposition parties regarded it as a direct condemnation of the electoral laws of 1935. The Socialist newspaper *Robotnik* wrote on September 15: "We do not hesitate to state that the decision of the President is important and wise." Nevertheless, the issue of the 1935 electoral law continued to create an impasse. Dominated by Sławek, Parliament was unwilling to change this law; and the opposition — particularly the Peasant party, the Socialists, and the National Democrats — declaring that this law was fundamentally unfair, decided to boycott the November 6 elections.

In the summer of 1938 Parliament provided that local elections would take place in December 1938 (December 18 for the City Council of Warsaw) and in the first months of 1939. It also voted a new electoral law for the local self-governing bodies that controlled the nominations to Parliament under the 1935 law. The Prime Minister decreed that these local elections should be free of administrative interference, " clean and honest." This statement indicated that for the first time since the *coup d'état* of 1926 the nation would be given an opportunity freely to express its views.

While grateful for this change, the opposition pointed

out that the Parliamentary elections called for November would precede the elections to the self-governing bodies, and therefore would not be fair. The President had indicated, in his decree, that the main task of the new Parliament would be to change the electoral law. The opposition parties asked that the work of the new Parliament be limited to this task, and that once a democratic and liberal law had been enacted, the legislature should be dissolved and new elections held. The government declined to accept any such commitment, going so far as to enact a decree punishing anyone who advocated abstention from the election. Thus the effort to reach agreement between government and opposition failed. The Parliamentary election was held on November 6, 1938 in the face of an opposition boycott. The government groups consequently obtained the majority, and Colonel Sławek was defeated.

Although nearly 35 per cent of the voters abstained from the election, the régime won a much greater victory than in 1935. Pro-government newspapers went so far as to say that the elections had demonstrated that the opposition parties were negligible, some putting them at less than 10 per cent of the electorate. In his greetings to the new Sejm on December 1, 1938, Prime Minister General Składkowski said: "You were elected by the largest masses which have yet participated in elections in the reborn Poland. Of the seventeen million citizens entitled to vote, more than eleven million have accorded you their fullest confidence. These are unprecedented figures in Poland." [33]

The victorious *Ozon* received a surprise, however, when the first municipal elections, held in fifty-two cities in December 1938, gave a decisive victory to the opposition

[33] In fact 78.3 per cent of the voters took part in the 1928 election, and 74.8 per cent in the 1930 election.

parties. They won 639 seats in contrast to the 383 seats of the *Ozon*. In Warsaw the opposition won 61 of the 100 seats in the municipal council, in Łódź the *Ozon* elected only 12 of the 80 members of the City Council. The *Endeks* were unsuccessful, except in the west, although they campaigned on the "Polonization of the cities" issue. The *Naras* also met with complete defeat, electing only four city councillors in Warsaw. Łódź elected a Socialist majority, and in Warsaw the Polish Socialist party won 27 seats, and the Jewish "Bund" 16 seats. Among the Jews, the Socialists increased their numbers at the expense of the Zionists and more conservative groups. Although these elections were technically local, they were the first fair plebiscite of Polish opinion on the régime in many years, for these elections were relatively free from interference by the administration. They showed that the critics were right in saying that the government did not command widespread respect and that Poland was a "dictatorship without a dictator."

Notwithstanding its weakness, the government can fail to come to terms with the opposition without running into immediate danger. For it has three great assets. The first is the division of the opposition. If Right and Left could unite against the government, its position would be critical. But although a number of such coalitions were formed before 1926, the only type of coalition discussed in 1939 was that between the peasants and Socialists. Despite the optimism felt in some quarters regarding such a coalition, these two groups are divided over economic policy, although they can momentarily unite on the question of restoring democracy. The division of the opposition works to the advantage of the present government.

The second asset of the government is the international

situation. Poland realizes that a civil war would inevitably mean the intervention of Russia and Germany, and the consequent loss of independence. No Pole wants Poland to become a second Spain, because the consequences to Polish independence would be even more serious — namely, a new partition. This situation again plays into the hands of the government. Realizing that the opposition is too patriotic to embark on revolution or some other form of disturbance under present circumstances, the government might feel free to ignore the demand for a fair election and a democratic constitution.

Finally, the government enjoys the support of the army. The Colonels' group continues to occupy important political posts; the "second citizen" of the country continues to be the Inspector-General. The army is exceptionally patriotic and well-disciplined, and its independent position established by Piłsudski after a long struggle with the Sejm seems to have been maintained. The army, suspicious of Left governments, would undoubtedly step in at the first sign of political disintegration should a Peasant-Socialist government conceivably come to power. The fact that the present régime represents the army, or a large part of it, is an element of strength.

Despite these assets, the Polish government remained in a precarious position at the beginning of 1939. The German success in Czechoslovakia increased the danger to Poland and made more important than ever the establishment of a government which could command national confidence. The absence of such a government was an element holding back private investment in the country.[34] No doubt there was some merit to the official contention that, in the existing international situation, free elections would be danger-

[34] Cf. p. 186.

ous. But this contention did not apply to the argument that a government understanding with the peasants had become essential to Polish security as well as to the solution of Poland's serious economic and social problems. Achievement of such an understanding depends on whether the heirs of Piłsudski are dominated by his patriotism to the extent of sharing their present monopoly of patronage. While from the tactical point of view the government occupies a strong position, it must broaden its base soon, otherwise lack of confidence — leading to demagogic dictatorship — may result. No country in Europe can now ignore the danger of the growth of Fascist sentiment. Poland still seems to have a greater chance to escape the totalitarian danger than the nations of the Danubian area. The greater the danger of German domination, the more suspicious Polish youth — which is essentially nationalist — may become of Nazi intrigue and propaganda. The highly individualistic nature of the Polish people, and the presence of such a large proportion of non-Polish nationalities, reduce the prospects of complete totalitarianism in this country. The Catholic Church in Poland, which is unusually strong and comparatively enlightened, does not wish to suffer the fate of the Church in Germany. The Polish government has time to broaden its base if it really wishes to do so. Nevertheless the heirs of Piłsudski will make a grave mistake if they believe they can ignore the importance of solving the internal political problem, which in some respects is the most important of all problems confronting the country.

CHAPTER V

THE ECONOMIC DILEMMA

1. Europe's Distress

UNTIL recently the mastery of the world has been in the hands of Europe. Despite its division among numerous rival units, Europe developed vast industrial and political power during the nineteenth century. By the end of this period it had succeeded in dominating about two thirds of the area and population of the world and placing the remainder under some degree of financial and economic control. Under Europe's leadership, world agricultural production multiplied five times during the past hundred years, industrial production twenty times, and world commerce fifty times. The real income of the European wage-earner quintupled during the same period.[1]

This vast economic development made it possible for the European continent to support a population increase from 200,000,000 to 400,000,000 during the nineteenth century.

[1] Cf. a valuable volume translated from the German, Reithinger: *Le Visage économique de l'Europe*, pp. 15, 20, 25.

It is estimated that by the middle of the present century this population will have reached nearly 600,000,000 people. For the most part, the population increases are taking place in the agrarian zone of Eastern Europe and in the Mediterranean area. Between 1900 and 1930 the population of Eastern agrarian countries increased nearly 39 per cent, in comparison with only 11 per cent for the Western democracies.

Until recently Europe could absorb these vast increases by means of world trade, international loans, and colonial empires and migration. But now that the world economy has collapsed, that Europe is divided between twenty-five or more nearly air-tight units, that immigrants are no longer wanted, that the two great extra-European powers of Japan and the United States have challenged European supremacy — the problems confronting this continent have become exceedingly grave. Unless Europe can organize itself, and reach agreement with non-European countries over the question of markets and raw materials, the outlook for world peace is not bright.

Although Western Europe is, for the most part, heavily industrialized, the continent as a whole is largely agricultural. At least half of the half-billion people of the continent derive their livelihood from agriculture, in contrast to a quarter, including artisans, who derive an income from industry; another quarter live from commerce, service, and government employment.[2]

The maladjustments of Europe are increased by the fact that the agricultural regions of Eastern and Central Europe are less productive and more densely populated than similar agricultural areas in the West. In agrarian Europe the density of the peasant population is about twice that in

[2] Ibid., p. 44.

France or Germany; and the disparity is increasing. The agricultural yield in Eastern and Central Europe is only a third or a half of the corresponding yield in the West. As a result of this great density and lower yield, the purchasing power of the peasant in agrarian Europe is only a quarter or a sixth that of the peasant in the West.[3]

In a large part of agrarian Europe the wage of some farm workers is little more than twenty-five cents a day — about that paid to native labour in many tropical colonies. When one adds to this fact the excessive price of manufactured goods due to protection, it can be realized that at least half of the people of Europe live on the very margin of subsistence. The population of agrarian Europe is increasing more rapidly than its income.

If the countries of Central and Eastern Europe are to solve their problems, they must increase the purchasing power of the peasant. This can be done by increasing the yield of agriculture and finding export outlets. It can also be done by the industrialization of these countries so they can support existing densities of population on a higher standard of living than is possible under an agrarian economy. If the world were organized on a basis of relative free trade, such as existed before the World War, the task of halting the deterioration of Central and Eastern Europe would not be insuperable. For the industrialized countries of Western Europe should import large quantities of agricultural produce. If the people of these countries had adequate purchasing power, they would consume vast increases of milk, vegetables, and eggs, not to mention other foodstuffs. To supply such foods for Western Europe, as well as for itself, agrarian Europe would have to supplant to a large extent its present extensive agriculture with an inten-

[3] Ibid., p. 32.

sive system.[4] Increased purchasing power can be achieved only if the countries of Europe — and of the whole world — are willing to accept the principle of division of labour and to remove the constant fear of war by achieving political appeasement. But the prospects for such development today are not encouraging. The agrarian policies of many of the relatively industrialized countries of Europe work against the interests of agrarian Europe. Since the depression Germany, France, Italy, and Czechoslovakia have maintained domestic wheat prices about three times above the world price; and the policy of many Western countries with respect to sugar and meat has been the same.[5] The unwillingness of the great powers (at least before the conclusion of the Anglo-American trade agreement of November 1938) to lower trade barriers, together with the collapse of the world capital market and the closing of migration outlets, all contributed to the difficulties of agrarian Europe. Divided by historic political and cultural antagonisms, trade barriers and military fortifications, the countries of Central Europe failed to develop any real form of unity during the post-war period, partly because of the diplomatic and economic policies of France and Britain, and even of the United States. The situation thus created played into the hands of Nazi Germany. As a result of the Munich agreement of 1938, Germany has secured virtually a free hand to impose some form of economic unity on Central Europe. Whether Hitler will succeed or not, no one can predict. It is safe to say, however, that if Germany uses

[4] *Final Report of the Mixed Committee of the League of Nations on the Relation of Nutrition to Health, Agriculture and Economic Policy* (Geneva: League of Nations; 1937); B. Ohlin: *International Economic Reconstruction* (Paris: Joint Committee, Carnegie Endowment, International Chamber of Commerce; 1936), p. 128.

[5] Reithinger, op. cit., p. 40. However, Poland has recently been receiving from Germany prices above world prices. Cf. p. 199.

its new position to reduce these countries to a position of economic servitude to the Third Reich, the misery of Europe will remain.

2. *Poland's Resources and Financial Policy*

The difficulties experienced by Poland typify the problems confronted by Eastern Europe as a whole. In certain respects its economic dilemma is more serious. Not only does it have the greatest population problem of any large European country, but, as a result of the Period of Captivity, it virtually lost a whole century in the task of building up an economic system adequate to grapple with this problem. Now endeavouring to make up lost ground, it finds that former outlets for its immigrants have been closed, and that world-wide economic and political nationalism obstructs its foreign trade. The development of Poland's purchasing power depends largely on internal possibilities of improving the efficiency of agriculture and building up industry. These possibilities, in turn, are controlled to a marked extent by the international situation. World agricultural surpluses depress Polish agricultural prices and hinder exports. World trade barriers prevent Poland from obtaining the foreign exchange needed to pay for imports essential for industrialization of the country. General lack of world political confidence deters the possibility of foreign investments. Meanwhile the Polish population is increasing more rapidly than production, which means a constantly lowered standard of living. Such is Poland's economic dilemma.

Had Poland the natural resources of Russia or the United States, it could ignore the international situation. But geography has not been as generous to Poland as to other countries. Its nucleus is the basin of the Vistula, which rises in the Carpathian Mountains and empties into the Baltic.[6] While the country is mountainous in the south, the central and north sections consist of a large lowland of less than six hundred feet in elevation. The soil of eastern and southern Poland is relatively rich, but that of the western lowland, stretching from Poznań to Vilna, is sandy and lacking in phosphates and calcium. The isolated and marshy districts of Polesie are known as one of the " poverty corners " of Europe. While the country is mainly agricultural, twenty-two per cent of the area is forest.

Poland, however, has a number of other natural resources. Thanks to the Peace Conference, it received part of the great mineral wealth of Upper Silesia, as well as the oil of Eastern Galicia. Poland, Russia, and Rumania are the only countries in Europe which have important petroleum resources,[7] although the best oil fields are becoming exhausted.[8] Poland also has a low-grade iron ore which can be mixed with imported ores, as well as scrap.[9] Poland's greatest mineral asset is coal, and it ranks fourth in Europe as a coal-producer. It has no manganese, nickel, copper,

[6] Cf. *Poland: Human and Economic Characteristics in Their Geographic Setting* (Birmingham University Service on Slavonic Countries, Monograph No. 1, December 1936).

[7] Leopold Wellisz: *Foreign Capital in Poland* (London: George Allen & Unwin; 1938), p. 35.

[8] In the opinion of some experts, Poland will be obliged soon to import crude oil to keep certain refineries in operation. C. W. Wright: " Poland's Raw Material Surplus Production and Requirements," *Mineral Trade Notes* (U.S. Bureau of Mines, Special Supplement No. 5, February 20, 1937).

[9] The extent to which such mixtures take place depends on the price of coke. As the price of coke did not change during the depression, while the price of foreign minerals declined, the import of such minerals increased. J. Zagórski: *Les Matières premières importées dans l'industrie polonaise* (Prace Instytutu Badania Konjunktur Gospodarczych I Cen., 1933, Zeszyt I, Tom II).

tin, or aluminum, and lacks cotton, wool, and rubber. Official sources estimate that out of twenty-four essential raw materials, Poland possesses only ten, and those in insufficient quantities. As a result, about half of Poland's imports consist of raw materials.[10]

Unlike other European countries which settled down to work on the conclusion of the armistice in November 1918, Poland used up its resources in fighting the Bolsheviks in a war which lasted two years longer. It is difficult to exaggerate the debilitating effect which this new campaign had on Poland's economy. As a result of the burden of reconstruction, Poland depreciated its currency, giving itself up to an uncontrolled inflation which made the formation of internal capital as well as the contracting of foreign loans impossible. The Polish mark, which had been made legal tender in 1920, depreciated by 1924 from its par value of 120 marks to the dollar to 6,400,000 marks to the dollar. In 1924 the Polish Parliament enacted monetary reforms, establishing the zloty as a new monetary unit at the rate of the gold franc. Unfortunately, a crop failure in the next harvest made large food imports necessary. Owing to lack of adequate reserves in the Central Bank, Poland could not prevent the zloty from depreciating as a result of the unfavourable balance of trade. Although the expiration of the German trade agreement in 1925 led to a drop in coal exports, in the next year the British coal strike gave Poland a new opportunity to export its coal. Moreover, there was a good crop in 1926 and, for the first time, Poland showed a surplus in its budget.[11] Following the report of a commission of American experts headed by Professor E. W.

[10] Communiqué of Iskra Agency, September 4, 1936.
[11] Cf. Charles S. Dewey: *Combined Reprint of the Quarterly Reports of the Financial Adviser to the Polish Government* (Warsaw: Printing Office of the Bank of Poland; 1930), pp. 227, 231, 268.

Kemmerer, the Polish government adopted the stabilization plan of 1927 under which, with the aid of a loan of about $71,000,000 based on customs receipts as security, the zloty was stabilized at a lower figure. At the same time, fourteen Central Banks extended a reserve credit to Poland up to $20,000,000.[12] Moreover, the government undertook to maintain a budget surplus and to revise its system of taxation. It also agreed to employ a foreign financial adviser to the government for a period of three years, who was to serve as a Member of the Council of the Bank of Poland.[13] Mr. Charles S. Dewey, former Assistant Secretary of the United States Treasury, was appointed to this post.

Following the 1927 stabilization, Poland enjoyed several prosperous years. Internal capital began to accumulate. Agricultural prices were high, largely because of world conditions. Poland proceeded to rebuild itself and made progress toward industrialization. Machinery and apparatus imports increased 42 per cent in 1928 over the previous year; and raw-material imports also showed large advances. As a result of these imports, Poland had an adverse trade balance between 1927 and 1929, for which it paid partly with the proceeds of foreign loans and emigrant remittances. Polish exports, however, reached the high point of 2,813,-000 zlotys in 1929. The average wage of common city labour increased from 4.72 zlotys in 1927 to 5.52 in 1929. There was a general improvement in labour productivity; thus, the daily efficiency of blast-furnace workers increased 77 per cent between 1924 and 1929.[14] By 1928 there were

[12] Wellisz, op. cit., p. 69.
[13] For text of the stabilization plan, cf. Dewey, op. cit., p. 22. Mr. Dewey repeatedly called the attention of the government to its undertaking to revise the tax system; cf. also Mildred S. Wertheimer: "The Reconstruction of Poland," Foreign Policy Association, *Information Service*, June 11, 1930.
[14] Dewey, op. cit., pp. 99, 217, 219.

about 25,000 industrial concerns in the country, employing a total of 845,100 workers, 22 per cent of whom were women.[15]

If, in many respects, Poland had a more difficult task of reconstruction than other countries, in one respect it enjoyed a more fortunate position. Before the stabilization of 1927 its debt burden was only 108 zlotys or $12 per capita. As of July 1, 1926 the total public debt amounted to $312,000,000, of which $245,000,000 consisted of debts due to foreign governments, largely for advances made in the early days of Polish independence, the greater part being owed to the United States as a "war debt." About $36,000,000 represented Poland's share of the old Austro-Hungarian debt. A total of $70,000,000 was owed to private creditors in the form of four loans from foreign organizations and three foreign bond issues, namely the six per cent dollar loans of 1920, the seven per cent Italian loan, and an eight per cent Dillon loan, all payable in dollars except the Italian loan. Poland's foreign debt at this time would have matured by 1950, except for the United States debt, which, according to the funding agreement of 1924, would be retired only by 1984.[16] The Polish internal debt in 1926 amounted to less than ten per cent of the external debt. Although Poland borrowed a further

[15] Ibid., p. 216. In 1926 the Kemmerer commission expressed the view that Polish industry was probably over-developed rather than under-developed, in relation to agriculture and raw-material production. "Poland's greatest opportunity would now seem to lie in the production of agricultural products and raw materials for industrial markets." E. W. Kemmerer: *Reports Submitted by the Commission of the American Financial Experts* (Warsaw: Ministry of Finance; 1926), p. 526. This view seems to overlook the fact that an agricultural economy cannot possibly support as many people as an industrialized economy, even though the latter is comparatively inefficient from the theoretical point of view.
[16] Ibid., p. 532.

$71,000,000 in the stabilization loan of 1927, before the depression the government had contracted few public loans for constructive economic purposes.

Nevertheless it did secure a number of intermediate credits from foreign concerns making sales to the Polish government.[17] Moreover, private capital sought investment in the Polish private economy in amounts which exceeded the indebtedness of the state and local governments. In 1929 this private indebtedness amounted to a total of 5,654,000,000 zlotys. Foreign capital participated in 446 out of a total of 1,118 joint-stock companies in the country. It constituted more than half the capital in 290 large companies; and between 25 and 50 per cent in 141 other concerns. Taking the capital of all Polish corporations as a whole, foreign capital contributed a total of 38.4 per cent. The largest sums were invested in mining and foundries, followed by the chemical and electrical industries. Despite the large proportion of foreign capital in Polish corporations, the total capital of such corporations was small in comparison with other countries. It was only 7 per cent of the German figure, 20 per cent of the Italian, and 3 per cent of the British.[18] These statistics indicate that, notwithstanding the assistance of foreign capital, Poland was still far behind other countries in the employment of corporations as a method of industrialization. One reason was the fact that the moneyed classes traditionally preferred to keep their money in land or real-estate mortgages.

Since Poland was a predominantly agricultural country, it suffered severely from the fall of world farm prices and the depression generally. In 1930–1 the budget again

[17] Cf. Wellisz, op. cit., pp. 88 ff.
[18] Ibid., pp. 147 ff. At the end of 1935 there were also forty-six branches of foreign enterprises in Poland.

showed a deficit, aggravated no doubt by the decision of
the government to grant subsidies to needy industries and
the unemployed. In the next budget salaries were cut 15
per cent,[19] the situation being relieved by the match monopoly loan of 1932 and the construction of the Silesia-
Gdynia Railroad. As the crisis deepened, the government
decided to adopt a policy of rigorous deflation. Severe
economies were introduced in the years 1931–4, the budget
being cut more than 30 per cent, cartel prices by 20 per
cent, and railway rates by 20 per cent. The monetary circulation was also reduced, and the government rigorously
refrained from increasing the public debt.[20] While this
policy made Poland one of the "cheapest" countries in
Europe, unemployment increased from 220,000 in 1932
to 414,000 in 1934. The general standard of living declined
and government revenue diminished more rapidly than
expenditure. The reverses suffered by numerous state enterprises [21] imposed a greater burden on the government
than in countries where the economic system remained in
private hands.

During 1934 the budget deficit continued because of military demands, while the stock of gold held by the Bank
fell off in the following year. Believing that the floating of
new loans was impossible, the Kościałkowski government
which came to power in the fall of 1935 made a new effort
at balancing the budget. Heroic measures increased the
income tax and levied an impost on government salaries,

[19] Machray: *The Poland of Piłsudski*, p. 284.
[20] Cf. Ignacy Matuszewski: *Próby Syntez* (*Essays of Synthesis*)
(Warsaw, 1937). M. Matuszewski was the Minister of Finance in the
government responsible for this policy. The government deficit during
this period was covered by reserves, treasury bills, an internal loan (1933)
which was subscribed to as a patriotic duty, and profits from the issue
of token coins.
[21] Cf. p. 158.

as a result of which the six-year deficit came to an end.[22] Since then the ordinary budget has been annually balanced. For 1938–9, revenue and expenditure are estimated each at 2,475,000,000. The 1937–8 receipts, however, are only 88 per cent of receipts for 1927–8, as compared with expenditures which stand at 99 per cent.[23]

The result of these deflationary efforts was further to depress private enterprise and the standard of living. By 1936 the consumption of electricity had fallen off by twenty per cent in comparison with 1929, while the number of automobiles declined by ten thousand in comparison with 1921. The railways also showed a deficit of about six million zlotys a month. The deflationary policy could endure as long as the population did not protest against a continually declining standard of living. While for a time "confidence" returned to the business class, the general condition of the trade balance and of business again led investors to hoard or invest large sums abroad, further weakening the resources of the Bank of Poland.

Although Poland during the boom could afford to import more than it exported, the situation suddenly changed with the depression. Foreign capital began to flee the country, with the exception of several loans mentioned elsewhere. Moreover, emigrant remittances began to dry up, while emigration itself declined 91.2 per cent from 1929 to 1932.[24] At the same time, nearly every government began to erect new trade barriers, which particularly injured the efforts of debtor countries to discharge their obligations with goods. The serious drain upon Poland is indicated by

[22] *Report of the Directors for the Financial Year 1936* (Warsaw: National Economic Bank; 1937), p. 13.

[23] *Bulletin Statistique du Ministère des Finances,* No. 4 (1937), p. 5.

[24] S. Fogelson: "International Migrations during the Economic Crises," *Baltic Countries,* Vol. II (1936), p. 201.

the fact that, during the first five years of the crisis, Poland paid out in capital and interest to foreign creditors more than 1,500,000,000 zlotys, of which a billion came from the gold and foreign exchange of the Central Bank.[25] Under the circumstances Poland could no longer contemplate an import surplus financed by foreign loans. It became necessary to build up an export surplus. Otherwise the Central Bank would have soon been drained of its gold and currency reserves. Confronted by a similar situation, many other countries resorted to exchange control or devaluation so as to increase exports. Devaluation was proposed in Poland as early as 1932. But the fact that the depreciation of the dollar automatically reduced Polish foreign obligations, and that devaluation might increase the cost of living, caused the idea to lose support. Fearing a recurrence of its earlier financial history, Poland determined, at all costs, to maintain the stability of its currency and to continue foreign debt payments, except for the war debts suspended by the Hoover moratorium. Nevertheless, it decided to push its exports by means other than devaluation while cutting down on all " unnecessary " imports.

Long before the depression, Poland had endeavoured to promote its foreign trade by exempting export industries from taxation, granting exports preferential freight rates, and concluding commercial agreements, usually based on most-favoured-nation treatment. A tariff war with Germany and difficulties with Russia blocked the development of two of Poland's most logical markets; but by 1930 it had arranged trade agreements with most of the other

[25] " The Polish Balance of Payments During the Crisis," *Monthly Review, National Economic Bank*, July 1935; " Polish Balance of Payments for the Years 1934 and 1935," ibid., January 1937.

European countries. Despite its trade war with Germany following termination of the commercial provisions of the Treaty of Versailles in 1925, Poland's exports until 1928 went chiefly to Central European countries, Germany taking priority.[26] When the depression began, all of these countries introduced severe controls, so that Britain — despite the conclusion of the Ottawa pacts — came to assume first place as the purchaser of Polish goods. Between 1928 and 1931 the volume of Poland's exports to Britain doubled. This market was particularly important for Polish bacon and timber, although the Scandinavian countries continued to buy large quantities of Polish rye, timber, and coal.[27]

Meanwhile Poland endeavoured to protect its foreign trade with treaty arrangements. Thus on February 27, 1935 it signed an agreement with Britain reducing the injury to Polish bacon exports caused by the Ottawa pacts. Poland agreed to grant adequate import quotas to British goods; in return, Britain guaranteed that Polish bacon exports should continue at least to the extent of 41.1 per cent of the imports in 1932, and that Polish egg exports should be not less than 13.5 per cent of the total imported into Britain.[28] This agreement in fact made possible an increase in volume of Polish exports to Britain.

In May 1937 Poland concluded an agreement with France, taking account of the fact that Paris was an important source of credit. In this agreement France granted Poland most-favoured-nation treatment and accepted the principle that henceforth the value of French exports to Poland should be fixed at eighty per cent of the value of

[26] *Annuaire*, p. 157.
[27] J. Zagórski: "Poland's Export Trade to the United Kingdom," *Baltic Countries*, Vol. I (1935), p. 65.
[28] League of Nations, *Treaty Series*, No. 3740, Vol. CLXII, p. 182.

Polish imports to France.[29] France and Britain, together with the Scandinavian countries, have provided Poland with nearly all of its active balance of free exchange.

Following the political rapprochement of 1934, Poland and Germany succeeded in terminating their trade war and concluding a commercial agreement on November 4, 1935. After the treaty entered into effect, Poland found it impossible to collect payment on German purchases of Polish butter and pigs owing to German exchange restrictions. As a result, Poland accumulated large quantities of frozen credits in Germany, which caused it to reduce exports. German exchange restrictions also precipitated a crisis over the transport dues on German traffic across the so-called Corridor. These differences were finally liquidated in a new agreement of February 1937, which provided that the trade between the two countries should be balanced at 176,000,000 zlotys a year. The agreement increased trade about 35,000,000 over the previous year. At the end of 1936 it was also agreed that Germany would liquidate a large part of its railway-dues debt by supplying, outside the clearing agreement, German goods such as machinery and other capital goods.[30]

The Polish-German agreement was a clearing arrangement, under which Polish exports to Germany are annually balanced by German exports to Poland, allowance being made for the payment of credits. Prices are fixed in terms of the legal parity between the two currencies, which means that Polish exporters to Germany receive as a rule a price higher than the world price. Although Germany

---

[29] S. Rousellet: "Negotiations Commerciales Franco-Polonaises," *L'Europe Nouvelle*, December 4, 1937.

[30] C. B. Jerram: *Report on Economic and Commercial Conditions in Poland* (London: Department of Overseas Trade, March 1937), No. 670, p. 11.

agreed to buy Polish goods amounting to a total of 176,-
000,000 zlotys a year, at fixed prices, Poland merely promised to allow equivalent amounts of German goods to enter,
without giving any guarantees as to prices or sales. If Poland found that its market could not absorb this amount
of German goods, however, Germany would correspond-
ingly reduce Polish purchases.[31] The arrangement increased German-Polish trade, and was favourable to Poland in so far as prices were concerned; but it did not
give it any free exchange.

While endeavouring to increase its exports by trade agreements and certain types of subsidy,[32] Poland early began to
eliminate unnecessary imports. In 1925 Poland extended
tariff protection to many agricultural products,[33] increasing
duties on imports of grains and fats again in March 1931.
In the same year the customs-handling tax was raised from
10 to 20 per cent of the duty on the usual shipment. In
August 1932 customs duties were increased 300 and 400
per cent. Following the study of a special committee into
the changes deemed necessary by world conditions, a new
tariff law was adopted on October 11, 1933. This law established a maximum-minimum tariff, on the understanding
that conventional rates below the minimum would be given
to countries having trade agreements with Poland. About
twenty such agreements granted conventional duties which
have been passed on to countries receiving most-favoured-
nation treatment from Poland, including the United States.
But the advantages of this tariff were, to a certain extent,

[31] For the 1938 agreement and the effect of the annexation of Austria,
cf. p. 148.
[32] Cf. p. 195.
[33] The tariff changes of Poland are summarized in Haily H. Conrad:
Farm Aid in Poland (Washington: U.S. Department of Agriculture,
Bureau of Agricultural Economics; September 1938).

nullified by the adoption of a system placing all imports under licence. A decree of December 29, 1931 declared that permits would be necessary for any import, and that the government would exercise its permit granting authority to see to it that no non-essential imports entered the country. As a result, a virtual embargo was placed on imports of cereals, flour, starch, macaroni, vegetables, fruits, certain vegetable oils, condensed milk, many manufactured goods, and other items. Subsequently, the list of " non-essentials " was amended, and it was provided that the quotas of the articles on the list could be imported if Poland had a favourable balance of trade with the country of origin. Meanwhile the long tariff war with Germany, terminated only in 1934, had served to develop new industries in Poland.

In 1935 the Polish government also adopted a " domestic raw-materials program " under which nearly every important agricultural raw material was excluded by restrictive quotas, while the production of synthetic wool and other materials was encouraged. Moreover, refiners were required to buy domestic oil seed at prices above the world price. As a result of such measures, Poland became nearly self-sufficient so far as raw materials for oil-production were concerned, and some progress was made in stimulating domestic production — at a heavy cost to the consumer.[34]

As a result of the decline of world prices, the general decline of Poland's purchasing power, and these restrictive measures, imports fell from 3,111,000,000 zlotys in 1929 to 799,000,000 in 1934.[35] In that year, however, Poland succeeded in developing an active trade balance of 176,000,-000 zlotys. In 1935 the favourable balance declined to 64,-000,000 and almost disappeared in the first quarter of 1936 owing to large imports of raw materials, reflecting a nervous

[34] Ibid.   [35] *Petit Annuaire*, p. 154.

condition in industry. Meanwhile the rigorous deflationary policy of the government had not produced the desired results. And in various parts of the country, no longer ruled by the firm hand of Piłsudski, signs of unrest appeared. In Cracow, Łódź, and Upper Silesia strikes took place in March 1936. Elsewhere the workers vented their displeasure against economic conditions. Withdrawal of foreign currency from the Bank of Poland and hoarding increased. When it became known that the effort to raise a loan abroad to strengthen the currency had failed, public confidence declined still further. The Bank of Poland's fund of gold and foreign currency decreased from 531,000,000 zlotys in 1934 to 471,000,000 in 1935; and in the following quarter in 1936, it fell even more rapidly to 395,800,000. The gold coverage had now fallen to 39 per cent, which was nine points above the legal minimum. The army was urging increased expenditure on armament, while the workers and peasants demanded relief from their distress.

3. The New Recovery Program

Confronted by a serious crisis, the government decided to abandon the semi-orthodox policy hitherto followed. But it rejected the solution of devaluation which had been applied by Britain and the United States and was subsequently to be applied by France. Instead, it adopted measures in many respects similar to those already applied in Germany. Between April and July 1936 it issued decrees providing for three important steps: it (1) introduced exchange control, all transfers of currency being left to the discretion of an Exchange Committee; (2) placed all imports and exports under severe control; and (3) suspended payments on its foreign debt. It also developed the use of clearing agreements [36] so as more nearly to balance imports by exports with each country concerned. By 1938 Poland had made a total of ten such clearing agreements, covering about 28 per cent of its foreign trade.[37]

Poland also reduced its foreign obligations by going into default. In April 1937 Parliament passed a law authorizing the conversion and exchange of the external obligations of the government into 4.5 per cent zloty state bonds.[38] The Polish government now proceeded to conclude refunding agreements with foreign creditors, cutting down interest payments,[39] and resuming debt payments upon the new basis. As a result of the saving in the service of foreign loans, the gold reserves in the Bank of Poland increased by 42,000,000 zlotys in 1937.[40]

While decreasing its dependence on foreign capital, the Polish government now embarked on a program of internal public investment. In 1936 Parliament approved a State Investment Plan and, in addition, authorized a National Defence Fund for Rearmament. Both of these projects call for the expenditure of a total of from 2,650,000,000 to 2,800,000,000 zlotys between 1936 and 1940. These com-

[36] Cf. *Enquiry into Clearing Agreements*, C.153.M.83.1935.II.B. (Geneva), p. 73.

[37] *Annual Report of the Bank Polski for the year ending December 31, 1937* (Warsaw, 1938), p. 11. Poland also concluded a number of tourist agreements controlling the amount of money which Polish tourists might spend in foreign countries. Cf. "Poland's Tourist Agreements," *Monthly Review, National Economic Bank*, June 1937.

[38] Most of the foreign issues affected by this law ranged from six to eight per cent. Foreign Bondholders Protective Council, Inc., *Annual Report, 1936* (New York, 1937), p. 675.

[39] After negotiations with the Polish authorities, the Foreign Bondholders Protective Council of the United States recommended to American bondholders that they accept a settlement of the American issues along the general lines of the 1937 Act. Cf. releases of May 31, June 30, and August 1, 1938 of the Foreign Bondholders Protective Council.

[40] *Report of Directors for the Financial Year 1937* (Warsaw: National Economic Bank; 1938), p. 13.

paratively large sums are being used for the construction of housing, new railways, roads, electrification projects, waterworks and extension of the port of Gdynia. The National Defence Fund for Rearmament is being used to develop the Central Industrial District in eastern Poland for the purpose of creating war industries in a relatively invulnerable part of the country. About twenty-five per cent of all state investments are being expended in this district.[41] This sum of 2,800,000,000 zlotys to be spent in four years is larger than the ordinary budget for 1938–9. If one includes the investment expenditure from the ordinary budget and credits available for foreign goods arising out of frozen sums due for Polish exports, the total amount available for public investments in 1937 was about 800,000,000 zlotys and a billion zlotys in 1938.[42] In 1936 about 20 per cent of the public investment came from foreign capital, largely from the French loan.[43] But in 1937 foreign participation was reduced to 10 per cent, the remainder coming from long-term internal loans, the resources of the state banks, treasury bills, and other similar channels.

Chiefly as a result of this growing public investment, Poland's internal debt showed large increases during recent years, at the time that foreign capital showed a marked decline. While the total debt of the Polish government increased from 4,170,000,000 zlotys in 1929 to 4,762,000,-000 in 1937, the foreign debt decreased from 3,810,000,000

[41] Cf. p. 160; also "The Four-Year Public Works Plan," *Monthly Review, National Economic Bank*, January 1938.

[42] The billion zlotys for 1938 is not to be expended until March 31, 1939. *Report of Directors* (Warsaw: National Economic Bank; 1936), p. 14; ibid. (1937), p. 12; cf. also speeches of February 5, 1937 and December 1, 1937 of Vice-Premier and Minister of Finance Kwiatkowski, in the Polish Sejm. For an account of Poland's housing program, cf. "The Financing of Housing from Public Funds," *Monthly Review, National Economic Bank*, December 1937.

[43] Cf. p. 334.

to 2,632,000,000.[44] In contrast, internal debt increased from 360,000,000 to 2,130,000,000 zlotys — an increase of nearly 600 per cent. The reduction in foreign debt was due to devaluation of foreign currencies and to refunding operations. As a result of these various factors, interest on the foreign debt declined from 102,000,000 zlotys in 1928–9 to 51,000,000 in 1936–37.[45]

The recovery measures adopted in 1936 brought certain immediate results. Stocks increased about thirty per cent, and the value of land properties rose. Poland diminished its dependence on foreign capital. For the time being, its balance of payments showed an improvement. Most important of all, internal business activity displayed considerable increases. Private capital, the type which had hitherto remained idle or fled the country, now began to embark on building and other investments. In this it was encouraged by a policy of liberal tax exemptions, as well as by continued fear of devaluation.[46] Industrial production in 1937–8 showed progress, followed by lesser gains in the case of consumption goods. In comparison with 1928 a number of industries actually increased output. Thus the production

[44] *Petit Annuaire*, p. 358; Wellisz, op. cit., p. 80. In fact, the decline is much more since it is estimated that about one third of Poland's foreign bonds have been repatriated by Polish capitalists for sums below their par value. The Stabilization bonds of 1927 were quoted on the New York stock market as 51 in 1932, 84.4 in 1936, and 69.7 in 1937.

[45] *Petit Annuaire*, p. 359. In part this decline was due to default on the United States war debt. It appears also that the percentage of foreign capital in Polish stock companies declined from 45.4 per cent in 1933 to 38.4 per cent in 1936. Ibid., p. 98.

[46] For example, certain new enterprises are given an exemption for fifteen years from the payment of taxes on immovable property or buildings erected. Anyone who buys a motor car or airplane may deduct 20 per cent, and 15 per cent during the next two years, of the purchase price from income-tax payments. For a review of this legislation, cf. "Facilities for Private Capital Investments in Works and Expansion Programmes," *Monthly Review, National Economic Bank,* May 1938.

of pig iron increased 24 per cent; steel 27 per cent,[47] electric power 28.2 per cent; cellulose 58.4 per cent, paper 68.8 per cent; hydrochloric acid 31.9 per cent; rayon (yarn) 159.4 per cent.[48] Nevertheless, the production of zinc and lead showed marked declines, while the production of coal, one of Poland's leading commodities, was considerably below the pre-depression figure.[49] In comparison with 1928, the industrial production index climbed to a maximum of 133.6 in the first eight months of 1938, although foreign trade remained far below the pre-depression figure.[50]

Notwithstanding this industrial expansion, the number of employed remained about the same. Maximum employment reached 859,000 in September 1938, in contrast to the pre-depression maximum of 850,000 in 1928. Despite the decrease in unemployment of 39,000 workers in September 1938 compared with September 1937, the unemployed for 1937 was still 470,000, or more than half of the number holding jobs.[51] Thus, while Poland since 1936 had adopted many of the German methods of recovery, it had not yet achieved the same results. The government had expended vast sums on rearmament and public works, but as yet had failed to generate private investment or activity to provide full em-

[47] *Report of Directors for the Financial Year 1937*, p. 9.

[48] *Annual Report of the Bank Polski, for the year ending December 31, 1937*, p. 7.

[49] The monthly average of output in 1929 was 3,853 tons; in August 1938, 3,139 tons. *Monthly Review, National Economic Bank*, September 1938, p. 15.

[50] In the first half of 1937 the general wholesale price index stood at a maximum of 59.4 for the depression period, while the agricultural index stood at 49.2. On the other hand, the nominal wage index stood at 66 during 1937, in comparison with 109 in 1929, while the real wage was 106 in comparison with 109 for large and average-sized industry. *Petit Annuaire*, p. 259.

[51] This includes the quarter of a million employed on public works. Cf. p. 153.

ployment. Meanwhile, the population has continued to increase at the rate of about 400,000 a year.

Moreover, it does not appear that Poland has advanced
as much as other countries since 1929, judging by the latest
available indices of employment and industrial production.

EMPLOYMENT INDEX

1937	100 = 1929
Poland	88.0
Hungary	104.0
Estonia	144.4
Sweden	117.3
Czechoslovakia	90.0
Italy	104.5
Yugoslavia	112.4
France	78.6
Latvia	116.8

INDUSTRIAL PRODUCTION INDEX

1937	100.2 = 1929
Poland	85.3
Rumania	131.7
Czechoslovakia	96.3
Latvia	155.9
Estonia	138.7
Hungary	137.3
France	82.8
Sweden	149.0
Germany	117.2

According to these two tests, Poland had made considerably less progress by 1937 in getting back to pre-depression

conditions than most other European countries, except France.[52] The reasons for this relatively slow progress are complex. In comparison with industrialized countries, the opportunities for expansion in Poland are virtually unlimited; and from this point of view it should have shown the vast increases realized in Soviet Russia. Nevertheless, it has failed to make as great advances as other Central European countries because of the deflationary policies followed until the spring of 1936, its lack of raw materials, a difficult situation with respect to foreign trade, and the continued handicap caused by the nineteenth-century division of the country into three parts. In addition Poland suffers from an agrarian and feudal background, depriving it of an adequate middle class. Since 1936 Poland has begun to make up lost ground, but the public investment policy now being followed is largely concentrated on rearmament and public works and has not yet succeeded, possibly for reasons beyond the control of the government, in stimulating private enterprise.

It is undeniable that Poland has made some progress toward both industrialization and self-sufficiency during the past several years. Nevertheless, of its 235,000 industrial establishments, judging by the number of industrial licences, 208,000 employ only from one to four workmen.[53] In other words, Polish industry is still predominantly in the handicraft and small-scale stage. Many of these concerns are in the hands of Jewish owners whom the nationalists want to eliminate.[54] Moreover, income even of the city workers is extremely low. In the comparatively prosperous year of 1929, it was estimated that the Polish worker had to spend

[52] *Statistical Year-Book of the League of Nations* (Geneva, 1938), pp. 61, 176.
[53] Wellisz, op. cit., p. 150.
[54] Cf. p. 299.

nearly seven out of every ten zlotys for food, as compared with the Czechoslovak worker, who spent only half his wage for this purpose.[55] In 1935 a survey indicated that more than two thirds of representative working families in Warsaw had less than 12.50 zlotys a week, or $2.50, and it was estimated that 40 per cent of these families had incomes insufficient to buy adequate food, particularly dairy products, fruits, and vegetables other than potatoes.[56] As a result largely of overcrowding and malnutrition, the death-rate from tuberculosis is high — 13.4 deaths per 10,000 inhabitants in 1936, in comparison with 4.6 for the United States. The rate of infant mortality during 1935 was 127 deaths during the first year of life per thousand live births, in comparison with 56 for the United States, 47 for Sweden, 69 for France, 152 for Hungary, 192 for Rumania, and 123 for Czechoslovakia.[57]

4. Opportunities for Investment

These conditions are not due to lack of opportunities for economic development. There are many new industries which could be created by enterprise provided with initiative and capital, while the efficiency of Polish agricul-

[55] Dewey, op. cit., p. 217.
[56] *The Workers' Standard of Living*, International Labour Office Studies and Reports, Series B (Economic Conditions), No. 30 (Geneva, 1938), p. 82.
[57] *Statistical Year-Book of the League of Nations* (Geneva, 1937), p. 39. A table analysing nutritive properties of workers' diet in a number of European countries and the United States shows that the diet in Italy is somewhat superior to that in Poland in most respects; and that the diet in Germany, Austria, Czechoslovakia, Norway, Sweden, and the United States is definitely superior. *Workers' Nutrition and Social Policy*, International Labour Office, Studies and Reports, Series B (Social and Economic Conditions), No. 23 (Geneva, 1936), p. 68. The pneumonia-rate in Poland is 10.4, in contrast to 9.2 in the United States.

ture could be greatly increased. To lay the foundations for such a development there is still a vast need for public works.

Poland has only 8.5 miles of railway line per 100 square miles of total area, in comparison with 15.6 in Czechoslovakia and 12.5 in France. The Polish Ministry of Communication estimates that about 3,500 miles of new railway lines are necessary to meet existing economic needs, at a cost of about $200,000,000. Poland has an even greater deficiency in highways, having only 25.0 miles per 100 square miles, in comparison with 56.6 miles for Czechoslovakia, 141.2 for France, and 44 for Germany. Only Hungary, Albania, Lithuania, Latvia, Estonia, and the Soviet Union show lower figures. To build the necessary road and highway system, the sum of $750,000,000 will be necessary according to official estimate. While the number of telephones has increased from 60,000 in 1922 to 245,000 in 1936, Poland has only 7 telephones per 1,000 inhabitants, in comparison with 12 for Czechoslovakia, 34 for France, and 49 for Germany.[58]

In Poland there are still about 1,250 miles of waterways to be rendered navigable, an area of 1,250,000 or more acres of land to be drained,[59] and 175,000 acres to be protected against floods by dikes. While Poland has large reserves of water-power, it utilizes these resources only to a limited extent. Poland consumes only 74 kilowatts of electrical power per capita, in comparison with 180 for Czechoslovakia, 348 for France, and 408 for Germany. Polish agriculture could be improved by the development of a system

[58] Wellisz, op. cit., pp. 207, 221. The backward condition of Poland is further indicated by the fact that Poland has 0.7 motor cars per 1,000 inhabitants, in comparison with 8.2 in Czechoslovakia, 43.4 in Britain, and 205 in the United States. Per capita consumption of sugar and coffee is far less than in other countries.

[59] Cf. p. 217.

of grain elevators and by an increase in the number of refrigerating plants designed for the export trade.[60] In Poland there are only about 20 such plants per million inhabitants as compared with 290 in Denmark, 50 in Holland, and 80 in Germany. Polish cities and towns are still in need of waterworks and sewerage systems. Only 152 of 603 Polish towns have satisfactory sewerage equipment; and only 11 of the 25 largest cities and towns have a street-car system. Warsaw has no subway system. Thus the field for expanding capital investment in Poland is still large. It may be argued that opening up new roads and otherwise improving local means of transport will automatically stimulate standards of living and private enterprise. Thus, a recent French writer points out that a century ago the peasant of Brittany lived as miserably as the peasant of Volhynia does now; but today the situation is far different. The French peasant is prosperous because every farm in France today is within reach of a reasonably good road. With 11,000,000 rural inhabitants, France has twice as many kilometres (600,000) of roads as the ten states of Eastern Europe, which have 60,-000,000 peasants.[61] Nevertheless it does not follow that the construction of public works will be automatically accompanied by the creation of purchasing power which will generate a continuous productive process. The building of an elaborate road system will not lead immediately to the mass production and consumption of motor cars, for in Poland there are only 25,000 people who have incomes of $4,000 (20,000 zlotys) a year. The investment of capital will yield

[60] Cf. p. 202.

[61] Francis Delaisi, quoted by Prof. N. F. Hall: *Preliminary Investigation into Measures of a National or International Character for Raising the Standard of Living*, A.18.1938.II.B., p. 54. One obstacle to the development of local transport is oppressive taxation. But Poland has made some progress in removing this burden by initiating a plan for the progressive abolition of tolls charged upon local transport. Ibid., p. 58.

productive returns only if it enters those fields which promise to raise the general standard of living. The construction of a road or building may temporarily give employment, but unless it increases the economic capacity of the country, it can hardly be called productive. This increase depends upon whether the road-building stimulates private initiative, and whether such initiative is supplied with capital.

Although Poland has continued to accumulate a certain amount of internal capital even during the depression, it is not likely to increase by its own savings the production of goods as rapidly as population grows. Consequently the country finds itself confronted by a vicious circle. If Poland, however, could obtain foreign loans, it might be able to equip itself with an industrial machine, within five years, which it could not acquire with its own resources within fifty. With the aid of this machine, Polish enterprise might quickly develop so as to raise the purchasing power of the whole country, bringing with it a slowing-up of the birthrate as well. By means of the right kind of outside aid, Poland could really grapple with its over-population problem in a way which is not possible so long as it is compelled to rely on its own internal strength.

Moreover, wholly apart from capital investment to prepare for the future, the industrialization of Poland requires certain types of machinery and raw material which can be obtained only from abroad. Poland's capacity to pay for such imports, as well as its capacity to raise foreign loans, depends partly on the international political situation and partly on its economic productivity.

Unless Poland can sell exports and services abroad in large enough quantities to pay for needed imports to service foreign loans, it will not be able to obtain adequate foreign capital. But it is the Polish balance of payments that, next to agricultural prices, constitutes Poland's most serious immediate problem.

5. Foreign Trade Difficulties

Lacking adequate outlets for its agricultural surpluses [62] and industrialized exports, the foreign trade of Poland in 1937, on a per capita basis, stood fourteenth in Europe.[63] Coal and wood in 1937 were responsible for about 32 per cent of Polish exports, but in amount coal was hardly half, and wood one third, the value exported in 1928. Forty-four per cent of the total exports consisted of agricultural products in comparison with 40 per cent in 1928.[64] Bacon and ham exports showed astonishing increases during the depression period. Exports of Polish iron and steel also doubled between 1928 and 1937.

More than half of Poland's imports are raw materials. Its most important import remains raw cotton, which in 1937 constituted 11.4 per cent of the total; machinery and electrical equipment take second place, or 9.4 per cent.

As far as destination is concerned, Poland has endeavoured with some success to increase its exports to Britain, the United States, and other countries. Although in 1928 Europe absorbed 97.3 per cent of Polish exports, in 1937 80 per cent of Polish exports went overseas. For political reasons, Poland has attempted to prevent more than 20 per cent of its foreign trade from going to Germany; but, as a result of the annexation of Austria in March 1938 and the final division of Czechoslovakia by the Nazis and Hungary,

[62] Cf. p. 202.
[63] Total exports were less than half those of 1929. *Petit Annuaire*, p. 154.
[64] Ibid., p. 170.

Germany's percentage has increased.[65] The direction of Polish foreign trade in 1937 as compared with 1928 was as follows: [66]

	Per Cent of Imports from		Per Cent of Exports to	
	1928	1937	1928	1937
Britain	9.3	11.9	9.0	18.3
Germany	26.9	14.5	34.3	18.3
United States	13.9	11.9	0.8	8.4
Belgium	2.0	4.5	2.3	5.8
Austria	6.6	4.6	12.4	4.9
France	7.4	3.2	1.7	4.1
Russia	1.2	1.2	1.5	0.4
Czechoslovakia	6.3	3.5	11.8	4.3

If one includes Czechoslovakia, Greater Germany dominates 27.5 per cent of Poland's exports, while Poland purchases from this source 22.6 per cent of its imports. As a result of the agreement of November 1938, these proportions should increase even further.

If this situation involves political dangers, what is even more serious is the fact that Poland is confronted with an adverse commercial balance. Although in 1936 it had an active trade balance of about 23,000,000, in 1937 it had a deficit of 59,000,000. During the first nine months of 1938 this adverse balance increased to 144,000,000.[67] During 1937

However, the percentage of German capital in Polish joint-stock companies decreased from 25 per cent of the total in 1931 to 13.8 per cent in 1937. This was because Polish interests took over several large companies in Upper Silesia. French capital leads in joint-stock companies, constituting 27.1 per cent, which contrasts with the low proportion of Polish foreign trade with France. American capital is second, having 19.2 per cent of the total. Wellisz, op. cit., p. 151.

[66] *Petit Annuaire*, p. 157.

[67] *Przegląd Gospodarczy*, November 1938.

the trade deficit did not adversely affect the reserves of the Bank of Poland because increased imports were paid for partly by Polish balances frozen abroad, and partly by goods credits granted in increased amounts over previous years.[68] Moreover, Poland in that year received part of the proceeds of the 1936 French loan. Nevertheless, the gold and bullion cover declined from 35.97 per cent in October 1937 to 26.8 per cent in September 1938, the legal minimum being 30 per cent.[69] While in " free " countries this decline would be alarming, in Poland the stability of the zloty has not been impaired, owing to the existence of exchange control. Today the gold reserve is of importance largely as a mobilization fund.

Poland's foreign trade figures are as follows: [70]

FOREIGN TRADE
(millions of zlotys)

	1929	1933	1934	1935	1936	1937	1938 (9 mos.)
Imports ..	3,111	827	799	861	1,003	1,254	983
Exports ..	2,813	960	975	925	1,026	1,195	839
Balance ..	−298	+133	+176	+64	+23	−59	−144

Poland's imports in 1937 showed about a 25 per cent increase over those of 1936. Exports did not, however, advance as much as imports.

As a defensive measure, Poland has resorted to barter

[68] *Annual Report of the Bank Polski, for the year ending December 31, 1937*, p. 24.

[69] Poland's total balance of payments does not seem to offset this conclusion. The balance of payments for 1937 is not yet available, but in 1936 income from services, principally emigration remittances, amounted to 135,300,000 zlotys, as opposed to payments due on interests, dividends, and profits of 125,000,000, leaving a balance of only 10,300,000 to be applied elsewhere. *Petit Annuaire*, p. 222.

[70] *Petit Annuaire*, p. 154; *Polityka Gospodarcza.*

with countries which insist on bilateralism, while endeavouring to obtain free exchange elsewhere. From the immediate standpoint, barter agreements have produced certain desirable results, at least as far as individual economic interests are concerned. Thus the Polish rye-exporter receives from Germany a far better price under a barter agreement than he would receive in a " free " market such as London. Nevertheless, if Poland extends its barter agreements with European countries, its active balance declines, and along with it the free exchange necessary to buy raw materials from overseas countries which are not able to import Polish goods in return. Thus the more Poland resorts to bilateralism, the more difficult the problem of securing raw materials becomes.[71]

Whether it resorts to barter or the free market, Poland must increase its exports, for it cannot reduce imports without arresting the course of industrialization. Today, however, the growth of Poland's foreign trade is held back by the general world situation. Poland has as much to gain as any other country from the development of a world economy such as that envisaged by the Hull trade program. But such an economy does not exist. Achieving its independence much later than other powers, Poland has entered a world of regimented autarchies, in which international trade is dominated less by economic than by political considerations. The totalitarian powers all practise dumping, in one form or another. Moreover, several of them, such as Italy and Japan, have lower labour costs, particularly because Poland has a relatively advanced system of social legislation.[72]

[71] Cf. Gilbert Maroger: *L'Europe et la Question Coloniale* (Paris: Sirey; 1938), p. 256.

[72] During the Ethiopian war Poland was able to drive Italian textiles out of part of the Mediterranean area and British India; but Italy re-

Despite these handicaps, Poland should be able further to increase its foreign trade. The most hopeful prospect lies in developing closer relations with Soviet Russia, which offers a potential market for Poland's iron and steel. As far as foreign trade methods are concerned, Poland can expect to exploit foreign markets, particularly that of the United States, only if it maintains agencies abroad, preferably in the hands of private interests assisted by the Ministry of Commerce, which will make a detailed study of the possibilities of expanding Polish exports.

Moreover, despite the growth of public banks in Poland, the extension of short-term credits to industry, particularly in the export trade, is still largely in the hands of the private banks. These banks by themselves cannot take the political or economic risks involved in financing many exports under modern conditions. To handle such risks Britain, France, and the United States have created, in one form or another, government guarantees of export credit. Poland might imitate this example.[73] Likewise, Poland may feel obliged to follow the example of Britain and consider whether it is not necessary to meet the dumping of Germany and other totalitarian states by export subsidies. At present Germany has a double advantage over Poland in many foreign markets; first, it has in effect depreciated the mark for export purposes; second, it provides the export trade with a large subsidy, amounting to thirty or forty per cent of the value of this trade. Poland does not have the resources to grant a general export subsidy; but it is possible that, if no other means is found of meeting unfair

captured the market after the war by resorting to extensive subsidies. Poland is handicapped in textile competition, because of the difficulty of financing cotton imports.

[73] Henryk Taubenfeld: *Finansowawnie i Kredytowanie wywozu* (*Financing and Crediting of Exports*) (Warsaw, 1937).

German competition, it might successfully subsidize certain finished goods, such as linen textiles.[74] Even by improving its foreign trade methods, Poland is not likely to meet its economic needs until the fetters now holding back world recovery are swept away.

NOTE

The Labour Fund

In 1935 the government established a Labour Fund which centralizes the direction of public unemployment agencies, unemployment insurance, and the public works program intended to give work to the unemployed. When a person loses his job, the Labour Fund attempts to get a new one for him through the state unemployment bureaus. If the worker has been insured by unemployment insurance, he draws his indemnity for thirteen weeks, and when this is exhausted, and he cannot find other work, the Fund endevours to find a place for him in its public works program. Three quarters of the burden of unemployment insurance falls on the employer, one quarter on the worker. The fund is supplemented by subventions from the Treasury. The Fund makes loans to various ministries or municipalities, and so forth, desiring to undertake public works, the financial aid being aimed at covering the expense of the worker, the cost of the material being borne by the entrepreneur. In 1936–7 the Labour Fund had an income of 161,800,000 zlotys. Of the 165,000,000 expended, 95,700,-000 went to public works, and 31,800,000 to workers' unemployment insurance. In 1937, 1,375,000 workers were

[74] It could not of course resort to such a subsidy in the case of the United States because of the American countervailing system. Cf. p. 357.

insured for unemployment; while 2,171,000 were insured for health. In the same year, 79,021 received benefits from the unemployment insurance. While in 1936 a maximum of 164,000 workers were employed by the Fund, more than a quarter of a million were employed on public works in 1938.

CHAPTER VI

STATE CAPITALISM

DESPITE an effort to adhere to orthodox monetary policy, Poland has developed state capitalism perhaps to a greater extent than any other country in Europe outside of Russia and Sweden. The policy of maintaining monetary parity and balancing the budget presumably has as its purpose the establishment of confidence, so that private investment will take place. Such a policy presupposes maintenance of a system of competitive private enterprise, making full use of Poland's cheap labour supply, with opportunities to sell freely at home and abroad. But a competitive system of this type does not exist in Poland today, for the government has embarked on an unusually large number of industrial activities of its own, and has established severe controls over private industry.

1. Government Ownership

This development is not new. The three empires which governed Poland during the nineteenth century all followed policies of rigorous state intervention in economic life. In Germany the ideas of List led to a policy of industrial protection from the west and agricultural protection from the east. Such protection greatly benefited the agricultural interests of Posnania and Pomerania. Tsarist Russia followed a mercantilist course in the nineteenth century. Industrial enterprises were so closely connected with the state that they were almost considered to be state institutions.[1] Russia's effort to industrialize its eastern and southern provinces worked to the advantage of Congress Poland.[2] Austria, for its part, deliberately retarded the economic development of certain of its provinces for the benefit of others. Thus Galicia during the nineteenth century was one of the poorest and worst-treated provinces, economically speaking, in the Austro-Hungarian Empire.[3] Perhaps an equally great factor causing the industrial backwardness of the Polish areas was the Polish aristocracy, whose position depended on agricultural feudalism.

State capitalism in Poland is explainable not only in historic, but in geographic, social, and economic terms. In view of the vulnerability of the country's frontiers, " Poland needs first of all munitions factories," as one Polish economist put it. To meet this need and to prepare for a régime of self-sufficiency, necessary in time of war, Poland must have a controlled economy. More popular as an argument in defence of *étatisme* is the social composition of the country. Poland has not developed a strong native bourgeoisie. The Polish ruling classes — gentry, state officials, and professional men — until recently despised commerce.

[1] Adam Heydel: " Dążności etatystyczne w Polsce " ("Étatiste Tendencies in Poland "), in *Etatyzm w Polsce* (*Étatisme in Poland*) (Cracow, 1932), p. 28.

[2] Cf. p. 58.

[3] Stanislaw Pawlikowski: *Nędza Galicji* (*The Misery in Galicia*).

As a result, the opposition against state intervention in economic life, which in Western countries comes from a large middle class, has hardly manifested itself in Poland. The parties which represent the Polish middle class, such as the National Democrats, are anti-Semitic, and believe that state capitalism is an excellent instrument with which to deprive the Jews of their economic position. On the other hand, the Left parties, which at the beginning of the Republic exercised considerable influence on the thought of the country, regarded *étatisme* as a step toward complete Socialism. M. Moraczewski, the labour leader and first Premier of Poland, estimated that about a hundred enterprises a year fell under state control and that at this rate the Polish economy would be entirely socialized within a relatively short period of time.

Long before the depression of 1929, *étatisme* was justified on economic grounds. In a new country such as Poland, particularly one formed out of disparate parts of three empires, the government necessarily had to take the initiative in organizing economic life. If it had not been for government intervention, many of the industries, particularly those directed by non-Polish interests, would have gone into bankruptcy in the early years of the new state. In the absence of a business class and of adequate private capital, the government had to step in. Britain and France had developed their colonies primarily by means of government initiative, and Poles contended that, since they were wrestling with what was originally an essentially colonial economy, government inevitably paved the way, in the hope that private enterprise would follow. The American Financial Adviser, Mr. Charles Dewey, while advising a change in the policy, nevertheless declared: "There is no question but that the government followed the only course possible for developing the country and its achievement has been remarkable as well as creditable." [4] The exigencies of the world depression, which made government intervention necessary in every country in the world, naturally intensified this tendency in Poland.

All together the Polish government owns about a hundred industrial establishments composed of more than a thousand units. What a Polish author calls the " state concern " consists of railroads, forests, post and telegraph, mines, factories, and banks which are either owned by the state or controlled by it.[5] Moreover, in about fifty corporations the state owns between 67 and 100 per cent of all the stock. The state owns 93 per cent of all the railroads, 100 per cent of the commercial aviation, and 95 per cent of the merchant marine, the post, radio, telegraph, and telephone. It possesses 70 per cent of the iron production, 30 per cent of the coal output, 99 per cent of the salt mines, 80 per cent of the capital invested in the chemical industry, 20 per cent of the oil refineries, 50 per cent of the metal industry, and three eighths of the forests of the country.[6] It owns the armament industry, and manufactures automobiles and airplanes.

The state, moreover, has five monopolies: the alcohol, match, tobacco, salt, and lottery industries. State institutions write almost half of all insurance policies. In addition to operating or controlling many private industries, state banks dominate the credit situation. The principal state banks are the Bank of Poland, which is the Central Bank; the National Economic Bank, which makes long-term credit

[4] Dewey: *Combined Reprint*, p. 120.
[5] Tadeusz Bernadzikiewicz: *Koncern państwowy w Polsce (The State Concern in Poland)* (Warsaw, 1938).
[6] *Tygodnik Illustrowany*, September 1937.

loans to local government institutions, larger agricultural holdings, and housing projects; the State Land Bank, which finances agrarian reform and makes loans to small farmers; and the Post Office Savings Bank, which has about 3,000,-000 savings accounts. In 1937 the state banks granted 36.4 per cent of all credit in Poland; if one includes the semi-official saving and other banks, 47 per cent. In 1936, 62.3 per cent of the borrowers from the National Economic Bank were state institutions, associated local authorities, co-operative societies, or communal savings banks, and so on.[7] Moreover, while deposits in the state banks in 1929 only about equalled those in private banks, they were three times as large in 1936. This growth of the state banks during the depression has been due in part to the systematic flight of deposits from private institutions. The enlargement of the role of the state banks had an inflationary effect which tended to offset the deflationary trend of private institutions dominated by considerations of profit.[8]

The extent to which state enterprise has gone may be indicated by the fact that the Polish government today has on its pay-roll about a million employees including the monopolies and state enterprises but excluding the army, and this exceeds the number of industrial workers.

The greatest economic achievement of the state to date is the port of Gdynia — constructed out of current revenue. The Polish government, concerned over the munitions strike at Danzig in 1920 during the Bolshevik war, determined to establish a Polish port on the Baltic. Although construction began in 1924, the first section of the harbour was completed

---

[7] *Report of Directors, National Economic Bank, 1936,* p. 25.
[8] Cf. M. Breit: "Les Changements dans la capitalisation en Pologne pendant la crise," *Prace Instytutu Badania Konjunktur Gospodarczych I Cen.,* zeszyt 4, Tom III.

only in 1930. The Polish Council of Ministers authorized the Ministry of Industry and Commerce to entrust construction of the port to private enterprise, and an agreement to this effect was made between the Polish government and a Franco-Polish consortium.[9] In 1933 a railroad, built under similar auspices, was opened connecting Gdynia directly with Upper Silesia, and saving about forty miles over the route via Danzig. Today Gdynia is the largest port on the Baltic and one of the most important ports in Europe.[10]

In 1936 a second state venture, in some ways resembling the Tennessee Valley Authority in the United States, was launched by the government. This is called the Central Industrial District, located at the confluence of the Vistula and San rivers — an area lying between Warsaw, Cracow, and Lwów.[11] Before the Partitions of Poland this area was the centre of Polish activity, but was subsequently divided up into several economic units and neglected. The District covers over 23,000 square miles and has a population of about five and a half million people. The area has considerable raw material and is close to deposits of petroleum, natural gas, and water-power. By taking the initiative in equipping the area with communications, electricity, and gas the government hopes to encourage the development of

[9] Smogorzewski: *Poland's Access to the Sea*, Chapter viii.

[10] According to the 1938-9 estimates, the expenditure on the port of Gdynia will be 14,232,000 zlotys for the year, while it will yield a revenue of 8,859,600 zlotys. The port is under a Port Authority directly responsible to the Ministry of Commerce and Industry and not a state enterprise like the railroads or forests, for example, which have their own budgets. Cf. "Port of Gdynia," *Monthly Review, National Economic Bank*, February 1938.

[11] Cf. Mieczysław Wajnryb: "The Economic and Social Importance of the Central Industrial District of Poland," *International Labour Review*, November 1938; M. Wańkowicz: *C.O.P.* (Warsaw, 1938); J. Rakowski: *Rola Centralnego Okręgu Przemysłowego* (Warsaw, 1938).

private industry and also to improve the quality of local agriculture. Through this district, the government also wants to link up the industrialized district of Silesia in the south with the undeveloped province of Volhynia in the east, and hopes to establish an international network of water communications linking up Poland and Rumania, via the Vistula, San, Dniestr, and Seret. A state steel plant has already been erected, and state munition factories are contemplated. A cellulose factory, a synthetic-rubber factory, a motor works, and other establishments have also been built. The government denies any intention of monopolizing the development of the area. To encourage private capital it exempts establishments built in the area from taxation, while state banks grant such establishments credits on liberal terms. So far, however, few private enterprises have taken advantage of these opportunities. Doubtless the situation will change, once the pioneering stage is passed, provided adequate capital for both public and private ventures can be found.

Many reasons led to the selection of this region of Sandomierz as the scene of an industrial experiment. It was believed that, by virtue of its location in the interior, it might become the home of many industries now concentrated in the vulnerable frontier regions, particularly in Upper Silesia. Moreover, this province is one of the most densely populated in Poland, having more than a hundred inhabitants to the square kilometre, and the peasants live in great misery on dwarfish holdings. It was here that the peasant strikes of 1936 and 1937 were most widespread and led to the greatest disorders. From the agricultural point of view, the land is comparatively poor, and industrialization is urgently needed as an outlet for the surplus population of the region.

Hitherto, Polish industry has been based mainly on coal and petroleum, found only in the frontier regions of Upper Silesia and Eastern Galicia. The Central Industrial District, however, hopes to develop electrification as well as natural gas, since it is in the neighbourhood of mountains which will supply new motive power for industry. Thus it is believed that this District may prove important both from the military point of view — by creating in the heart of Poland an industrial region — and from that of population — by providing employment for surplus peasants unable to find a living on the land. If the government succeeds in this venture, its prestige of course will be greatly enhanced. It is estimated that the new industries projected in the District will give employment to a total of 125,000 workers — a considerable number when compared with the total of 850,-000 now employed in Polish industries.

In a speech of December 2, 1938 Vice-Premier Kwiatkowski, author of the Central Industrial District plan, enlarged the public investment program into a fifteen-year plan, which would develop not only the Central Industrial District but industry, agriculture, and commerce in other sections as well. The fifteen-year plan, as outlined by M. Kwiatkowski, will be divided into five three-year periods. The first three years (1939–42) will be devoted to the increase of the Polish war potential; during the next three years (1942–5), special emphasis will be placed on the development of transportation facilities such as railroads and bridges. The third three-year period (1945–8) will be devoted to the improvement of the agricultural situation, intensification of production, and popular education. The fourth period (1948–51) will deal particularly with the problems of industrialization and urbanization; and, finally, in the last three years (1951–4) of this gigantic plan, an at-

tempt will be made to balance and complete the upbuilding
of the new economic structure of the country.

2. Profit and Loss of State Enterprise

The extent to which the state directs economic life may
be indicated not only in economic but in financial terms.
One economist estimates that these state enterprises, including the monopolies, have a capital of more than eighteen
billion zlotys, or between 15 and 25 per cent of the total
national wealth. These concerns in 1932-3 had a turnover
of about 17 per cent of the general turnover of commerce
and industry, and it is estimated that this has since increased
to 20 per cent.[12]

Today about 27 per cent of the national budget, including the special public-investment budget, goes to public
investment, as compared with 19 per cent in France, 20
per cent in Belgium, and 15 per cent in Italy.

Ostensibly, however, state enterprises not only pay for
themselves but yield a profit to the government. One third
of government revenue comes from its enterprises and
monopolies. According to the 1938-9 estimates, the five
state monopolies are the most productive source of revenue, yielding a total of 692,000,000 zlotys, in contrast to
state enterprises proper, such as railways, forests, chemical
factories and mines, which yielded only 137,552,000 zlotys.
Revenue from both these sources totalled 830,000,000
zlotys, out of a total state revenue of 2,475,000,000 zlotys.

When these items are broken down they prove even

[12] Adam Heydel: *Czy i jak wprowadzić liberalizm ekonomiczny?*
(*A Liberal Economy: Shall It be Introduced, and How?*) (Cracow, 1932),
p. 78. Professor Lulek estimates the value of the state enterprises at the
end of 1931 at thirteen billion zlotys. Tomasz Lulek: *Przedsiębiorstwa
Państwowe* (*State Enterprises*) (Cracow, 1932), p. 311.

more revealing. Of the total of 137,552,000 zlotys from state enterprises proper, the state forests yielded 58,700,000 zlotys, the railroads 42,000,000, and the post office 32,000,-000, or a total of 132,700,000. This leaves a revenue of less than 5,000,000 zlotys for the numerous other state enterprises.

The question whether these state enterprises are really profitable to the budget depends on whether the net profit paid to the government is greater or less than such enterprises in private hands would pay in the form of taxes. It also depends on whether the government gives to state enterprises privileges not accorded to private concerns; even though these concerns are a charge against the budget, they may be profitable to the country, but this depends on whether state enterprises in a monopolistic position charge higher prices than would be fixed on a competitive private market.

In answer to the first question one economist estimates [13] that, in the nine years 1929–38, the state enterprises paid to the government in profits an average of 55,000,000 zlotys a year, or 0.5 per cent of their capital value. Leading private corporations, however, paid to the government in taxes the equivalent of 4.6 per cent of their capital, whether making profits or not. On the basis of this comparison, the economist contends that if the state turned its enterprises over to private entrepreneurs, they would yield greater returns to the government in the form of taxation than they do now without increasing prices. It is charged, moreover, that state enterprises unfairly compete with private industry and are inefficiently managed.[14]

[13] T. Bernadzikiewicz: *Przerosty Etatyzmu* (*The Overgrowths of Étatisme* (Warsaw, 1936), p. 147.
[14] For charges as to the inefficient operations of the state forests, cf. the budget debate in 1935. Jerram: *Economic Conditions in Poland*, p. 23.

State enterprises are liberally supplied with credit from state banks, in contrast with private enterprises, which have to pay high interest-rates and often are unable to borrow at all. Professor Tennenbaum, in his monumental work on Polish economy, summarizes his view of the situation by saying that " each state enterprise is a privileged enterprise." [15] The general rapporteur of the 1937–8 budget, Deputy Duch, estimated that the actual return of the state enterprises was only 0.74 per cent, and that if all the tax and other privileges of the state enterprises were taken into consideration, they would actually be a liability for the Treasury.[16]

Many complaints are also directed against the government monopolies, particularly against the high prices charged for salt, tobacco, matches, and alcohol.[17] Before the World War the alcohol monopoly existed only in Russian Poland, being unknown in Germany and Austria. The tobacco monopoly, on the other hand, existed in Austria, but not in Germany or Russia. None of these countries monopolized the production of matches. On achieving independence, Poland extended the monopoly policy. While these monopolies provide a large proportion of the state revenue, many critics insist that their management is uneconomical and often disregards the purchasing power of the population. The policy of high prices followed by the monopolies is an example for private industry, especially for the cartels, and lowers living-standards. A characteristic example of lack of understanding of market conditions was indicated in the report of the State Control for 1931–2. In 1930, when agricultural prices fell alarm-

---

[15] Henryk Tennenbaum: *Struktura gospodarstwa polskiego* (*The Structure of Polish Economy*) (Warsaw, 1932), Vol. I, p. 504.

[16] Budget Committee of the Sejm, February 4, 1937.

[17] For the match monopoly, cf. p. 181.

ingly and the depression set in in Poland, the alcohol monopoly increased its prices. The State Control says on this point: " The increase was introduced at a time of considerable decrease in prices of raw materials used in the production of alcohol (wheat, potatoes), which on the one hand lowered the purchasing power of the people, and, on the other hand, contributed to the increase of illegal production." [18]

Many other examples could be given showing inefficiency and lack of businesslike outlook on the part of the monopolies. Not only are the financial results for the state monopolies unsatisfactory, but economically the management of the monopolies is often harmful. It is also pointed out that the monopolies are used as a source of patronage, and that people who know little about business receive licences, while others who have been in the trade for generations are driven out. Often the persons who receive licences rent them to those with experience. Thus the monopolies create a class who really do nothing but live on the country by offering their connections for sale.

Before the war the now existing monopolies were largely in private hands; prices were lower then, and it is estimated that these industries paid more in taxes than the monopolies bring in today. A peasant now has to sell between two and three times as much of his products as in 1913–14 in order to buy the same amount of tobacco, salt, or alcohol. In terms of corn, for instance, a peasant in 1914 could get 10 kg. of salt for 6 kg. of corn, 1 litre of alcohol for 11 kg. of corn, and 1 kg. of tobacco for 115 kg. of corn. In March 1938, in order to get the same quantities of the monopolized

[18] This statement is cited by Bernadzikiewicz: *Przerosty Etatyzmu*, p. 147.

articles, he had to sell 16, 21, and 379 kg. of corn, respectively.[19]

In addition to maintaining these state enterprises and monopolies, Poland has embarked on an impressive public-investment program. These various activities are financed by the state, and, together with other public charges, constitute a heavy drain on the country. In the absence of foreign capital, Polish taxes are excessive, and internal capital, as Professor Grabski states, is "almost entirely absorbed by the state."[20] As early as 1930 the Financial Adviser stressed the lack of business capital and reserves, and suggested that the burden of development be transferred from current revenue to foreign loans and that government spending be reduced.[21] The advent of the depression made the adoption of such advice impossible, and during the past two years the government has resorted largely to the internal market to carry on public investment, while government expenditure has consumed an ever-increasing part of the national income.

Some Polish writers have contended that the budget as a whole consumes a smaller proportion of the national income in Poland than in any other country. Thus one economist estimates that in 1929 taxes in Poland consumed only 13.5 per cent of the national income, as compared with 23.1 per cent in France, 21.3 per cent in Britain, and 26.6 per cent in Germany.[22] These statements by themselves do

---

[19] *Annuaire*, p. 236.

[20] Stanisław Grabski: *Ku Lepszej Polsce (Toward a Better Poland)* (Warsaw, 1937).

[21] Dewey, op. cit., pp. 122, 172.

[22] Paweł Michalski: *Zagadnienia etatyzmu (The Problem of Étatisme)* (Warsaw, 1929), pp. 11, 96; cf. also L. Landau: "La Part de l'Administration et des Impositions dans le Revenu National de la Pologne," *Prace Instytutu Badania Konjunktur Gospodarczych I Cen.*, zeszyt 3.4, Tom IV.

not mean very much, for they overlook the fact that the per capita national income in Poland, even for the prosperous year of 1929, was far less than in these other countries.[23] A tax of 100 zlotys paid by a person having an income of only 900 zlotys is a much heavier burden than a 900-zloty tax paid in Britain on an income of 4,200 zlotys. When a Pole pays such taxes, he deprives himself of necessities in addition to savings, in contrast with an Englishman, who merely deprives himself largely of luxuries, while keeping a part of his income for capital purposes.[24] Professor Krzyżanowski, one of Poland's leading economists, is correct in stating that " it is an absolutely undoubted fact that the Polish nation is too heavily taxed." [25] If the Polish people were taxed too heavily in 1929, this situation was made worse during the depression, when the income per inhabitant fell from 900 zlotys in 1929 to 500 zlotys in 1933, while the state budget declined in the same years by only 20 per cent. The total Polish national income fell from 28,300,000,000 zlotys in 1929 to 15,500,000,000 zlotys in 1933.[26]

According to a statement of Senator Evert, rapporteur of the 1937–8 budget, made before the Budget Committee of the Senate on February 26, 1937, the national income for 1934–5 amounted to about ten billion zlotys, of which state and local taxes consumed half. Finance Minister Kwiatkowski challenged this statement, maintaining that the national income was far above ten billion zlotys. But

[23] 900 zlotys in Poland, 2,100 zlotys in France, 2,500 zlotys in Germany, 4,200 in Great Britain, 5,800 in the United States.
[24] Heydel: *Czy i jak wprowadzić liberalizm ekonomiczny?* p. 35. Cf. *Concise Statistical Year-Book, 1937*, p. 55.
[25] Adam Krzyżanowski: *Bierny Bilans Handlowy (The Unfavourable Trade Balance)* (Cracow, 1932), p. 58.
[26] *Concise Statistical Year-Book, 1937*, p. 55.

he did not challenge the assertion that the state and local taxes consumed five billion zlotys. On the basis of the official figure of 15,500,000,000 zlotys for 1933, this would indicate that taxes consumed more than thirty per cent of the national income. While the national income has increased since 1934, the budget has also increased, and, with the adoption of the public-investment program, state and local authorities probably consume a greater proportion of the national income than ever before. Thus, as a result of an expanding *étatisme* monopolizing the savings of the country, and of excessive taxes, private enterprise in Poland seems in a state of stagnation, constantly losing ground to the state.[27]

The tendency of the state to encroach on private enterprise is illustrated by the fact that today state munition factories are manufacturing typewriters and bicycles for

[27] By a law of January 1, 1936, Poland adopted the progressive income tax in which all incomes below 1,500 zlotys are exempt, but income of that amount pays 44 zlotys a year, while an income of 25,000 zlotys pays 3,131 zlotys, etc. The tax is increased by 14 per cent for bachelor taxpayers having incomes above 3,600 zlotys a year, and is lowered for taxpayers who support more than one member of the family. The income tax was estimated to yield 295,000,000 zlotys in the budget of 1938-9 out of a total revenue of 2,475,000,000 zlotys. Moreover, industrial and commercial enterprises and the professions are subject to an industrial tax, based on the law of July 15, 1925 and decrees of May 30 and December 11, 1936. The tax consists of payment of a certain percentage of business turnover or purchases of licences according to category. The export trade is exempt from the turnover tax. In 1938-9 the budget provided for a yield of 270,000,000 zlotys from the industrial tax. According to decrees of November 4, 1936 and March 31, 1937, land is subject to a tax, varying according to quality and location. The land tax in the budget of 1938-9 was estimated to yield 68,000,000 zlotys. There is also a real-estate tax of eight per cent on all city buildings, and rural buildings not connected with agricultural activities. The tax is increased on buildings assessed at more than 10,000 zlotys. The real-estate tax was estimated to yield 85,000,000 zlotys in the 1938-9 budget. There are a few other direct taxes; the total yield of all direct taxes was estimated to be 751,500,000 zlotys out of a total budget of 2,475,000,000 zlotys in 1938-9.

the general market. Business men resent the manufacture of these articles by the state. The government replies that it is unwise to produce in peace-time enough matériel to give full employment to the mechanics and other employees needed to man the munition factories when war comes; yet, in the interest of preparedness, these employees must be occupied in the production of articles requiring the same technical skill as munitions. Thus the demands of the international situation have accentuated the trend toward state capitalism. Public enterprise has become necessary as a preparedness measure. It has also become inevitable in view of the unwillingness of private enterprise to make long-time commitments under existing political conditions.

Nevertheless, the Cabinet decided on January 17, 1936 to create a special commission to investigate the state enterprises. The commission was also authorized to make suggestions which would limit the scope of such enterprises and reduce their privileges in comparison with private industry. This commission, composed of outstanding economists, business men, and others, prepared a report of twenty volumes which the government has so far refrained from publishing. It is believed that the report is critical of many state activities and suggests their limitation. State intervention, however, has meanwhile steadily increased.

3. The Cartel System

In addition to *étatisme*, the Polish economic system is characterized by a cartel system into which nearly every important industry, except textiles, is organized. In 1930, 56 cartels controlled about 37 per cent of the total industrial production in the country, in contrast to the state monopolies, which controlled 3.9 per cent.[28] The cartels agree on quotas of production and sometimes fix prices. While keeping up prices at home, they may dump surpluses abroad.

The cartellization process began on Polish territory long before the resurrection of an independent Polish state. The first cartels were formed as early as 1880 in the heavy industries such as coal and iron. Other cartels followed, and became quite numerous in independent Poland. Following the economic crisis of 1930, the tendency to cartellization increased, and the process still continues despite the fact that the government has dissolved quite a number of cartels.

The tendency to cartellization has been facilitated by Poland's high protective-tariff policy and the more recent controls established over every item of foreign trade. As a result of such controls, Polish industry need not fear foreign competition and is therefore in a position to combine so as to eliminate internal competition as well. Through the cartel, domestic prices can be maintained at a point high enough to recoup the losses occasioned by dumping, a practice deemed necessary by the state in order to secure adequate foreign exchange.

Moreover, when Poland regained its independence, it was confronted with the problem of over-capacity, particularly in the case of coal and sugar beets.[29] Costs of production in these and other industries varied greatly, according to area; and had Poland allowed the law of supply and demand to operate, invested capital in the least efficient

[28] M. Kalecki: "La Part des cartels dans l'activité industrielle sur le marché polonais," *Prace Instytutu Badania Konjunktur Gospodarczych I Cen.*, zeszyt 3, Tom II.

[29] It is estimated that the margin of surplus capacity in the case of coal amounts to one half in Poland. *The World Coal-Mining Industry*, International Labour Office, Studies and Reports, Series B (Economic Conditions) No. 31 (Geneva, 1938), Vol. I, p. 74.

areas would have been destroyed and thousands thrown out of work. In a country lacking capital, the law of competition could not be allowed to operate so as to destroy existing plant, even though it was comparatively inefficient.[30] All these factors operated to encourage the development of the cartel system.

The legal basis of cartel activities in Poland is the cartel law of March 28, 1933, as modified by Presidential decree of November 27, 1935.[31] By cartels the law understands all "agreements, decisions, and regulations which tend through reciprocal obligations to control production, prices, or the conditions in which goods ought to be exchanged in the industrial, mining, or commercial fields."

Government control over cartels is exercised chiefly through the cartel register kept at the Ministry of Commerce and Industry. All cartel agreements must be registered in a public register within fourteen days after their conclusion, under a 50,000-zloty penalty. A further means of controlling the activities of cartels is the right of officials in the Ministry of Commerce and Industry to look into all books and records of the cartels. The most extreme form of control provided by the law is the right of the government to dissolve the cartels.

Articles 4 and 5 of the cartel law state that, if the Minister of Commerce and Industry believes the cartel agreement, or its administration, is harmful to the public interest, or if he considers the regulation of production and the cartel prices economically unjustifiable, he can dissolve the

[30] Cf. Walter Rosenbusch: *Die Polnische Kartellwirtschaft und ihre Probleme* (Freiburg, 1936), p. 8.

[31] Dz. U.R.P. Nr. 31, poz. 270; also Nr. 86, poz. 529. Three ordinances — one of the Minister of Justice of June 28, 1933, and two of the Minister of Commerce and Industry of July 4, 1933 — complement the cartel legislation. Dz. U.R.P. Nr. 48, poz. 381; Dz. U.R.P. Nr. 48, poz. 382.

cartel either completely or partially, and free the members of the cartel from all obligations assumed in the cartel agreement. All such decisions of the Minister are immediately executed, even if the dissolved cartel uses its right to appeal within fourteen days to the Cartel Court.

The Cartel Court is composed of five members: three judges of the Supreme Court, one representative of the government, and a Chamber of Commerce expert in industrial and economic problems. The decisions of the Cartel Court are final.[32]

Except for the cartel register, the Polish cartel law of 1933 closely follows similar legislation in Germany. The law does not endeavour to grant special protection to members of the cartel, nor to those concerns which remain aloof from the cartel. But while it does not oppose monopolistic practices, as do the anti-trust laws in the United States, Polish legislation is concerned with the maintenance of "economically justified prices." This interpretation of the meaning of "the public interest" as used in the cartel law was given by the Cartel Court in its first and most famous case, dissolving the Cement Cartel.[33]

It soon became evident that the cartels were maintaining their prices at a time when the country was going through a drastic deflation. In an endeavour to correct this situation, the government during 1935 utilized its powers of dissolution with a vengeance. "All leading manufacturers and a large number of cartels and syndicates were in December forced to reduce their prices either by voluntary agreement or the dissolution of the syndicates responsible for price maintenance. In dealing with these car-

[32] Julusz Braun: *Ustawa Kartelowa* (*Cartel Law*) (Warsaw, 1933).
[33] Adam Daniel Szczygielski: *Polska Ustawa Kartelowa w Świetle Wyroku sądu Kartelowego* (*The Polish Cartel Law in the Light of the Decision of the Cartel Court*) (Warsaw, 1934).

tels the Government threatened that if Polish industrial prices were not brought into line with international prices and with the purchasing capacity of the Polish market, which depends largely on the prices received for agricultural produce, the protective customs duties would be suspended and foreign goods allowed to enter the markets at low rates of duty, enabling the population to satisfy its requirements for industrial goods at a reasonable cost. This action resulted in the dissolution of 79 manufacturing and trading cartels and syndicates out of 154 such cartels and syndicates dealt with.

" The reduction in price of a large number of commodities, including State Monopoly goods, as well as reduced State Railway freights on most of the products subject to price reductions, became effective during the last half of December. These reductions were, however, not all passed on to the consumers, and a plain hint was given by the Minister of Commerce in his budget speech that Government action would be taken to control traders' profits unless the merchants and distributors themselves reduced their profits in a measure corresponding to the general reduction of prices." [34] These drastic measures did not wholly succeed in correcting the disparity between industrial and agricultural prices.

Subsequently the Minister of Commerce and Industry dissolved 93 cartels, among them being 19 local agreements between wholesalers. In 1936 and 1937, 25 more cartels were dissolved by the authorities, mostly for keeping up economically unjustified prices. Since some cartels, when threatened with forcible liquidation, prefer to dissolve themselves, the number of cartels dissolved as a result

[34] Jerram, op. cit., p. 7.

of government action is really higher than the official figures might indicate. In spite of government action, the number of cartels is not decreasing. While in 1919 there were only 9 cartels and in 1929 100 cartels, at the end of 1936 the number of cartels rose to 266, 77 having been liquidated during the course of the year, while 69 new ones were created. One reason for the increase of the cartel during the depression is that it offers a convenient method of dumping exports, and thereby contributing to maintenance of the proper balance in Poland's international payments. Poland assists the export of coal by unusually cheap railway rates from the mines to the port of export.[35] During the depression the export of leading commodities, such as coal, iron, and sugar, was usually possible only at dumping prices — that is, prices below the domestic price, or the cost of production. Moreover, the cartel provides a means by which foreign trade quotas can be allocated among the interested concerns.

The sugar and coal industries are perhaps the best illustrations of the cartel system in both the international and the export field. Following the example of many other countries, Poland exercises one of the most extreme forms of control over the sugar industry. Before the World War both the German and the Russian governments subsidized the beet-sugar industry, in contrast with the Austrian government, which hampered its development in Galicia. At the beginning of the war there were 86 factories producing about 6,348,000 quintals (699,740 tons) of sugar — 48.8 per cent in the German area, 47.8 per cent in the Russian provinces, and 2.9 per cent in Austrian Poland.

[35] *The World Coal-Mining Industry*, International Labour Office, Studies and Reports, N. Y. 31 (Geneva, 1938), Vol. I, p. 162.

During the World War, production decreased, many factories being destroyed. Unlike France and Belgium, where government initiative restored destroyed factories, Poland left this task to be assumed by private enterprises. Today about 400,000,000 zlotys of capital are invested in the Polish sugar industry, which has a total of 58 factories, producing, in 1937, 4,574,000 quintals (about 504,192 tons) of sugar.

The Polish sugar industry experienced serious difficulties immediately after the World War. Its operations were hindered by devaluation of the currency, and exports were hampered by an export tax of four pounds per ton. When, in addition, the world price made export unprofitable, factories tried to dispose of their entire production on the interior market, demoralizing the industry. The government then decided to intervene, and in the law of July 22, 1925 it was given authority to regulate the production and price of sugar. Each factory is now assigned a quota of production to be sold in the interior, and another to be exported. Following the example of many countries, Poland sells sugar abroad at less than the domestic price. Owing to sugar exports, the Polish industry has received a credit of about £3,000,000 a year from English importers, which has contributed to the development of the industry. In 1929 the government insisted that the industry form a single cartel as a condition of securing a price increase. A sugar cartel and a Bank of the Sugar Industry now control the whole production. Nevertheless, the government not only regulates production and prices, but imposes a heavy consumption tax on sugar, which in 1937–8 yielded to the budget the sum of 141,000,000 zlotys. Largely as a result of this tax, internal consumption of sugar declined, until Poland became for a time one of the lowest per capita con-

sumers of sugar in the world.[36] In 1932 the government
took steps to lower the price and the consumption tax, so
that sugar consumption in Poland increased 33 per cent
between 1932–3 and 1937–8.[37] Poland participated in the
Chadbourne plan, and also signed the international sugar
convention of 1931, which allotted it an export quota of
308,000 tons. This quota, so far, has not been reached.
Although exports fell from 186,000 tons in 1928 to 42,400
tons in 1936–7, they increased to 75,000 in 1937–8.

Particularly important for Polish economic life is the export of coal. Cartels in the coal industry are the oldest existing on Polish territory, but before 1925 they had a regional rather than a national scope.

The Polish coal industry became quite prosperous in the
years after the war, largely because the Treaty of Versailles
obliged Germany to import 500,000 tons of Polish coal
annually, free of duty. With the expiration of these treaty
provisions after five years, together with the stabilization
of the Polish currency at a comparatively high level, the
situation underwent a drastic change. A ruthless fight for
markets occurred, as a result of which the price of coal
fell from about 30 zlotys a ton in 1924 to 13 zlotys in the
middle of 1925. Poland's strongest competitor was Great
Britain, especially on the Scandinavian markets. In order
to increase the competitive power of the industry a general
Polish cartel, called the Polish Coal Convention, was formed
in 1925, with headquarters in Katowice. The three existing
regional cartels were united, and all the thirty-four important corporations adhered to the new organization.

[36] In 1932–4 Poland consumed 8.9 kg. of sugar per inhabitant, in comparison with 50.4 kg. for Denmark, 49.3 for Great Britain, 45.1 for the
United States, 45 for Sweden, and 36.1 for Holland. *Petit Annuaire,*
p. 151.
[37] *Petit Annuaire,* p. 147.

When the 1925 convention was revised in 1931, the powers of the cartel were increased. Today it fixes output quotas for each colliery, and the exports as well as the internal sales of all its members.

In 1926 Polish coal won a predominant position on the Scandinavian markets because of the British miners' strike. But shortly afterward British coal recaptured its lost position, aided by the depreciation of the pound and the refusal of Poland to devaluate the zloty. The Polish mines, in order to defend their exports, were forced more than ever into a dumping policy.[38] The importance of that dumping can be seen by comparing the internal and export prices: [39]

COAL PRICES

Year	Internal Price	Export Price
1926	.... 14.31 (reichsmarks)	14.53
1927	.... 15.30	14.55
1928	.... 16.63	13.25
1929	.... 18.13	12.48
1930	.... 18.09	12.45
1931	.... 18.09	11.57
1932	.... 18.09	9.63

This dumping constituted a considerable burden on the Polish economy, the proportion of Polish coal exports to internal consumption being higher than in any other coun-

[38] For a time the coal industry was subject to a tonnage tax, the proceeds of which went into a fund to subsidize exports. Manufactured goods enjoyed export premiums in the form of " export certificates," issued with respect to exports by the customs office; these could be sold to Polish importers of goods who required " compensating trade certificates " for their imports. Jerram, op. cit.

[39] Rosenbusch, op. cit., Table IV.

try.[40] Despite that policy, however, Polish coal lost ground in Scandinavia: in 1935 only 28 per cent of the Polish coal exports went to Scandinavian countries, in contrast with 58 per cent in 1932. The situation was improved, however, with the conclusion of the Anglo-Polish Coal Export Agreement of January 1, 1935, between the colliery-owners of Great Britain and Poland. This agreement provided that Poland's coal exports to a specified group of markets should not exceed 21 per cent of the British shipments to the same markets. Although Poland thus gave assurances that its exports to a number of markets would not exceed a certain maximum, it received in return an assurance that coal-export prices would improve, which reduced the difference between the domestic and the export price.[41] Poland also concluded coal agreements with France, Denmark, Norway, Finland, and Sweden — countries which import the greater part of Polish coal. As a result of these agreements and the general improvement of the economic situation, Polish coal exports showed a marked increase. From 8,362,000 tons in 1936, they rose to 11,003,000 in 1937, and the internal consumption of coal increased from 21,200,000 tons in 1936 to 24,800,000 in 1937.[42]

In its cartel system Poland is merely imitating the example of nearly every other country in Europe. But most of these countries are at a much more advanced industrial stage than Poland; and the question is whether the imposition of this system — which industrialists want as much as the government — on a new country will retard the ra-

[40] In March 1933 a decree reduced internal sales prices for coal eighteen per cent, but compensated the mines by reducing by three zlotys per ton shipments of export coal to the Baltic ports. *The World Coal-Mining Industry*, Vol. I, p. 243.

[41] For further details, cf. ibid., Vol. I, p. 249.

[42] *Petit Annuaire*, pp. 145, 163. Exports still remained below 1929; cf. p. 148.

pidity and scope of industrial progress. Cartels inevitably tend to restrict production, when Poland's greatest need is for increased production. Moreover, the policy of dumping exports, while assisting the balance of payments, constitutes an added burden on the country as a whole. For the losses suffered by these exports must be retrieved from internal prices, which are increased by high tariffs and import contingents. However much the Cartel Court may endeavour to force prices down, it cannot force them below the costs, which are increased by the very nature of the system.

If a competitive world economy existed, Poland might take advantage of its cheap labour costs to improve efficiency and increase exports at the expense of other competitors. For example, the Polish mines in Upper Silesia have the greatest output per man-shift of any European country, including Great Britain.[43] But in the absence of such an economy, Poland has endeavoured to protect itself by adhering to international cartels. While it receives a certain quota of exports from a cartel arrangement, it can hardly hope to obtain a quota larger than its share in 1929 trade. It thus gives up the possibility of expanding exports by taking full advantage of its competitive position.[44]

[43] *The World Coal-Mining Industry*, Vol. I, pp. 167, 177.

[44] Poland's relatively advanced social legislation is a further obstacle to its expansion in competition with Japan and Italy. One of the most extreme social measures, impeding the working of deflation in Upper Silesia, is the Demobilization Law. This system was created by the German Republic to prevent widespread unemployment after the cessation of hostilities. Although the law was repealed in 1924 in Germany, it has continued in effect in Poland in two areas ceded by Germany, Upper Silesia and Pomerelia. The Commissioner of Demobilization in Polish Upper Silesia may prevent for four months and a half the complete liquidation, and for six months the partial liquidation, of any establishment giving employment. He may occupy an enterprise threatening to close down, and decide equally whether any workers shall be discharged. The activities of the commissioner prevented a serious situation from

Nevertheless, in a period of world recession, the international cartel system has proved useful to Poland. For example, when it adhered to the international steel cartel, it was able to dispense with the subsidy hitherto expended on the export of steel. In the absence of adequate capital resources, as well as free export markets, cartels form an inevitable part of Poland's economy, despite the fact that they tend to restrict production and give the bureaucracy control over economic life.

In addition to the cartel system, the Polish government has resorted to the monopoly or special concession, not only in the case of public utilities but in other enterprises as well. Apart from the state monopolies already described, it created a State Match Monopoly in 1925, which in the next year was leased to the Swedish-American Joint Stock Company, a Krueger subsidiary. This company agreed to meet the domestic need for matches, maintain exports at thirty-three per cent of domestic production, and provide sums whereby the state could buy out existing private match enterprises. In return for this concession, the company agreed to pay the government an annual fee of 5,000,000 zlotys, plus half its profits. At the end of twenty years the match properties were to revert to the state without compensation. At the same time the match company made a loan to the Polish Treasury of $6,000,000 at seven per cent. In 1930 the agreement was revised, the Polish Treasury receiving a new loan of $32,400,000 at six and a half per cent, and the lease being extended to 1965. The obligation to export matches was dropped, and the amounts which the state was to receive were decreased. Following this agreement, the price of matches was raised; during 1938

---

coming into existence when, at the end of the Polish-German coal convention of 1925, Germany stopped its imports of coal.

the consumption of matches in Poland was still less than half the pre-depression level.[45]

An equally important concession was granted in 1931 for the construction of a railway linking Silesia and Gdynia, a total length of 321 miles. This concession was granted by the government to a French company, the Société Anonyme Compagnie Franco-Polonaise de Chemins de Fer de Paris, which was formed for the purpose of building the road. Eight of the fifteen million French francs constituting the stock of this company was provided by the Banque des Pays du Nord and M. Schneider & Co., and seven million by the Polish State Railways. The concession will expire in 1975. The government guarantees the service on the bonds and has the right to participate in the profits. Owing to the difficult financial situation in France, it was only in 1937 that the company was able to issue the necessary bonds, and then it received the aid of the French government. In 1934 this line yielded a profit of more than four million zlotys, which went to the Polish State Railways in accordance with the agreement between the company and the government.

Even the manufacture of motor cars takes a monopolistic form. The story of the so-called motorization of the country is particularly interesting. After the first unsuccessful attempts to create an automobile industry, the question of motorization was turned over to the State Engineering Works created in 1928. In 1930 this institution concluded an agreement with the Swiss factories, "Saurer," to construct a motor-truck assembling plant in Poland, with parts imported from Switzerland, together with parts made in Poland. Despite their high quality, these trucks turned out

[45] Wellisz: *Foreign Capital in Poland*, pp. 102 ff.

to be wholly unsuitable for Polish needs according to some critics.

In 1931 the State Engineering Works made another agreement, this time with the Italian Fiat Company. The state exempted the Fiat, or any Fiat parts, from all customs duties, until the State Engineering Works was able to begin production of the " Polish Fiat." In practice this meant that the State Engineering Works imported Italian cars without duty and sold them in Poland. At the same time, on October 10, 1932, new and heavy duties were imposed on all other automobiles, which in some instances proved prohibitive. The State Engineering Works, as a result, acquired a monopoly on the Polish market.

While the State Engineering Works succeeded in constructing the " Polish Fiat " in 1935, many Poles complained that the cost of the automobile was excessive. The government, in reply, justified its policy on the ground that these Fiats were designed primarily for military use. Despite the government's effort to motorize the country, Poland witnessed a return to the " horse and buggy days." In Warsaw taxicabs decreased from 2,447 in 1929 to 1,629 in 1935, while the horse cabs, or *droshkies*, increased from 1,282 to 1,682 in the same period. According to official statistics, Poland had nearly 26,000 cars in 1936, but an expert believes that only 15,000 motor cars were actually in use, because the cars were too old and the roads too difficult.[46] The same expert calculated that the state could have bought from forty to sixty thousand excellent motor cars and given them away free of charge for the sums it lost in the pro-

[46] Wacław Bóbr: "Motoyzacja i Zapotrzebowanie Produktów Naftowych" ("Motorization and the Consumption of Oil Products"), *Przemysł Naftowy*, 1936, pp. 352 ff.

duction of automobiles. Even those who did not join in this criticism believed that the government defeated the cause of motorization, first by excessive road taxes, and second by fixing bus fares so that they would not compete against the railways, which have comparatively high rates.

Since 1935 the situation has somewhat improved. In the trade treaty with Great Britain of February 27, 1935, the duties on motor-car parts were reduced by about seventy per cent, and this reduction applied to all countries having trade agreements with Poland containing the most-favoured-nation clause. A Presidential decree of May 7, 1936 granted tax reductions to those acquiring new motor cars. Those measures, together with the improvement in the economic situation, brought an increase of automobiles to 34,324 on January 1, 1938, which is, however, still below the 1931 figure of 39,391 motor cars.[47]

Moreover, under a decree of 1935 the government granted a concession to the Lilpop, Raw, and Loewenstein Co., to construct a motor-car assembling plant in co-operation with General Motors. This plant may produce motor cars by assembling parts imported from the United States, together with parts which Poland can produce. By virtue of such a concession, the foreign company is permitted to import under favourable conditions, but is obliged to utilize certain Polish materials and labour. Although the importer could buy the whole product abroad more cheaply, this method reduces Poland's dependence on foreign exchange. Nevertheless the concession system, together with import licences, impairs the development of the dynamic economy of which Poland is in need.

Generally speaking, Polish bureaucracy maintains strict

[47] *Petit Annuaire*, p. 185.

control over private enterprise. Thus it is necessary for a business man to get a permit to erect a new factory, purchase land, or import goods. The granting of these permits is not automatic; it involves the discretion of the government department concerned. Polish business men complain that officials interfere with the internal operations of their plants to a greater extent than similar officials in Germany, but that the Polish bureaucracy lacks the initiative and dynamic qualities which exist in Nazi Germany. As a result of *étatisme*, the cartel system, and state monopolistic concessions, private enterprise in Poland is on the defensive and virtually stagnant. The state is coming to occupy a more and more predominant part in economic life, despite the protestations of the government in favour of private enterprise. The government continues to absorb the greater part of private savings, although Poland has not gone as far as Germany in closing the private capital market.

There is little doubt that, under ordinary circumstances, private enterprise could increase the production of wealth more effectively than a policy of *étatisme* and regimentation. It does not follow, however, that should the Polish government abolish state enterprises or state monopolies and return to the system of economic liberalism — as France under the Reynaud decrees is trying to do — private capital and managerial ability would step into the breach and keep the economic system alive. In a country as poor as Poland, private enterprise will always lack opportunities to make profits large enough to justify the risks involved. In contrast, the state can be content with a much smaller return because it can spread losses over the country as a whole. Some critics believe that a different monetary policy, and a more friendly attitude toward private enterprise, might alter the situation, but this is improbable.

Whatever the avowed policy of the Polish government, private enterprise is likely to be held back by (1) excessive taxes, (2) lack of confidence in a government which apparently fails to command popular support, and (3) the ever-present fear of a general war. These same fundamental factors deter the investment of foreign capital in Poland, at least for long-time projects. Until the world situation is clarified, Poland seems destined to cling to its present system of state capitalism.

One school of thought believes that Poland can industrialize itself and improve living-standards by its own resources, on the pattern of Italy or Germany.[48] A moderate form of this point of view is that Poland should completely abandon the gold standard and that the state should draw up a twenty-five-year plan to be financed by state investment. It is argued that Poland should increase its monetary circulation, and that this will not lead to inflation unless the amount of money exceeds economic needs. Foreign capital is difficult to obtain and gives the foreigner too great an influence on the life of the country. While, according to this view, state capitalism is not the alternative, the state should encourage private enterprise and develop an active, in contrast to a passive, capitalism by a cheap-money policy.[49]

[48] Before 1932, international restrictions on exports were not numerous, and the percentage of Polish industrial products exported in relation to industrial production increased from 16.5 per cent in 1928 to 25 per cent in 1931. While domestic sales declined 38 per cent, volume of production declined only 31 per cent. The situation changed, however, after 1932, when trade barriers began to block Polish exports. The proportion of exports to industrial production fell from 25 to 21 per cent. Industrial exports were hurt more than agricultural exports, but prices of the latter fell more rapidly than the former. Ludwik Landau: "Exportations Polonaises pendant la Crise," *Prace Instytutu Badania Konjunktur Gospodarczych I Cen.*, zeszyt 2–3, Tom III.

[49] Stanisław Grabski: *Ku Lepszej Polsce.*

A more extreme program is advocated by the National-Radical party, which broke off from the National Democrats several years ago. It asks that the national economy be directed by a national organization according to a general plan through professional corporations. While independent peasant holdings should be encouraged, wholesale trade and all credit institutions should be nationalized.[50]

A more detailed presentation of this type of nationalism is made by one of the intellectual leaders of the nationalist youth, Jan Mosdorf.[51] After attacking the predominant role played by foreign capital in Polish life, he contends that Poland does not live under the capitalistic system known elsewhere, and that its problems are very different from those of the Western world. Poland must increase its total national income at a rate exceeding the natural increase of the population. To do this, the country should adopt a policy of *autarkie*, becoming independent of the three "menacing economic imperialisms" — Hitlerism, Bolshevism, and the "gold international" dominated by Jews and Masons. A state monopoly of foreign trade should be established; and the state should nationalize all industries now dominated by foreign capital. As a rule such capital should be confiscated, since the budget cannot afford to pay an indemnity. Production should be decentralized by the aid of electricity. Private commerce should give way to co-operatives or state agencies. Even these measures, the author admits, would not take care of the population increase. But since the great majority of people cannot reduce their present consumption, Poland should adopt

[50] Przełom Narodowy: *Zasady programu Narodowo-Radykalnego* (*National Revolution, Principles of the National-Radical Program*); cf. also p. 109.
[51] Jan Mosdorf: *Wczoraj i jutro* (*The Past and the Future*) (Warsaw, 1938).

the slogan: "The wealthy classes must lose." Sums now spent on luxuries should be diverted to the consumption of necessities by expropriating the rich.

Dissatisfied with the slow rate of development under the present policies, the nationalist thus wants an increase in the power of the state, the expulsion of foreign and Jewish capital from Polish life, and the adoption of a policy of self-sufficiency or autarchy. It is much easier to adopt the repressive features of such a program than its constructive part; the danger in the nationalist program is that it will still impoverish Poland.

Capitalists, Socialists, and a certain type of nationalist all find much to criticize in an economic system which rests largely on exchange control, cartels, government price-fixing, and other interferences with private enterprise. The system yields considerable returns to the bureaucracy, who enjoy social prestige and power, even though their salaries are extremely low. But the capitalists make only meagre profits, and the productivity of the country is not increasing as rapidly as its population.

Although Poland has a directed economy, which in certain respects already resembles the system existing in Germany and Italy, it does not follow that Poland can fully imitate the Fascist states. The regimentation of private enterprise in Germany and Italy is far less difficult than in Poland, because of the nature of the people and the organization of society. The very existence of a semi-feudal economy, marked by landed estates, a mass of semi-literate peasants, and large national minorities, makes the development of a totalitarian economy along German lines extremely difficult to envisage. The divisive forces latent in the social organization and history of Poland increase the difficulty of arousing the type of emotionalism which

Fascism has found it necessary to develop for its success in Germany and Italy. Piłsudski was the one modern Pole who might have been able to do it — but he is no more. Yet Poland cannot return to a system of free enterprise so long as the present international tension exists, and so long as it cannot count on the world market for exports, emigrants, or loans. Until the great powers compose their differences, Poland seems doomed to oscillate between a totalitarian and a free economy, just as it must oscillate in the political sphere between Russia and Germany. It seems clear that until the European situation becomes stabilized, the state will have to maintain a predominant authority over economic life, doing little more than combat the pressure of a rapidly increasing population on an already extremely low standard of living.[52]

[52] One critic writes as follows concerning the above section: " I believe the trouble with Poland to be that she did not start enough industries on the basis of government ownership. For start them she must in view of her over-population. And private capital could never start them, as industries in very poor and over-populated countries cannot yield any return. . . . The government should therefore have bent all resources to industrialization in such a way as to offer cheap goods to the masses. Instead, the whole industrialization in Poland, as well as in the rest of South-East Europe, has served the purpose of finding sources of income for a parasitical upper and middle class, with the result that industrial products become more expensive as more industries are built. A decent government in these countries, which would not have been influenced by the feudal nobility, would have industrialized completely and exclusively on the basis of government ownership. As it is, they did not do it; consequently Totalitarianism, which will expropriate the big landowners and wipe the middle classes from their positions in industry and government, will be definitely more beneficial to the Polish masses than any ' democratic régime ' which they have ever known. It will of course not solve the Polish problem; but it might mitigate it, whereas the present régime can only make things worse."

CHAPTER VII

THE AGRICULTURAL QUESTION

THE WORLD depression of 1929 brought to Poland the worst agricultural crisis in eighty years. Prices fell to abysmal levels and purchasing power in the rural areas was destroyed. The price of wheat declined from 51.65 zlotys per 100 kilograms in 1927–8 to 18.84; rye from 42.50 zlotys to 13.02; and barley from 39.66 zlotys to 12.38; oats fell off nearly as much.[1] While many peasants managed to keep alive on a very meagre diet, they probably suffered greater privation as a result of the depression than employed workers in the city.

The general condition of the peasant village has been recently described as follows by the Social Policy Council of the Primate of Poland: " The bad situation of the Polish village in economic and social matters is expressed in the following elements: (a) the extremely low level of agricultural culture and technical equipment; (b) the feeble rate of return of peasant farming; (c) the dwindling size

[1] The low figure in each case was for 1933–4; but subsequently prices fell even lower. *Concise Statistical Year-Book of Poland, 1937,* p. 214.

of farms; (d) the truly catastrophic situation of the common lands; (e) over-population. This last element is due above all to the fact that it is impossible to employ in other branches of the economy the excess population of the villages.

"As a result of this situation the agrarian question takes in Poland extremely acute forms, particularly in that which concerns peasant property. This question provokes social troubles, threatens interior peace, menaces the structure of the state, and becomes an arena where every subversive action exercises an evil influence . . . the actual state of affairs is certainly contrary to social justice and leads to a lowering of the moral level of the rural population and as a result to the weakening of the religious sentiment and attachment to the Church." [2]

From the financial point of view, the agricultural situation is little better. On 482 farms ranging from 2 to 50 hectares (5 to 125 acres), the net receipts over the period from 1931–2 to 1934–5 averaged less than one per cent of the capital invested. On farms of five hectares or less, net receipts were less than one half of one per cent.[3] According to the Polish Minister of Finance, in 1934–5 the average cash income of the peasant was eleven grosze (about two cents) a day; and the farm population, although nearly 70 per cent of the total, contributed only 15 per cent of the budget.[4]

Polish agriculture naturally suffered from the World War and the subsequent campaign against Russia. Never-

[2] For the French text, cf. J. Rappaport: "Chronique polonaise," *Le Monde Slave*, February 1936, p. 278.

[3] *Concise Statistical Year-Book, 1937*, p. 62; Conrad: "Farm Aid in Poland," *Foreign Agriculture*, September 1938.

[4] Cf. H. E. Reed: "The Hog Industry in Poland," *Foreign Crops and Markets*, March 23, 1936.

theless, as a result partly of government encouragement, pre-war levels of production were soon restored and in most cases surpassed, as the following table shows:

CROP PRODUCTION

(*millions of quintals*)

	Wheat	Rye	Barley	Oats	Potatoes
1909–13 average ...	16.8	57.1	14.9	28.1	247.9
1931–5	19.8	63.9	14.5	25.1	310.5
1936	21.3	63.6	14.0	26.4	342.8
1937	19.3	56.4	13.6	23.4	402.2

1. Agricultural Price Policies

Polish agriculture is largely devoted to the production of cereals, with livestock — particularly hogs — occupying second place. Poland produces 14 per cent of the world's output of rye, ranking third after Russia and Germany. It produces 15 per cent of the world's potatoes, and is the fifth largest producer of oats. Next to Russia, Poland leads the world in the production of flax. It is one of the five largest producers of pigs, and has great quantities of cattle, horses, and sheep. It is the fourth largest exporter of timber in Europe.[5]

Beginning in 1928, Poland developed substantial agricultural exports. In a period in which Polish foreign trade declined as a whole, Polish farm exports were as follows:

FARM EXPORTS

(*in thousands*)

	1928	1929	1930–4	1935	1936	1937
Rye, including flour	$448	$6,717	$6,685	$10,008	$9,060	$3,974
Barley	5,157	9,179	4,278	6,231	8,682	7,559

[5] Cf. Conrad, op. cit.

	1928	1929	1930–4	1935	1936	1937
Wheat, including flour ...	112	336	2,405	3,021	4,530	1,325
Oats	336	1,231	535	2,077	2,076	946
Total	$6,053	$17,463	$13,904	$21,337	$24,348	$13,814

Despite the decline in 1937, cereal exports during the depression showed large increases over 1928. Great gains were also registered for hams and bacon.[6] On the other hand, sugar exports declined from $15,000,000 in 1929 to $1,703,000 in 1937. Thus in the major staples Poland, given its low standard of living, not only is self-sufficient but has an export surplus.

Confronted by a serious agricultural crisis arising from the drop in world prices, Polish authorities — unlike the United States under the A.A.A. — did not limit production in order to raise internal prices. Instead, it extended high protection to domestic agriculture while subsidizing exports. With the possible exception of rye, Poland supplies such a small proportion of the world's agricultural produce that a unilateral restriction policy would have had little or no effect on world price levels.

Polish agricultural policy has taken a number of forms. Since 1928, high tariffs have protected the Polish peasant from grain grown in neighbouring countries.[7] The Polish government has also reduced the agricultural debt burden by providing a form of debt moratorium, and by reducing interest rates — a measure benefiting the large estate-owners more than the peasant.[8] Polish peasants went heavily into

[6] Cf. p. 148.
[7] Cf. p. 135.
[8] One authority estimated that, by the conversion of long-term credits,

debt during the boom period, purchasing fertilizers and agricultural machinery, and thereby increasing the costs of production. The government's efforts to reduce the interest rate during the depression have not succeeded in accomplishing the desired result. Today a fully mortgaged peasant farm " has to meet charges equivalent to about one-third of its productive capacity. Very few of these farms are able to avail themselves of long-term mortgages, the cheapest form of credit, with the result that actual charges borne by peasant farms may be even higher." [9] Despite attempts at debt reduction, one recent survey of 2,400 farms indicates that, as compared with 1932, indebtedness on farms of more than 124 acres increased by about 5 per cent, whereas on smaller farms it increased nine per cent. In 1936 a medium-sized farm in Poland was worth less than half its 1929 price. It is clear that the government's efforts to reduce debt charges or write off tax arrears has not gone far enough to give substantial relief to Polish agriculture.

The government, in addition, has granted credits for withholding crops, to relieve peasants of the necessity of selling their grain at distress prices during the most unfavourable season of the year. In order to stabilize prices on an annual basis, the State Grain Company began purchasing grain as early as 1930-1. Farmers were encouraged to store grain on their farms until the spring months. Grain acquired by the State Grain Company was sold or exported at current prices. When world prices increased in 1936, the Polish government reduced its purchases but continued to make loans on stored grain. The government now plans

farmers have been relieved of 40 per cent of their debt burden. Roman Górecki: *Poland and Her Economic Development* (London: George Allen & Unwin; 1935), p. 114.

[9] Cf. Conrad, op. cit., p. 426.

to erect grain elevators at Gdynia and elsewhere, which may exercise an influence on the grain trade.[10] The alcohol monopoly uses surplus grain in the manufacture of alcohol; and the government fixes the extraction ratio for the milling of flour in order to conserve grain for export — for instance, rye.

Moreover, the government encourages exports by export premiums. These take the form of negotiable customs receipts issued on certain exports. They can be applied to the payment of import duties; in certain cases they have a fixed cash value. These subsidies are intended, first, to check the fall of internal prices, and, second, to meet the competition of foreign subsidies.[11]

Poland suffered a drought in 1937 which led the government to abolish subsidies, except on barley, from March 15, and in April it prohibited the export of grain except by permit. Grain exports for 1937 dropped to 354,000 tons, in comparison with 1,076,000 tons for the previous year.[12]

In 1929, owing to expansion, Poland developed a large export trade in rye, which offered keen competition to German government-subsidized rye in the Baltic and Scandinavian market. To meet the German subsidy, Poland felt obliged to adopt the same methods. Poland and Germany together produced about 60 per cent of the rye in Europe, Russia excluded. To eliminate subsidized competition the two governments concluded an agreement in February 1930 creating a Polish-German Commission at Berlin which fixed minimum prices and divided the export market between them — 60 per cent going to Germany and 40 per cent to

[10] Ibid.
[11] *Report of Directors*, National Economic Bank, 1937, p. 8.
[12] For a report of M. L. Pluciński on organization of exports of agricultural products in Poland, cf. *Conférence Internationale Agricole de Varsovie* (Warsaw, 1930), p. 73.

Poland.[13] This agreement was subsequently terminated owing to the competition of the U.S.S.R., but a new agreement was reached in November 1933, the purpose of which was " to influence the world price of rye and rye flour." Sales were to be controlled by an agency established by each government; and neither agency was to sell below the price agreed on jointly. But if one agency failed to make a sale on two consecutive days, the other would have to agree to reduce the price or purchase the stock at the existing level. No provision was made at that time for a definite allocation of exports between the two countries. In August 1934, however, the agreement was expanded to include exports of wheat and wheat flour. And in October 1934 the Soviet Union became party to the agreement as far as rye and rye flour were concerned. One interesting provision of this agreement declares that no one country can store, in a European port, more than 28,000 tons of unsold rye and rye flour without the consent of the others. The agreement was renewed on July 31, 1935, but it is not believed that it has materially controlled rye prices.[14]

Finally, the government has endeavoured to equalize the position of industry and agriculture by dissolving a number of cartels, such as the cement cartel, and lowering the prices charged by certain state monopolies, as well as the price of sugar and certain artificial fertilizers.[15] Nevertheless, until 1937 there was serious disequilibrium between the price of goods bought and sold by farmers, as the following table shows: [16]

[13] Conrad, op. cit., p. 423; also Pluciński, op. cit.
[14] Ibid.
[15] Cf. p. 173.
[16] Prepared by the United States Consulate General, Warsaw; cf. also Conrad, op. cit.

INDEXES OF PRICES IN POLAND, 1929–37

(1928 = 100)

Year	Goods bought by farmers	Goods sold by farmers	Excess of goods bought over goods sold
1929	100.7	89.5	11.2
1930	98.5	67.6	30.9
1931	90.4	59.5	30.9
1932	81.0	48.9	32.1
1933	72.6	42.6	30.0
1934	70.3	37.0	33.3
1935	66.3	35.8	30.5
1936	64.6	38.7	25.9
1937	66.1	49.2	16.9

During 1936 and 1937 Polish agriculture experienced a remarkable recovery, owing largely to the rise in world prices and internal industrial activity. But the 1937 improvement was to a certain extent illusory because it was accompanied by a short crop in Poland, which meant a reduced income. Even in 1937 the disparity between the agricultural and industrial indices was greater than in 1929, while the prices farmers received in 1937 were less than half those of 1929. In the following year, moreover, Polish farm prices, like those of the United States, suffered a severe decline.[17]

The question of farm prices is important because nearly two thirds of the Poles are engaged in agricultural work. It is difficult for Poland to be really prosperous and to

[17] In France, Germany, and the Netherlands, the agricultural index was higher than the industrial index in 1937. In the United States the agricultural index was higher than the industrial index during the first part of 1937, but subsequently fell more than 10 points below. *The Annalist,* July 20, 1938, p. 111.

develop the purchasing power necessary to stimulate industries unless farm prices are high. The government attempted a degree of deflation, but it did not succeed in eliminating the scissors between farm and city prices. Ruthless deflation means a dissolution of the cartels, abandonment of *étatisme*, wage-cutting in the cities, and drastic modification of the Polish system of social legislation. But no government could seriously consider carrying deflation to such a logical conclusion, particularly under existing political conditions. Devaluation might have been a simpler and more effective way of increasing farm prices, since industrial prices are relatively inflexible. Devaluation, however, would have increased the cost of living in the cities, and might have led to new barriers against Polish exports.

The Polish government declined to consider this alternative. The new conditions which developed in the summer of 1938, however, forced the government to take another step in the direction of the German type of planned economy. By the law of August 5, 1938 it established an " optimum price " for rye at 20 zlotys a quintal (96 cents a bushel), with the prices of other cereals fixed in proportionate ratios. Apparently adopting the idea of the American processing tax, this law provided that the funds for maintaining prices should come from a tax on grains sold to the Polish consumer at a maximum of 3 zlotys per quintal.[18]

Several months later Poland took a further step which should ensure a relative degree of success for this price-fixing policy. In November it concluded a barter agreement with Germany, providing for the importation, over

[18] Cf. *Foreign Agriculture*, October 1938, p. 483. The price of rye had fallen from 21.36 zlotys a quintal in January 1938 to 13.63 in October. This " optimum " price represents a considerable increase.

the next four years, of German industrial machinery to the value of $23,000,000, in exchange for German purchases of a like value of Polish cereals. The amount of cereals Germany will take in payment for this machinery is to be in excess of normal imports, and is to liquidate the debt over a period of nine years. It is believed that during this period Germany will import about half of Poland's grain export surplus at a price which will enable Poland to abolish its export subsidy on rye.[19] Should Poland sell its rye on "free" markets, it could expect to receive only the world price, which is far lower than the Polish price, and even then have to resort to subsidies. The barter arrangement with Germany is attractive as a short-term measure, because Germany pays the Polish exporter a price above the world level. His return is therefore greater than it would be if he sold his rye in London. Moreover, the government is relieved of the subsidy burden, even though it must receive German imports in return. This example shows that, in the absence of a fully functioning world economy, such barter arrangements achieve practical results.

Poland has also participated in more ambitious efforts, associated with the idea of European Union, to increase world grain prices and bring pressure on the industrialized countries of Western Europe either to abandon their own agrarian protectionism or to grant Poland and the Danubian countries a preference over grains from overseas. Numerous agrarian conferences of Central European states were held between 1930 and 1933 for the purpose of discussing these questions. In August 1930 a conference, consisting of such states as Bulgaria, Estonia, Hungary, Latvia, Rumania, Czechoslovakia, Yugoslavia, and Poland, having a

[19] In the following May, however, it was reported that Germany had failed to deliver the promised machinery, with the result that there was a $7,500,000 balance on Poland's side.

combined population of about a hundred million people, met in Warsaw. Apparently envisaging an international A.A.A., these states expressed a desire to eliminate competition and to rationalize the export of agricultural products. The quantities of agricultural exports, the final resolution stated, should correspond to the needs of the import markets. Each export country should organize a system of silos in which crops could be stored, and establish organizations to make financial advances to farmers and unify sales. The Conference suggested that the League of Nations negotiate an international convention for the abolition of export subsidies on farm products; that steps be taken to frame a plan for intermediate agricultural credits; and that preferential treatment be given by European importing countries to cereals and other products of European origin.[20]

None of these agricultural conferences led to any constructive result, partly because overseas countries opposed the principle of European preference, and partly because Poland believed that its agricultural interests coincided with the interests of Germany rather than with those of the Danubian countries. Should a measure of appeasement be achieved in Europe, it might be possible to revive these ideas.[21]

2. The Livestock Industry

In addition to promoting grain production, the government has done a good deal to encourage the livestock in-

---

[20] *Conférence Internationale Agricole de Varsovie;* cf. *Memorandum consacré au problème du credit agricole à terme moyen,* Session des Experts du Sud-Est de l'Europe (Warsaw), November 1, 1930.

[21] Cf. Elemer Hantos: "Le Régionalisme économique en Europe Centrale," *Affaires Danubiennes* (Bucharest: Institute Social Rouman, Centre des Hautes Internationales; July 1938), p. 13.

dustry. Next to Denmark, Poland at times ranks as the most important hog- and pork-exporting country in Europe.[22] Owing to the high prices received for Polish pork in Britain and Germany, hog exports may prove more important than grain. The number of hogs per square mile and per inhabitant, however, remains low, and the country can export large quantities of pork products only because of the low level of domestic consumption. The peasant usually is too poor to slaughter a hog for food; and the farm population eats little meat except during the summer months, when both men and women work in the fields from twelve to fifteen hours a day.

Government experimental stations are endeavouring to perfect breeds, including that of a native hog known as the Golebska. Chambers of Agriculture, assisted by public funds, teach farmers how to improve breeding and feeding methods. A highly efficient veterinary inspection service has kept Polish livestock comparatively free from disease. In general, Poland endeavours to follow Danish production practices.

Nevertheless, hog production is held back because " Poland has the most inefficient and unsatisfactory marketing system of any important hog-producing country in Europe. The marketing system is largely the result of the small unit of hog production and the inadequate railway transportation and poor farm-to-market roads." [23] In outlying districts the peasant relies on the itinerant trader to market his hogs, and there is a considerable spread between the price the peasant receives and that finally paid by the consumer. Moreover, distances to market are so great, and the weather so bad, that many fat hogs die en route. No better illustration could be found of the importance of com-

[22] Reed, op. cit.   [23] Ibid., p. 345.

munications to national productivity.[24] The Chambers of Agriculture have encouraged farmers to make contracts selling their hogs direct to bacon factories. The Chambers endeavour to fix a price which ensures the farmer costs of production plus a fair profit; they also endeavour to maintain this price at a relatively stable level. The bacon factories, which have increased from six in 1926 to more than thirty-five in 1939, are organized into a Bacon Export Corporation. Partly as a result of the efforts of this corporation and of government supervision, Polish pork exports have shown a marked improvement in quality and uniformity during recent years.

Poland has many natural advantages in the production of hogs, such as low production costs, self-sufficiency in feed crops, and proximity to fat-deficit countries. In theory, Poland is thoroughly justified in endeavouring to convert itself into a pork-exporting rather than a grain-exporting country. Exploitation of these natural advantages, however, is held back not only by lack of capital, but also by the system of European trade under which importing countries insist that Poland accept their industrial products in return for Polish pork. The low standard of living in Poland imposes definite limits on its capacity to absorb such imports, and consequently on its ability to sell pork products abroad.

3. Agrarian Reform

While Polish agricultural prices are of fundamental importance, Polish authorities have also paid attention to two other aspects of the peasant problem: relatively low yield, and concentration of landownership.

[24] Cf. p. 147.

The agricultural yield in Poland in the case of wheat is inferior to that of fifteen European countries; in the case of rye, to that of fourteen countries; and potatoes, to that of eleven.[25] The Polish yield may be graphically presented as follows: [26]

Agricultural Population per km. of arable land	Yield in quintals per hectare average, 1931–6		
	Wheat	Rye	Potatoes
Poland .. 91	11.3	11.2	112.8
Germany 48	21.7	17.4	156.3
France .. 45	16.0	11.8	111.0

The relatively slow development of Polish agriculture may have been due originally to the attitude of the Polish peasant toward the land. To him, land was semi-sacred, an expression of the unique family group, which must never be mortgaged except to a member of the family. The purpose of the land was to give a living to the family; and if there was an excess of production, it should be distributed to the poor of the community and to guests. It was not exactly a sin to sell crops, but the peasant had a guilty conscience about it. He had a natural aversion toward the exploitation of nature on a large scale.[27] Although this attitude has now largely disappeared, Polish agriculture still has a comparatively low yield, because of lack of capital, the type of culture, and the land system.

In the western part of the country the intensiveness and efficiency of production, and the general level of farm life, are considerably higher than in the east. In former German

---

[25] *Concise Statistical Year-Book of Poland, 1937*, p. 71.
[26] Reithinger: *Le Visage économique de l'Europe*, p. 163.
[27] Cf. W. I. Thomas and Florian Znaniecki: *The Polish Peasant in Europe and America*, pp. 158, 167, 229.

Poland the agricultural yield has been considerably higher than in the rest of the country. This is not due to superior land, for in fact the land is sandy and requires artificial fertilizer. It is due to the superior methods of intensive cultivation employed by the Germans before 1914, and to the fact that this part of Poland was not devastated so much as the east during the World War.[28] Within recent years the yield of the former German territory of Poland has tended to decline as compared with other parts of the country. This seems to be due to lack of capital, and inability to compete with the more extensive and lower-standard areas of the east.[29]

Experts believe that with proper methods, which can be applied only under suitable conditions of land tenure, agricultural instruction, and capital investment, the yield in Poland might be increased as much as forty per cent. The government is aware of this problem, and in the areas of extensive cultivation in the east, progress has been made in agronomic experiment and instruction. In Volhynia the production of potatoes since 1918 has tripled, and milk production has increased eleven times.[30]

The second agrarian problem, related to the first, is the system of land distribution. When the 1921 census was taken, there were 3,262,000 farms in Poland, divided as follows: [31]

[28] O. S. Morgan (editor): *Agricultural Systems of Middle Europe* (New York: The Macmillan Company; 1933), Chapter vi, by Dr. Ponikowski and Dr. Leśniewski.

[29] Segal: *The New Poland and the Jews*, p. 111.

[30] J. Ancel: "Crise Polonaise? La Question Agraire et le Mouvement Paysan," *Politique Étrangère*, December 1937. Potato production may, however, indicate a lowering standard. Cf. p. 20.

[31] *Concise Statistical Year-Book of Poland, 1936*, p. 64.

Area in Hectares	Number of Farms	Per cent of number		Per cent of area
2 or less	1,109,000	34.0 ⎫	....	15.3
2–5	1,002,000	30.7 ⎭		
5–20	1,045,000	32.0	....	31.8
20–50	76,000	2.3 ⎫	....	9.9
50–100	11,000	0.4 ⎭		
over 100	19,000	0.6	....	43.0
	3,262,000	100.0		100.0

Approximately 65 per cent of the total number of these holdings consisted of farms of five hectares or less, comprising more than 15 per cent of the total area. Although 2,111,000 families live on these small farms, 19,000 owners held farms totalling 43 per cent of the total farm area. While Poland is not confronted with the problem of peasant tenancy, the concentration of ownership has been probably greater than in any other country in Europe except Hungary. In Poland, smaller farms (up to 50 hectares) constitute only 52.8 per cent of the total area, in contrast to 93 per cent in Holland, 80 per cent in Denmark, and 70 per cent in Rumania.[32]

While there is a difference of opinion as to how large a farm needs to be to support a family, there is general agreement that five hectares (12 acres) represents the minimum. If this figure is correct, nearly 65 per cent of all farms (called "dwarfish holdings") in 1921 were too small to support the families living on them. Moreover, there are four million peasants who own no land at all. The difficulty is increased by the system of strip farming which prevails throughout most of the country. Under the Polish

[32] Ancel, op. cit.

system of inheritance a father bequeaths his land equally among his heirs; and the result is that land is being constantly divided. The Polish countryside is literally a crazy-quilt of tiny cultures. Often single farmers may have sixty strips of land two yards in width scattered several miles apart. Such a system of land tenure — which prevailed in Russia before Soviet collectivization, and in England more than a hundred and fifty years ago — makes efficient farming impossible. Hours of time are consumed in walking from one strip to another; the use of agricultural machinery is virtually impossible; much land is wasted in boundaries; and countless time and money are spent in lawsuits over boundaries. One of the government's most fundamental agrarian measures has been the consolidation, or *commassation*, of these strips. Although the process is long and costly, more than forty per cent of the land involved (eight or nine million hectares) has thus been reorganized — a rather remarkable achievement.[33] As a result, production on these areas shows large increases. The "servitudes" once enjoyed by the peasants, such as rights of pasturage and gathering wood in the forests of the large estates, are also being liquidated, usually by purchase or grant of land by the owners.

Unable to make a living off these "dwarfish holdings," several million peasants must endeavour to supplement their income by working on the large estates or elsewhere, while many of their sons find their way into the towns. This constant pressure on the land explains the increasing competition confronting the Jewish merchant and makes the question of industrialization peculiarly acute. At the same time, many peasants do not relish being relegated to city

[33] A. Rose: "Le Problème de la population et des matières premières en Pologne," *Politique étrangère*, April 1938.

slums and warmly support agrarian reform at the expense of the large estates. In this attitude they echo the demands of peasants throughout Central and Eastern Europe.

Shortly after the close of the World War, the Polish Parliament adopted a resolution, on July 10, 1919, setting forth the principles of land reform. While this resolution recognized private ownership, it provided that no one should possess more than a maximum of 180 hectares (with two exceptions: 60 hectares if in the suburbs, and 400 hectares if in the eastern provinces). Moreover, the forests belonging to the large estates were to be nationalized. Land was to be distributed to farm workers who had lost their jobs as a result of the break-up of the large estates; to owners of "dwarfish holdings," to former soldiers, and to landless farm workers. The state was to divide up at least 200,000 hectares a year, providing long-term credit to the buyers.[34]

With the advance of the Red army on Warsaw, the Polish Parliament adopted the law of July 1920, which roughly followed the 1919 principles. It made the state the sole agency of subdivision; allowed a maximum area of 180 hectares in the country, subject to certain exceptions; but gave soldiers precedence over workers and owners of dwarfish estates. As far as compensation was concerned, the law of 1920 granted expropriated landowners the right to a sum covering only fifty per cent of the value of their property. Although less radical than similar legislation in the Baltic countries, Rumania, and Yugoslavia, this law eventually gave way to a more conservative measure adopted in 1925. The 1925 law no longer provided for the confiscation of half the land value taken, but provided that the agrarian offices established to carry out the land reform should determine the value of the land, subject to appeal

[34] Segal, op. cit., p. 106.

to the courts, and that half of this value should be paid in cash by the state, and the balance in government bonds. The beneficiary of agrarian reform is required to pay only five per cent down, and has forty-one years to pay off the remainder. The State Land Bank finances these reforms.

In addition to dividing up large private estates, the law provides for the partition of lands belonging to the state, the Catholic Church (as provided by the Concordat of April 23, 1925), and other public institutions, with the exception of cities and villages. In the suburban and industrial districts, lands in excess of 60 hectares may be partitioned. In the eastern parts of Poland, however, where the population is largely Ukrainian or White Russian but the estates mainly Polish, farms up to 300 hectares are exempted. For the most part, the land to be divided up·consists of large estates exceeding 180 hectares in the country, although land may be retained for industrial purposes. Forests and orchards are exempted from parcellation — which may explain why considerable land is now being converted into orchards. The law provided that 200,000 hectares should be parcelled annually during the next ten years, and that if this figure is not attained in one year it should be made up the next. In fact, the figure of 200,000 hectares was reached only in 1926, 1927, and 1928.

The government annually publishes a list in the locality concerned, giving the amount of land which each proprietor must part with. During the next twelve months he may sell this land to any buyer, subject to the approval of the agrarian office, but if he has not disposed of it, the government will acquire it through the procedure described above.

Following the establishment of the Piłsudski dictatorship in 1926, the government reached an understanding with the conservatives, as a result of which agrarian reform was slowed up. In an apparent effort to win the support of the peasants, however, the Kościałkowski government, in 1935, began to intensify agrarian reform.[35] The work is in the hands of Minister of Agriculture Poniatowski, who has been a member of the Cabinet since 1935. Although Poniatowski is a descendant of Poland's last King and a confidant of Marshal Rydz-Śmigły, he is bitterly attacked by the Right press as a radical because of his energy in pressing agrarian reform. Poniatowski and Kwiatkowski started several organizations, such as the *Zarzewie* and the Young Village movement, for the purpose of winning over peasants from the Populist, or regular peasant, party — but this latter effort does not seem to have met with much success.[36]

The total area of Poland suitable for agriculture is about 25,589,000 hectares, 4,606,002 of which consist of farms of 50 hectares or more. Between 1919 and 1937, 2,535,600 hectares were divided up into small farms, while 4,993,700 were consolidated.[37] Greatest progress has been made in the eastern and central provinces. All together about 698,400 families have benefited from parcelling; 768,700 by unification; and 272,200 by liquidation of servitudes.

More than two thirds of the land subdivided has been disposed of by the original owner by private sale, rather than by state expropriation. The tendency of the private owner is always to dispose of his inferior land, and when he sells it to satisfy the agrarian law, it usually passes to a comparatively well-to-do peasant rather than to needy families. Such a system does not fit into a broad agricultural plan.

It is estimated that about a million hectares of land are

[35] Communiqué of the Press Agency of August 19, 1936. *Bulletin Périodique de la Presse Polonaise*, No. 256.
[36] Cf. p. 112. Ancel, op. cit., p. 576.
[37] *Petit Annuaire*, pp. 65, 68.

still eligible for partition.[38] Agrarian reform is thus about two thirds complete, and may be finished within six or seven years. Probably only 100,000 new holdings can be further created as a result of the application of the law, bringing the total population benefited to about 800,000 families. One hundred thousand farms can support approximately 450,000 people — which represents the population increase of one year. Today, however, from six to nine million peasants cannot make a living from agriculture.

About half of the land so far divided has gone to create independent farm colonies, which opponents dub *Poniatowskis*,[39] while about a million hectares have merely enlarged dwarfish farms. Further progress in creating independent farms has been held back by lack of capital. It is estimated that 50,000 francs are required to equip a farm of 10 hectares; and to provide capital for the thousands of new farms needed in Poland, even on available land, is almost prohibitive. On the other hand, a hectare or two can be added to any existing farm without increasing capital outlay.[40]

Thus, despite the progress of agrarian reform, it does not seem that the fundamental agricultural maladjustments in Poland have been remedied, as there were fewer farms in 1931 than in 1921.[41]

[38] A. Rose: "Le Problème de la population et des matières premières en Pologne," p. 109.

[39] *Petit Annuaire*, p. 66.

[40] A. Rose: "Le Problème de la population et des matières premières en Pologne." 124,100 landless peasants; 61,000 non-agricultural workers; and 448,000 landowners have benefited from the reforms. *Petit Annuaire*, p. 6. The average size of the new farm is 9.4 hectares, but in Cracow province some such farms are as small as 3.2 hectares, while in Polesie province they go as high as 16.

[41] *Petit Annuaire*, p. 63.

Year	Total Number of Farms	Less than 2 hectares	2-5 hectares	50 or more hectares
1921	3,262,000	1,109,000	1,002,000	30,000
1931	3,196,400	741,000	1,136,200	14,700

But the number of tiny farms on the one hand, and very large estates on the other, showed substantial decreases. A levelling process has thus been going on; but there is no indication that population pressure has been removed to any great extent.

Indeed, a number of critics believe that agrarian reform, which takes the form of creating small farms, may make the situation worse. In their opinion, the large Polish estates are much more efficiently and productively operated today than small peasant holdings. Two leading Polish agricultural authorities expressed this view several years ago when they wrote: " The level of education, both general and professional, of persons managing estates is much higher than in the case of small holdings. The estate produces primarily for the market; it is in direct contact with the mercantile and social life of the country; it therefore perforce is directed on capitalist lines, where the greatest possible returns on invested capital are sought. The small holding is altogether different. It is foreign to the capitalist system of agricultural production, and to the needs which would bind it to the world market, etc. The purpose of the peasant owner is solely to provide food for himself and his family. Therefore, he has no idea of labor value, and has little regard for efficiency." [42] They point out that a small farm is relatively overburdened by capital investment and that such investment goes much further on large properties. Workmen on small holdings, they state, are worse off than

[42] Ponikowski and Leśniewski: " Polish Agriculture," in Morgan: *Agricultural Systems of Middle Europe*, p. 260.

on the large estates; " the estates are clearly superior respecting the level of animal husbandry. They are almost the sole pedigree breeders, and own the majority of registered animals. The productiveness thereof is also unquestionably greater on the estates. . . . Both the efficiency and intensity of the large holding are on a higher level than that of the smaller holding." [43] Statistics for 1936 indicate that on holdings under 50 hectares, rye production was only 10.7 quintals a hectare, in comparison with 12.7 quintals for the larger estates. In the case of wheat, the figures were 11.8 quintals and 14.0 quintals, respectively.[44]

The large estates are further justified on the ground that they pay higher taxes proportionately than the small farmer, and provide most of the agricultural exports, which are indispensable to the industrialization of the country. The peasants consume about 75 per cent of their wheat and 83 per cent of their rye; in contrast, the large estates market 78 per cent of their wheat, and 54 per cent of their rye. Thus the city and the army must rely on the large estates for their food. The abolition of the large estates would vitally impair national defense. Security would be endangered if Poland had to become an importer of grain.[45] These critics contend, moreover, that, except in the western districts, any parcelling will benefit national minorities more than the Poles. The Ukrainians, meanwhile, attack the agrarian reforms for exactly the opposite reasons. They insist that large Polish estates are being divided up and given to Polish colonists, at the expense of the Ukrainian farm

[43] Ibid., pp. 289, 295.
[44] Concise Statistical Year-Book, 1937, p. 66.
[45] Colonel Rostworowski and Colonel Stablewski: Rolnictwo i wojna (Agriculture and War) (Warsaw, 1937); Osiński Kazimierz Junosza: Polityka agrarna w Polsce a obrona kraju (Polish Agrarian Policy and National Defence) (Warsaw, 1938).

worker formerly employed on these estates. Other conservatives do not oppose agrarian reform as such, but insist that the goal should be a farm large enough to maintain
a peasant on an independent and dignified basis. They insist that at least 15 hectares, rather than 5, is the minimum
necessary for this purpose.

A number of replies are made to these arguments. It is
pointed out that ever since the abolition of serfdom, large
estates have been subdivided; and that since 1919 about two
thirds of the parcelled lands have come by way of private
sale. Critics believe this shows that economically the land
is worth more in small than in large units. It is argued,
moreover, that the burden of over-population falls on the
small holdings, for the large estates maintain only as many
workers as they economically need. If large estates are
more productive than small holdings, it is partly because
they have superior land. Large estates are also favoured
with more liberal credits, while the very fact of forced
sale under agrarian reform provides them with capital with
which they can intensify production. The late Ladislas
Grabski, former Premier, contended that while statistics
show the per hectare yield to be superior on the large estate, in fact such an estate does not cultivate its inferior
land.[46] If the total production of a holding in relation to its
size is taken into consideration, he estimates that the small
holdings produce 12 per cent more per hectare in grains and
44 per cent more in potatoes than the large estates. The
peasant will be able to feed the cities and army in time of
war, since he does not stop operations as quickly as the
large estate, and can adapt himself to the most difficult con-

[46] *Parcelacja wobec Struktury, Gospodarstwa i Dziejów Polski* (*Parcelling in face of Poland's Structure, Economy, and History*) (Warsaw,
1936).

ditions of production. It is contended that small farmers have survived the recent crisis much better than the large estates, many of which are still in bankruptcy. Some of those who favour agrarian reform ask that the minimum of 180 hectares be lowered, so as to increase the amount of land available for distribution.

Other defenders of agrarian reform, while admitting that the Poniatowski policy may be to reduce production of wheat and rye, and that in future Poland may even have to import grain, insist it will lead to increased production of dairy and animal products, and thus raise the peasant's standard of living and increase his capacity to buy industrial products. Moreover, the export of animal products is more profitable than that of cereals.

Such are the arguments advanced by advocates and opponents of agrarian reform in Poland today. It is difficult for an outside observer to pass judgment regarding the relative merits of the large estate versus the small holding. Two conclusions, however, seem clear. First, the Polish landed class cannot hope to resist the demand for agrarian reform which has swept over other European countries.[47] The peasant majority wants land for social and political reasons, regardless of the economics of the problem. Second, there is real danger, as the experience of other countries — notably Russia, Mexico, and Rumania — indicates, that mere redistribution of land among peasants lacking capital and technical competence may result in a decrease in agricultural yield. Other states are in a better position to pay this price for agrarian reform than Poland, which is one of the most densely populated and under-nourished

[47] Although in Poland the maximum estate allowed is normally 180 hectares, in Czechoslovakia it is 250 hectares, and in Rumania 500 hectares. Morgan: *Agricultural Systems of Middle Europe*, pp. 102, 317.

countries in Europe. Poland has already adopted many policies which restrict the production of wealth.[48] If possible, it should introduce that type of agrarian reform which offers hope of increasing agricultural wealth. This does not mean that it should abandon agrarian reform, but that it should endeavour to organize these farms, possibly on a co-operative basis, so that each farmer can benefit from the most efficient agricultural and marketing methods.[49]

Although Poland has a co-operative movement, it is doubtful whether, in the immediate future, the co-operatives can be expected to meet the country's need.[50] In eastern Poland the peasant is too illiterate, and in western Poland too individualistic, to participate in co-operative activity. Under the circumstances, the government should intensify its educational activities, laying the basis for co-

---

[48] Cf. pp. 136, 180.

[49] Cf. also *Problems of the New Cuba*, Report of the Commission on Cuban affairs, organized by the Foreign Policy Association (New York, 1935), Chapter xx.

[50] Before the World War consumer co-operatives developed primarily in Prussian Poland. But the war virtually destroyed the co-operative movement. During the reconstruction period the government made use of the consumer societies to distribute foodstuffs. This led to a rapid increase in membership — not out of conviction of the value of co-operatives, but as a means of getting food. Subsequently many members were stricken from the lists. In 1924 an amalgamation of all the consumers' co-operative unions took place in the Union of Consumers' Societies. The depression which commenced in 1929 dealt another blow at the co-operatives, and a good many went into liquidation despite government credit. As a result of the breakdown of many agricultural societies, the government enacted legislation giving it more control over the management of co-operative units. Since the reorganization in 1934, four Polish and six national minorities co-operative unions exist. Consumer co-operative societies rapidly increased in 1935 and the following years. The Consumers' Societies are " decidedly anti-capitalistic," and a group of Agricultural Societies profess similar radical aims. At the other extreme are the Schultze Co-operative Organizations, championing the "Third State " — i.e., the small merchants, craftsmen, and well-to-do farmers. Cf. *The Co-operative Movement in Poland* (Warsaw: The Co-operative Research Institute; 1936).

operation in the future, but making efforts of its own to improve agricultural and marketing skills. Until the educational level of the Polish peasant is raised, it would seem inadvisable to reduce the maximum size of estates permitted under the law. It is apparently the policy of the government to rely on such estates for the production of cereals, while encouraging peasant holdings to concentrate on animal products.

Although the agricultural situation in Poland has greatly improved during the past few years, partly because of the world situation and partly because of government policy, it seems clear that the completion of agrarian reform — which at its present rate should be achieved within seven years — will not solve the problem of Poland's over-populated countryside. It will help temporarily; but as the population increases and farms are divided on the death of the farmer, "dwarfish" farms too small to support a family will continue to multiply. Some Poles, realizing this danger, favour the enactment of legislation similar to that of the Hereditary Farms Law of September 1933 in Nazi Germany, limiting inheritance to the eldest son.[51] Predominant sentiment, however, seems to be against such action, on the ground that any measure suddenly interfering with long-established custom will do more harm than good. If legislation of this type is enacted, it will force an even greater part of the farm population into the ranks of the industrial unemployed.

4. The Marshes of Polesie

There is considerable waste land in Poland which might be reclaimed and " meliorated." Much of this land is under

[51] Mildred S. Wertheimer: "Economic Structure of the Third Reich," *Foreign Policy Reports*, September 26, 1934.

water and can be rendered arable by drainage and river diversion. The so-called marshes of Polesie offer, perhaps,
the greatest possibility. The total area of the Polesie marsh
lands is 1,676,000 hectares (about 4,141,400 acres). According to a committee of League experts, " a well-planned
and well-executed system of drainage would improve not
only the actual marshes directly drained thereby, but also
a large area in the vicinity of the marshes which, though
not actually swampy, suffers from excessive moisture. The
systematic drainage of Polesie would thus improve most of
the land and would considerably increase its value." In
support of this statement the committee quoted the results
of drainage undertaken by pre-war Russia. As a result of
an outlay of a million rubles, the income from the land so
improved in the next ten years exceeded that received in
a similar previous period by 2,453,864 rubles. The League
committee estimated that the cost of draining the Polesie
marshes would be 450,000,000 zlotys ($50,000,000), which
is less than the cost of the port of Gdynia.[52] Some are scep-
tical of progress in this direction, not only because of cost
but also because the co-operation of the Soviet Union appears necessary, since the marshes enter Russian territory.
In view of Poland's relations with Moscow, many Poles
favour keeping the marshes as they are since they constitute an obstacle to invasion. If the marsh lands were drained
and subdivided, the land would constitute about two thirds
of the area so far divided under agrarian reform, making
it possible to create over 150,000 new holdings.

The productivity of Poland's countryside is the heart
of the country's problem. If the purchasing power of the

[52] *Note by the Committee of Experts Placed at the disposal of the
Polish Government by the League of Nations on the Drainage of the
Marshes of Polesie.* League of Nations, Advisory and Technical Com-
mittee for Communications and Transit, C.24.M.17.1927.VIII.

Polish peasant can be augmented by increased exports and intensified yield, purchasing power will be created for the consumption of manufactured products. The demand for such products will then lead to the creation of new industries which will absorb surplus rural populations, and gradually develop an increased standard of living. In addition to producing grain more efficiently, a large part of the countryside should devote itself to the production of protective foods, such as eggs, fruit, milk, and vegetables. Denmark, for example, has concentrated on increasing production and export of animal products, yet has developed a high efficiency in wheat production. Thus it has an output of twenty-nine bushels a hectare of wheat, in comparison with 11.25 bushels, which is the average for Hungary, Poland, Rumania, and Yugoslavia.[53] Denmark " was fortunate in finding open to her during the period of development, wealthy industrial markets which needed large amounts of animal products. But there is no reason other than contemporary political policies and national rivalries why many regions of Europe should not find in the near future opportunities similar to those which Denmark has already seized on so successfully. With the steady forward drive of technological progress the industrial populations of Europe and, indeed, of the world as a whole, are likely to increase. They will need increased quantities of foods of all types and in particular the protective foods. They can offer in exchange the equipment which agricultural Europe will need if it is to improve its methods of production and, after these have been supplied, the increased earning capacity of agricultural Europe will set up a continuing demand for a large variety of consumption goods which will have to be produced by the industrial populations." [54]

[53] N. F. Hall: *Preliminary Investigation*, p. 51.   [54] Ibid.

As far as Poland is concerned, the realization of such a goal depends on an improvement in agricultural methods, which turns on agricultural instruction, adequate capital, and the proper system of land tenure. It depends also on whether the purchasing power of the city workers is increased. But this internal effort will be frustrated to a large extent unless it is accompanied by a co-operative attitude on the part of the outside world. Poland's effort to develop greater exports of cereals will probably fail unless the great industrialized powers — Germany, Britain, and France — drastically modify their own existing policies of agrarian protectionism, or at least grant to Poland and other agrarian countries in Europe some form of preference over non-European sources of supply. France's willingness to extend the quota of Polish agricultural imports in the agreement of May 1937, the German-Polish agreement of November 1938, and Britain's abolition of its six per cent duty on wheat in the agreement with the United States are minor indications of a desirable trend. But fundamental progress in this direction, making it possible for Poland to export increased quantities of agricultural as well as other produce in order to pay for necessary imports and service on foreign loans, awaits the political appeasement of Europe.

CHAPTER VIII

EMIGRATION VERSUS COLONIES

POLAND'S economic difficulties have been aggravated during the depression by the decline not only of exports but of migration. Poland can no longer count on foreign outlets for its excess population. To understand the maladjustments caused by the inability to export men as well as goods, one should remember that before the World War emigration was an important means of easing the population pressure. Every year about 250,000 emigrants found their way overseas, while about 600,000 Poles went to near-by continental countries, for the most part as seasonal workers.[1]

At first, emigration consisted largely of political refugees, forced to flee after the revolts of 1830 and 1863. But subsequently Polish workers began to go abroad to improve their economic situation. North and South America attracted most of those who went overseas. Today there are more than seven million "Poles" living abroad — or about a fifth of the country's population. Two and a half million

[1] *La Politique Sociale en Pologne, 1918–1936* (Warsaw: Ministère de l'Assistance Sociale; 1936), p. 68.

constitute minorities proper — more than a million in Germany and about a million in Russia. Most of the remainder are Poles and their descendants.[2] Four million of these live in the United States.

Immediately after the World War, a mass movement of Polish peasants took place toward northern France and Belgium. For a time there were about 800,000 Poles in France, where they were partly responsible for the rapid reconstruction of the devastated areas. During the depression, however, many returned to Poland, although some Polish workers remained as farm workers in the underpopulated French provinces. For a time German agriculture also absorbed large numbers of seasonal workers. The migration situation since the war has been as follows:[3]

MIGRATION (IN THOUSANDS)

Years	Emigration	Return	Excess or Deficit
1919–25	577.8	. . .	. . .
1926–30	964.1	459.7	+504.4
1931–5	229.3	232.5	− 3.2
1936	54.6	43.7	+ 10.9
1937	102.4	40.8	+ 61.6

In 1937 there was an increase of from 8,400 to 33,000 Polish emigrants to France. Of the total emigrants since 1919 about 60 per cent have gone to European countries — chiefly France and Germany — and about 40 per cent to non-European countries. The United States, South America, and Palestine, in the order named, have been the chief overseas outlets for migrants. Polish emigration reached its height in 1929, when 243,442 left the country, falling to its

[2] *Rocznik Polityczny I Gospodarczy* (Warsaw, 1938), p. 13.

[3] *Petit Annuaire*, p. 55. For the Jewish migration, included in these totals, cf. p. 311.

lowest point of 21,439 in 1932. In the latter year — and indeed for the whole depression period of 1931-5 — Poles returning to Poland outnumbered those leaving the country. Since then the situation has improved, but Poland today can no longer count on emigration as a solution of its difficulties.

Long before the depression, world-wide restrictions on immigration began to reduce Polish migration. Before the World War, more than 100,000 Poles annually went to the United States; but, as a result of restrictive immigration legislation and economic conditions, the average number of Poles entering the United States between 1930 and 1934 was about 3,300 annually [4] — only half the figure to which Poland was entitled under the American quota system. Between 1920 and 1924, nearly 37,000 more Poles left the United States than entered it.[5] In 1922 Germany also discontinued the practice of receiving seasonal agricultural workers from Poland. Seasonal migration, which before the war reached 600,000 in some years, had virtually disappeared by 1935. Only Latvia admitted such workers, beginning in 1928, owing to a shortage in labour caused by agrarian reform. The number of Poles going to this little Baltic country increased from 5,000 in 1933 to 22,800 in 1937.[6]

The decline of emigration has had a depressing effect on Polish economy. This is due not only to increased pressure of population at home, but to a decrease in emigrant remittances, which at one time constituted an important

[4] U.S. Department of Commerce, *Statistical Abstract of the United States, 1937*, p. 98.

[5] Ibid., *1933*, p. 96.

[6] *La Politique Sociale en Pologne*, p. 73. Poland has protected its immigrants abroad by a number of agreements, such as the Franco-Polish agreement of September 3, 1919 and the German-Polish agreement of November 24, 1927.

active item in the Polish balance of payments.[7] As a result
of this decline, the Polish government has shown increasing
concern about finding new outlets. It has supported the
development of international plans for assisted migration
and settlement; as well as propaganda in favour of colonies
for Poland.

In recent years the Polish government has been particularly interested in the Palestine question. The uncertainty
created by the ill-defined status of that country has seriously curtailed this outlet for Polish emigration. Polish
emigration to Palestine, which reached a high point of 30,-
533 in 1935, fell to 3,679 in 1937, and to 1,887 during the
first six months of 1938. At the League Council meeting
of September 1937, Foreign Minister Beck emphasized that
"whatever the future régime of Palestine might be, the
Polish Government's principal anxiety was to ensure for
that country a maximum capacity of absorption." [8] Uncertainty regarding the future of Palestine made it difficult
to develop a constructive policy concerning Jewish emigration. At a meeting of the sixth committee of the Assembly, the Polish delegate, M. Komarnicki, expressed his
government's view that the hopes raised by the Balfour
Declaration would be carried out, and that "this Jewish
National Home should constitute for the masses of Jewry,
and not only for a chosen few, a basis on which they could
build a durable national economic existence." [9] It is no

[7] The largest emigrant remittances have come from the United States.
These declined from a maximum of 166,800,000 zlotys in 1926 to 70,000,-
000 zlotys in 1937. France comes second, with a decline from a maximum
of 76,600,000 in 1930 to 35,400,000 in 1937. German remittances, reaching
40,000,000 in 1930, disappeared entirely after 1933.

[8] League of Nations, Minutes of the Council, Ninety-eighth Session,
Official Journal, December 1937, p. 903.

[9] League of Nations Council, Minutes of the Sixth Committee, Records of the Eighteenth Assembly, *Official Journal, Special Supplement*,
No. 174, p. 27.

coincidence that Poland looks with favour on the revisionist movement headed by a Russian Jew, M. Jabotinsky, who
hopes to move 100,000 Polish Jews to Palestine annually.

Poland has also made several efforts to find a new outlet
for Polish settlers in colonial areas. Following a conference
between the French Minister of Colonies, Marius Moutet,
and Colonel Beck, the Polish government sent a commission to Madagascar, to determine the possibilities of settlement in that French colony. In order to reassure the Polish
Jewish population, the government published a communiqué
in May 1937 stating that the question of eventual Jewish
emigration to Madagascar could not in any way compromise the " benevolence " of the government concerning the
development of Palestine as a Jewish national home. The
commission reported [10] that there were important areas
suitable for colonization by Jews and Poles proper, and
declared that Madagascar could absorb 30,000 Polish peasants at a cost of 30,000 francs per family. At the same time,
a former Governor-General of the colony wrote that because of its barren soil, insalubrious climate, and lack of
capital, the plateaus of Madagascar could not absorb any
large number of Polish settlers. In 1927 a Japanese mission
had reached a similar conclusion with respect to Japanese
settlement in Madagascar.[11] Even if the calculations of the
Lepecki commission are correct, Madagascar would accom-
modate all together only about a third of the minimum of
annual emigrants desired by the Polish government, at a
settlement cost of about 90,000,000 French francs.

The Polish authorities also carried on negotiations with

[10] Cf. Major M. B. Lepecki: *Madagaskar* (Warsaw, 1938). Cf. also
Marcel Olivier: " Madagascar — Terre d'Asile," *L'Illustration* (Paris),
February 19, 1938; A. Lahaque: " Colonisation Juive et Colonies Fran-
çaises," *Afrique Française*, January 1938.
[11] Olivier, op. cit.

Belgium, proposing to increase Polish imports of products from the Congo — such as coffee and cocoa — if, in exchange, the Katanga were opened to Polish colonization. An experiment of this type was carried out in Liberia, with unfortunate results.[12]

Finally, Poland, which since 1934 has declined to accept League intervention for the protection of its minorities abroad, has gone to the League for help in solving its migration problem. In September 1936 Colonel Beck asked the League Council to study the question of enlarging the Mandates Commission so as to include representatives of other states interested in the colonial problem.[13] Before the second committee of the 1936 League Assembly, Adam Rose, the Polish delegate, stressed the shortage of raw materials in Poland and presented a resolution asking that the question of emigration be studied by the International Labour Office. About the same time a semi-official communiqué stated that the defective social structure in Poland made necessary an annual Jewish emigration of about 80,000 persons, and that since Palestine did not furnish an adequate outlet, other areas should be opened for colonization.[14]

Meanwhile an International Labour Conference at Santiago in January 1936 adopted a resolution asking the Labour Office to investigate the question of emigration from Europe to America. After sending a commission of inquiry to Latin America to study the question,[15] the Labour Office

[12] Lahaque, op. cit. At one time the Monrovia authorities invited Poland to send two experts to Liberia, which gave rise to the suspicion in certain quarters that Poland had designs on this country. Polish representatives at Geneva carefully followed the efforts of the League of Nations for reconstruction of Liberia.

[13] League of Nations, Minutes of the Council, Ninety-third Session, *Official Journal*, November 1936, p. 1143.

[14] Communiqué of the Iskra agency, October 4, 1936.

[15] From the report of F. Maurette and Enrique Siewers; cf. "Immigration for Settlement in Brazil, Argentina, and Uruguay," *International*

convened an experts' conference on migration in Geneva in February and March 1938, attended by representatives of ten immigration and eight emigration countries: Argentina, Austria, Bolivia, Brazil, Chile, Colombia, Czechoslovakia, the Dominican Republic, Ecuador, Hungary, Japan, the Netherlands, Peru, Poland, Switzerland, Uruguay, Venezuela, and Yugoslavia. The Conference suggested that governments of immigration countries gather information regarding the types of immigrants desired and the opportunities open to them; and that the governments of emigrant countries gather similar information on the number of families wishing to migrate and many other questions. It also made a number of proposals relative to migration assistance, particularly credit facilities. Finally, it proposed that the International Labour Office establish a Permanent International Committee on Migration for Settlement.[16] Through such an agency, some international form of assisted emigration from Poland and elsewhere might gradually be developed.

Poland was not invited by President Roosevelt to participate in the Évian Refugee Conference of July 1938 as it was not a country which could receive refugees. Nevertheless, Poland felt some concern that an international agency should seek to relieve German refugees without paying similar attention to Poland's particular problem. Some Poles expressed the fear that this attitude might oblige their country to adopt Hitler's methods toward the Jews

Labour Review, February and March 1937. Also F. Maurette: *Some Social Aspects of Present and Future Economic Development in Brazil*, International Labour Office, Studies and Reports, Series B, No. 25 (Geneva, 1937).

[16] *Technical and Financial International Co-operation with regard to Migration for Settlement*, Technical Conference of Experts, International Labour Office, Studies and Reports, May 1938, Series O, No. 7 (Geneva, 1938), p. 165.

in order to obtain international assistance — a view reiterated after the anti-Semitic excesses in Germany in November 1938. The Évian Conference took the view, however, that the immediate task of meeting the German problem was so gigantic that it could not broaden the scope of its responsibilities.[17] Moreover, it could be pointed out that since Poland's problem was that of easing general over-population rather than that of relieving the distress of victims of anti-Semitism, the best hope of international assistance lay through the migration efforts of the International Labour Office.

It is difficult not only to find outlets for Polish emigrants, but also to finance expatriation. The day when Polish workers could sail for America reasonably sure of obtaining work has long gone by. No Polish settler can hope to succeed in a new home without capital of some kind, at least for a temporary period. But this means for Poland a drain of the wealth it desperately needs for industrialization purposes. For example, Jewish emigration, which did not exceed 30,000 persons in 1934 and 1935, cost the Bank of Poland from 45,000,000 to 50,000,000 zlotys. It is estimated that the cost of settling 20,000 Polish families abroad would be 100,000,000 zlotys — a very heavy drain on Poland's balance of payments.[18]

Plans are being studied in Poland which would make it possible for an emigrant to receive advances paid out of a loan from some foreign source, which would relieve Poland of the problem of transferring capital. An international bank for such a purpose might be established. These plans

[17] Cf. David H. Popper: "International Aid to German Refugees," *Foreign Policy Reports,* November 1, 1938.

[18] A. Rose: "Le Problème de la population et des matières premières en Pologne," *Politique Etrangère,* April 1938; also *Technical and Financial International Cooperation,* p. 97.

are theoretically sound, provided that Poland can increase its exports so as to service the loan, and that a loan from a foreign source is forthcoming. The best chance for this type of financing would seem to lie through the migration committee being created by the International Labour Office. But until a degree of political stability returns to the world, it is difficult to see how international loans for the purpose of financing assisted migration can be raised, or, for that matter, how Poland can increase its exports so as to service the loans. In the absence of such an arrangement, emigration from Poland inevitably involves a drain on its capital resources which it can ill afford.

Provided proper credit facilities can be found, some form of assisted migration would undoubtedly relieve the Polish situation. But to a neutral observer the present Polish emigration policy has several defects. The first is the emphasis placed on the emigration of Polish Jews.[19] In view of the great pressure of Jewish refugees from Germany and Austria, it is not likely that many places for Polish Jews can be found in foreign lands. The Polish peasant is best suited to take advantage of existing emigration opportunities, either in the French countryside, or elsewhere where agriculturists are lacking. The Polish peasant population is increasing more rapidly than the Jewish population; and before the depression several times as many non-Jews as Jews emigrated overseas. The resumption of non-Jewish emigration

[19] The communiqué of December 9, 1937, summarizing the conversations between Foreign Ministers Delbos and Beck, said: " The two ministers were in agreement in believing that this [emigration] cannot be exclusively raised on racial lines. It is known that the important annual increase of the Jewish element in Poland obliges the government to seek the possibility of establishing this part of the population on territories overseas. It is normal that the emigration to Palestine should be exclusively Jewish. On the other hand, this consideration is not involved if other territories are in question."

consequently cannot be ignored. Whether the Polish government wishes, for non-economic reasons, to reduce the strength of its Jewish population is another question, discussed elsewhere.[20] But if it concentrates its emigration efforts on the Polish Jew, it is likely to be disappointed. On the other hand, an emigration policy adapted to those classes of Poles, Jews and non-Jews, who are best fitted to emigrate may have some chance of success. The attitude of some Poles is that the Jews themselves, particularly in foreign countries, should finance the expatriation of Polish Jews — an attitude not likely to produce constructive results. If renewed emigration on any substantial scale is to become a reality, the Polish government will probably have to assume greater financial responsibilities.

In any event, it should be noted that there has been no year since the World War when Polish emigration equalled much more than half the annual population increase.[21] And it is hardly likely that the pre-depression figures will be reached in any predictable future. Emigration, therefore, can only be a partial palliative. The real solution of Poland's population problem depends on increasing the productivity of the country.

In addition to supporting international planning for migration, Poland has worked to secure international measures which would relieve its raw-material problem. At the Raw Materials Committee convened by the League of Nations in 1937, Polish representatives presented plans to give overpopulated countries economic concessions in colonial areas, which would enable them to develop raw materials by

[20] Cf. p. 307.
[21] A high figure of 243,442 was reached in 1929, as compared with an annual population increase of about 400,000. On the other hand, during the past five years the Jewish population has increased by 30,000 a year, in contrast to the top figure of 30,700 Jewish emigrants in 1936.

means of excess labour. The report of the Committee, however, did not go as far as Poland desired. And in a note of
June 22, 1938 the Polish government [22] criticized the report,
intimating that it did not pay adequate attention to the
" core of the problem," which " lies in finding means to
enable States lacking raw materials to exploit them direct
and to acquire them by exchanging them for such commodities as those States possess." While it believed that colonial
markets were valuable, the Polish government went on to
advocate the continuance of international action with a view
to arriving at a practical solution of the raw-material problem. It expressed the belief that a conference should be held
to draft a convention or lay down principles governing the
conclusion of bilateral agreements.

Theoretically, the solution of Poland's migration and
raw-material problem might be found in world recovery
along traditional lines. Under such a system Poland would
be able to buy and sell freely on the world market, while
the Polish emigrant could wander where he wished, attracted by the best wages. There is no prospect that this
kind of world will again come into existence; but there is
the alternative of international planning, which would open
up certain areas for limited numbers of emigrants and would
also work out plans whereby Poland and other over-populated countries could exchange their surpluses for colonial
raw materials without the necessity of acquiring foreign
exchange.[23] But with existing political conditions, it has

[22] "Commercial Access to Raw Materials," C.339.M.205.1938.II.B.,
September 24, 1938. Cf. also *Report of the Committee for the Study of
the Problem of Raw Materials*, A.27.1937.II.B.

[23] The Van Zeeland report declared: "With regard to raw materials
a most interesting proposal has been formulated tending to the supply of
colonial goods in exchange for industrial products. An agreement would
be concluded between a colony and an industrial State, and colonial goods
supplies would be carried to an account and paid for by the execution in

proved as difficult for Poland to obtain concrete international action with respect to planned emigration or raw
materials as to secure the return of a world economy func-
tioning on orthodox economic principles. Despairing of international action, and motivated by considerations of prestige, Poland has therefore developed a colonial movement.
The Poles believe that, if Poland is a great power, it should
have a colonial empire, as in the case of Britain, France, or
Italy.

The Maritime and Colonial League, founded in 1930, car-
ries on propaganda in favour of colonies. Although the
organization at first did not receive government support,
today every member of the *Ozon* is asked to join. The old
German Maritime League seems to be the model for the
Polish organization.[24]   Membership has grown from 40,000
in 1930 to 759,000 in 1937.[25] The visitor will see plastered
on factory walls huge placards in favour of the colonial
campaign. Nearly 6,000 local groups have been organized,
and colonial propaganda is carried on even among Poles in
the United States and South America. In January 1933 the
government asked the Maritime and Colonial League to organize a Fund of Maritime Defence, to be used to build war-
ships; and, as a result of a national subscription, amounting
to about 5,000,000 zlotys, a submarine was constructed.
The budget of the League totals nearly 2,000,000 zlotys annually. In addition to publishing large quantities of literature, the League organizes at Gdynia an annual Holiday of

return of important public works — bridges, railways, ports, etc. The intermediate finance would be provided by the metropolitan State." For
text, cf. *New York Times*, January 28, 1938; reprinted in *International
Conciliation*, March 1938 (No. 338).
   [24] Cf. Gilbert Maroger: *L'Europe et la Question Coloniale* (Paris:
Sirey; 1938), p. 249.
   [25] *Rocznik Morski I Kolonialny 1938 (Maritime and Colonial League
Annual)* (Warsaw), p. 415.

the Sea. In the fall of 1937 it sponsored colonial manifestations in every Polish city. At Warsaw, after singing "The Hymn of the Baltic," the audience passed a resolution expressing the view that "an energetic action should be pursued on the international terrain, in order to obtain colonies in Africa, so as to assure Poland a really free access to raw materials. We demand colonies for Poland!" The League also maintains camps for the purpose of arousing interest in the colonial question among the youth. The Colonial League has contributed sums to a Polish colony in Brazil, inspired by a desire to train future colonial administrators.

In 1933 Prince Radziwiłł, then president of the Foreign Affairs Commission of the Diet, advanced the interesting doctrine that if former German colonies were to be restored to Germany, Poland was entitled to receive a share, in view of the doctrine of state succession. Since Poland succeeded to 15 per cent of German territory, it is legally entitled, according to Polish writers, to 15 per cent of Germany's foreign colonies.[26] While the Polish government does not seem to have expressed this view, Poland has shown considerable interest in the Cameroon, because the Polish explorer Scholz-Rogodziński played an important role in its discovery. Leon Bułowski, author of *Poland and Colonies*, demands that Poland be given a mandate over Tanganyika in compensation for the services rendered Europe in the war against the Soviets in 1920.[27]

That the Polish government is in earnest about the colonial movement is indicated by the fact that Colonel Beck informed Foreign Minister Delbos, when the latter visited Poland in the fall of 1937, that Poland would formulate de-

[26] Maroger, op. cit., p. 263. Cf. Teitelbaum: "La Pologne devant le problème colonial," *L'Europe Nouvelle*, December 12, 1937.
[27] Cf. Teitelbaum, op. cit.

mands regarding colonies when the problem of a new redistribution was actually raised. In such a case, Poland would insist that account be taken of its own vital necessities. Poland was also interested, according to its Foreign Minister, in participating in any international companies to be eventually created for the exploitation of certain colonies. The French Foreign Minister replied, according to a communiqué issued at the time, that he could only recognize in principle the demands of Poland presented in this "moderate form." [28]

Moreover, in its note of June 22, 1938 criticizing the report of the League Raw Materials Committee, the Polish government said it was wrong to minimize the importance of colonial raw-material markets. "The present production of raw materials in colonial territories affords no sort of indication of their possibilities of exploitation and development in the future. It is precisely for the countries lacking raw materials that colonial markets may in certain circumstances constitute a valuable source for the supply of indispensable raw materials." [29] The Polish campaign for colonies may serve as a psychological diversion from in-

[28] Communiqué of December 9, 1938. *Bulletin Périodique de la Presse Polonaise*, No. 266.

[29] "Commercial Access to Raw Materials," cited. The Polish government representative on the Public Works Committee of the 1937 International Labour Conference proposed that an International Public Works Committee should "study the practical possibilities of an international system of financing public works, capable of supplementing the national planning of the public works, with a view to fighting unemployment and contributing to the re-establishment of satisfactory world economic conditions." He contended that in certain countries the adoption of a "pump-priming policy" would almost inevitably upset the balance of payments and involve measures of an autarchic character on the part of those countries unless loans could be raised abroad. The Committee recommended that this question be studied at the appropriate time. "Public Works as a Factor in Economic Stabilization," *International Labour Review*, December 1938.

ternal difficulties and as a means of furthering national unity around the ideal of Polish grandeur. Nevertheless, by advancing these demands, Poland poses one of the most important world problems. How is it possible to justify a colonial monopoly on the part of a few great powers unless all dependent colonies are placed under some form of international control assuring the principles of the open door as well as equitable treatment for native populations? Otherwise, agitation will continue for more equal division of colonies, and this agitation in itself may become a source of world unrest.

Should Britain and France decide to return Germany's former colonies to the Third Reich, it is likely that Poland will demand that its interests be considered. But it is doubtful whether either the Western democracies or Berlin would look with favour on Poland's claims. The former have been alienated by Poland's independent foreign policy, which contributed to the strengthening of Germany and the partition of Czechoslovakia. Germany, for its part, is in no mood to turn over part of its former colonial empire to Poland. If Poland should press its demand against Germany, relations between the two states might become embroiled over this issue as well as over the Ukrainian question, which in itself is a semi-colonial problem in the heart of Europe.[30]

Even if Poland were given colonies overseas, it would lack the capital, the merchant marine, and the navy necessary for their development. Capital raised for the purpose could be better employed at home. In any case, experience shows that tropical colonies cannot absorb any considerable number of European settlers. Poland has far more to gain from the development of plans for assisted migration and for

[30] Cf. p. 276.

placing colonial empires under international control than from any reallocation of colonies. For the moment, there is little prospect that either of these alternatives will be realized because of existing political tensions. Lacking exclusive colonial markets in which to find raw materials, deprived by trade barriers of the opportunity to buy such materials, and bereft of capital to develop its internal resources, Poland is confronted with a future which becomes more desperate as its population increases and autarchy sweeps the world.

Poland's position was eloquently if plaintively described in a speech of October 30, 1938 by Vice-Premier Kwiatkowski in which he said: "The situation in the world is becoming more and more complicated. Political and economic differences increase, international organization is being ridiculed. The permanent revolution now in progress does not permit a compromise solution of the most difficult problems of contemporary life. The world today does not want to go to the Left, but at the same time is unable to find the proper way to the Right. . . . Some nations have colonial empires a hundred times as large as their mother country, other nations live on too small territories, or in an atmosphere of hopeless misery and permanent unemployment. The rich nations call upon the poor and over-populated ones, exhausted economically and poisoned morally by misery, to observe and practise humanitarian principles. They ask the latter nations to give refuge to foreign peoples, while at the same time they themselves close the doors not only of their mother countries — this they have done for a long time — but even of their unexploited colonies before the superfluous Jews from Poland and before emigration from the over-populated countries of the Old World. . . . Is it possible to find basic elements of an equilibrium in a world in which the right to live and prosper is not given according to even the most modest needs of nations and their will to work, but according to historical accidents? Is it in agreement with the physiological laws of evolution that three states have accumulated 88 per cent of all the gold, while the other hundred nations have only 12 per cent? Under such conditions, what object do these three nations have in closing their credit markets and in their efforts to obtain a favourable trade balance, and thus further deprive the other nations of their gold? "

The answer to these questions must be given less by the European dictatorships than by the democracies of France, Britain, and the United States, who dominate the resources of the world.

CHAPTER IX

✿

THE MINORITIES: THE
GERMANS

ALTHOUGH it is customary to regard Poland as a state of 34,-
500,000 people, its Polish population numbers only about
23,000,000. The rest consists of national minorities which,
according to official statistics, constitute between 30 and 35
per cent of the population; unofficial observers believe the
percentage may be as high as 40. Now that Czechoslovakia
has been broken up, Poland has a larger minority population ratio than any other country in Europe.[1] The presence of these minorities offers unfriendly neighbours an
opportunity for intrigues and, if the Polish state does not
win the loyalty of at least some of these groups, they may

[1] The Polish census of 1931 does not reveal the nationality of its inhabitants, but it employs two tests for minorities — religion and maternal
language. According to the religion test, 64.8 per cent of the people are
Roman Catholic and presumably Polish. According to the language test,
68.9 per cent of the population is Polish. Cf. *Les Nationalités et les Con-
fessions en Pologne d'après le Recensement de 1931* (Warsaw: Institut
pour l'Étude des Questions Minoritaires; 1937). For the contention that
the minorities constitute 40 per cent of the population, cf. *La Situation
économique des Juifs dans le Monde*, p. 196.

become an element of weakness in time of war. Moreover, in fair elections the minorities might hold the balance of power, for they control about 30 per cent of the votes. A country with several "Sudeten" areas, Poland does not seem to have adequately considered the importance of winning the loyalty of its minorities.

Two of the minorities — the White Russians and the Ukrainians — are compact groups constituting the majority of the population in the larger part of the areas they occupy. The White Russians seem to have less sense of national consciousness than the other minorities. Most of them are illiterate and impoverished peasants, who tell the census-taker that their language is "the language spoken here." In the Treaty of Riga of 1921 Russia and Poland divided up the White Russian peoples, and between a million and a million and a half may be found in the eastern provinces of Poland today. This treaty contains reciprocal guarantees of the right of minorities to "intellectual development, the development of their languages, and the exercise of their religion." About 75 per cent of the people in the provinces of Nowogródek, Wilno, and Polesie are White Russians.[2] The leading White Russian political group, the White Russian Christian Democrat party, advocates the independence and unification of the White Russian nation with the help of its "natural allies," the Lithuanians and the Ukrainians.

The three most important minorities in Poland are the Germans, the Ukrainians, and the Jews. The Germans are the only minority which has a powerful national fatherland to which they may look for assistance; but they are scattered all over the country, and even in three western provinces they constitute less than 10 per cent of the population.

[2] J. Paprocki (editor): *La Pologne et le Problème des Minorités* (Warsaw: Institut pour l'Étude des Questions Minoritaires; 1935), p. 94.

The Jews are even more widely scattered, 80 per cent of the Jewish people being found in the cities.[3] In contrast, the Ukrainians form a compact majority with a solid social structure in the rural sections of Eastern Galicia and the eastern provinces. Aided by the Uniat Church and a growing co-operative movement, the Ukrainians are perhaps in the strongest position to safeguard their culture, despite the fact that they have no foreign government to plead their cause, with the possible exception of Germany.

1. The Minorities Treaty

As a condition of its independence, Poland, along with some other states, was obliged to accept certain international obligations with respect to its minorities. In the treaty of June 28, 1919 made with the Principal Allied and Associated Powers, Poland guaranteed toward all its inhabitants full and complete protection of life and property, without distinction of birth, nationality, language, race, or religion. Article 7 of the minority treaty says: " All Polish nationals shall be equal before the law and shall enjoy the same civil and political rights, without distinction as to race, language, or religion. Differences of religion, creed, or confession shall not prejudice any Polish national in matters relating to the enjoyment of civil or political rights, as for instance admission to public employments, functions, and honours, or the exercise of professions and industries. . . . Adequate facilities shall be given to Polish nationals of non-Polish speech for the use of their language, either orally or

[3] According to the census of 1931, about 27 per cent in the nine leading cities were Jewish. The largest percentage is in Łódż, where the Jews constitute 33.5 per cent; Warsaw comes second, with 30 per cent. In certain smaller cities, such as Równo, the Jews constitute more than half the population. Cf. p. 312.

in writing, before the courts." Article 8 further says that "Polish nationals who belong to racial, religious or linguistic minorities shall enjoy the same treatment and security in law and in fact as the other Polish nationals." In particular, minorities shall have an equal right to establish, manage, and control their own charitable, religious, social, and educational institutions, and to use their own language and exercise their own religion freely. Where the minorities form a "considerable proportion" of the population, adequate facilities for primary instruction in their own language is guaranteed, as well as an "equitable share" of any public moneys allotted for educational, religious, or charitable purposes. Special protection is accorded to the Jewish schools and to Jews wishing to maintain their Sabbath.

From the first Poland resented obligations which did not generally apply also to the other powers. M. Clemenceau, president of the Paris Peace Conference, defended this discrimination in a letter to M. Paderewski on June 24, 1919. He declared that it was a long-established principle of public law that, when a new state was established, the great powers could accompany their recognition by the requirement that such a state should comply with certain principles of government. Moreover, "it is to the endeavours and sacrifices of the Powers in whose name I am addressing you that the Polish nation owes the recovery of its independence. . . . It is on the support which the resources of these Powers will afford to the League of Nations that for the future Poland will to a large extent depend for the secure possession of these territories."[4]

This letter did not prevent the Polish Parliament, when ratifying the "Little Treaty of Versailles," as the treaty

[4] H. W. V. Temperley: *A History of the Peace Conference of Paris* (New York: Oxford University Press; 1920), Vol. V, pp. 432 ff.

of June 28, 1919 was called, from asking the government to take steps to reconcile its provisions with the full sovereignty of Poland.[5] The Polish constitution, however, extended ample guarantees to minorities. It provided that every citizen should have the right to preserve his nationality and cultivate his language and national qualities — provisions continued in the 1935 constitution. In 1924 the Parliament enacted a series of laws concerning minority languages and schools. One of these laws declared that Polish was the language of state, but that the authorities would accept requests presented in the maternal language of Polish citizens of Ukrainian, White Russian, and Lithuanian nationality and that such languages could be used in the deliberations of local bodies. Administrators would reply to requests in the state language and also in the language of the request. Another law protected the right to use the maternal language in the courts, while a third, regarding education, provided that there would be a single system of public instruction, but that the Ukrainians, White Russian, and Lithuanian nationalities had the same right as Poles proper to open private schools. In mixed districts the aim of the public school was to make good citizens of children of Polish and non-Polish nationality, at the same time respecting national particularities. In the public primary schools in communes possessing 25 per cent of a Ukrainian, White Russian or Lithuanian nationality, instruction in the maternal language was to be given at the request of the parents of forty children of the minority concerned. If parents of twenty children wished instruction in Polish, the school was to be bilingual, instruction being given half in one and half in the other language. In schools where the language of instruction was not Polish, the teaching of the

[5] S. J. Paprocki: *Minority Affairs and Poland*, p. 18.

Polish language and of Polish history was to be obligatory, both in public and in private schools. The law provided for a number of bilingual normal schools. At the request of the parents of a hundred and fifty children of Ukrainian or White Russian nationality in secondary schools, the state was to establish a secondary school giving bilingual instruction.[6]

The effort which Poland is making to fulfil these obligations with respect to schools is shown by the fact that, of the 28,337 primary schools in Poland (1936-7), 21,459, or 75 per cent, give instruction exclusively in the Polish language. Of the remainder, about 5,400 teach or employ Ukrainian; 2,274 use Polish as the language of instruction[7] but teach Ukrainian as a branch of instruction; 2,710 use both Polish and Ukrainian as languages of instruction. As we shall see below, the development of these bilingual schools has not proved popular with the minorities, who feel that under the minority treaty they are entitled to their own schools and teachers maintained at public expense.

So long as Germany was not a member of the League Council, it had no right to invoke the minority treaty against Poland. The Council, however, entertained countless petitions from German minority groups which Poland regarded as frivolous. A Polish authority writes: " Nine-tenths of the petitions received were simply a tissue of falsehoods and even of malicious slander." [8] A number of cases involving Poland's treatment of minorities were brought

[6] For the French text of these three laws, cf. B. Mirkine-Guetzevitch: *La Pologne* (Paris: Bibliothèque d'Histoire et de Politique; 1930), p. 99. The Jews are not covered by the guarantees of this law. Cf. p. 296.

[7] In addition there are 496 schools using Ukrainian exclusively, 428 exclusively German schools, and 166 Hebraic. *Petit Annuaire Statistique de la Pologne, 1938*, p. 314. Very few schools teach White Russian.

[8] Paprocki: *Minority Affairs and Poland*, p. 19.

before the Permanent Court of international Justice. In the most famous one of these, the court expressed the opinion that Poland had no right, on account of the minority treaties, to terminate land leases under which Germans had been colonized by Prussia on former Polish lands.[9] While no doubt legally sound, this decision did not make the Poles feel any more friendly toward the minorities treaty, which prevented the correction of what they regarded as a great historic injustice.

When Germany joined the League and became a member of the Council in 1926, it obtained the right to intervene on behalf of its minority in Poland. The Poles are probably right in saying that no other government abused this privilege as much as the government of the German Republic. In order to foster revisionist propaganda and to keep the "Corridor" question before world opinion, the Weimar régime brought innumerable complaints before the League Council and the World Court. In Poland's eyes, the German minority came to occupy quite a different position from that of other nationalities; the Germans were looked upon as enemies of the state, a docile instrument of German propaganda. Poland's resentment was increased by the fact that Germany had accepted no obligations to protect the Polish minority in Germany proper.

Polish apprehensions reached their height when the

[9] "It undoubtedly is true, as Poland has stated, that the persons whose rights are involved were settled upon the lands in pursuance of a policy of Germanization which appears upon the face of the legislation under which the contracts were made. The effect of the enforcement of the law of July 14th, 1920 would be to eradicate what had previously been done, so far as de-Germanization would result from requiring the settlers in question to abandon their homes. But . . . it is precisely what the Minorities Treaty was intended to prevent." Advisory Opinion No. 6, September 10, 1923. Manley O. Hudson (editor): *World Court Reports* (Washington: Carnegie Endowment for International Peace; 1934), Vol. I, p. 218.

U.S.S.R. became a League member in 1934. Remembering Catherine II's intervention on behalf of her Orthodox subjects in the eighteenth century,[10] Poland feared that under the guise of protecting minorities under the 1919 treaty, the Soviet Union would intervene even more than Germany in the domestic affairs of Poland. Fear of Russian intervention was one factor which led Foreign Minister Beck to declare at Geneva in the fall of 1934 that, until a general system of minority protection was adopted, Poland was "compelled to refuse all co-operation with the international organizations in the matter of the supervision of the application by Poland of the system of minority protection" under the agreement of June 28, 1919.[11]

A Polish commentator insists that the Polish declaration did not constitute a denunciation of the obligations of the minority agreement[12] but rather a refusal to co-operate in the minority procedure established by the League. In practice, the League of Nations, which, according to Clemenceau's letter to Paderewski, was to guarantee Poland's independence, was prevented from acting in Polish minority questions. With the virtual lapse of the 1919 agreement, Poland remained bound by the minority provisions of the Treaty of Riga and the Upper Silesian Convention of 1922.[13] Unlike the 1919 treaty, the obligations of these two agreements applied equally to both signatories and hence met Poland's demand for equality. The provisions of the Upper Silesian Convention represented an advance over the customary minority provision in that it granted an in-

---

[10] Cf. p. 45.
[11] Cf. League of Nations, Records of the Fifteenth Ordinary Session of the Assembly, *Official Journal, Special Supplement*, No. 125.
[12] Paprocki: *Minority Affairs and Poland*, p. 24.
[13] Cf. pp. 72, 79.

dividual the right to present a claim directly before an international body, without resort to diplomatic interposition.[14]

2. *The German Minority*

The 1931 census, unlike that of 1921, did not attempt to determine the nationality of the inhabitants of Poland but rather their mother tongue. Although the census noted down 741,000 persons with German as their maternal language, Germans believe that the number is larger. They declare that a person speaking both German and Polish, which is common in mixed areas, is likely, for political reasons, to tell the census-taker that his maternal language is Polish. While this may be true in some instances, such a practice would not radically affect the results of the census. Although the German minority organizations claim that there are a million Germans in Poland, the number of Protestants reported in the census is only 835,200.[15] There are many Catholic Germans, particularly in Upper Silesia, but they are outnumbered by Protestant Poles. Consequently, the religious test seems roughly to confirm the mother-language figures.

While the larger number of Germans is found in the former German provinces of Poznań, Pomorze, and Silesia, 153,000, or 20 per cent of the whole German population in Poland, are concentrated in the province of Łódź, which belonged to Russia before the World War. Germans and Jews settled in this province in large numbers to build the great textile industry of this area. Today the Germans in

---

[14] On the rights of individuals in international law in relation to the protection of minorities, cf. Georges Scelle: *Précis de droit des gens* (Paris: Sirey; 1934); S. Segal: *L'Individu en droit international positif* (Paris: Sirey; 1932).

[15] *Petit Annuaire*, pp. 22, 24.

Łódź continue to dominate textile production, providing a large part of the executives, engineers, and technicians and many of the textile workers, and constituting 8.9 per cent of the population. In the province outside Łódź they constitute 19.5 per cent.[16] Unlike the Germans along the frontier, the Germans of Łódź have never belonged to Germany nor had any irredentist tendencies; a majority of the workers, at least, are opposed to Hitler and the Nazi régime. In the former Austrian and Russian provinces apart from Łódź, 196,000 Germans also live isolated from their fatherland. They range from 0.01 of the Novogródek voivody — only 400 Germans — to 2.9 per cent of the total population of Warsaw province, which has 73,600 Germans. Of the 750,000 Germans living in Poland, 350,000, or about 45 per cent, live outside the former German provinces. They form German " islands," surrounded by huge non-German majorities. Their future is bound up with the fate of Poland itself. According to Polish statistics, the Germans in Posnania in 1931 numbered 193,100, in Pomorze 105,400 and in Silesia 90,600 — or 9.2, 9.8, and 7 per cent, respectively, of the total population.

The German minority in Poland is in many respects better off than the other national minorities. Under German rule the Germans possessed a large share of the wealth of the three western Polish provinces. While repeated complaints have been made to Geneva by the Germans that the Polish authorities are using agrarian reform as a means of depriving the German landowners of their possessions, in fact the Germans own large areas of well-cultivated land having a much higher yield per hectare than the average Polish farm. The Germans claim that between 60 and 70

[16] Dr. Alfons Krysiński: *Struktura narodowościowa miast polskich* (*The National Structure of Polish Cities*) (Warsaw, 1937), p. 22.

per cent of all the land parcelled in Posnania and Pomorze belongs to Germans,[17] and that virtually no German farmers ever receive any of the parcelled land. All together after 1921 about a million Germans left the provinces ceded to Poland. The situation of those who remain is generally better than that of other Polish citizens.[18]

The social and occupational structure of the Germans is better balanced than that of the Poles or the other national minorities. While the Ukrainians and White Russians are overwhelmingly a rural population, and the Jews live for the most part in cities, the Germans are farmers, artisans, workers, manufacturers, landowners, professionals and technicians. In Posnania and Pomorze the German city population emigrated to a large extent after the World War, so that large landowners and farmers form the bulk of the German population in those provinces. A relatively small number are in commerce and industry. In Upper Silesia the Germans are for the most part engaged in industrial occupations. Here German coal magnates, executives of large mines, engineers and technicians, miners and industrial workers are to be found; but there are also large German estates, such as the immense estate of Prince Pless, whose status has been debated before the Council of the League of Nations. Under the Geneva Convention those estates were exempt from the application of the Polish agrarian reform, but since that convention has expired it is expected that they will be at least partially divided. If the German farmers receive their share, along with Poles, little objection can be raised.

[17] Dr. K. Ballerstedt: *Gegenwartsfragen der ländischen Siedlung in Posen und Pommerellen* (Königsberg: Institut für Osteuropäische Wirtschaft; 1938), pp. 11 ff.

[18] Ancel: "Crise Polonaise? La Question Agraire et le Mouvement Paysan," cited.

Outside of the industrial centres of Łódź and Warsaw, the Germans in Congress Poland are mainly farmers, and in Galicia they engage almost exclusively in farming. The majority of the Germans, unlike Polish, Ukrainian or White Russian farmers, live on medium-sized, independent holdings; very few are landless or have dwarfish holdings. Thus the general Polish problem of a surplus farm population does not affect the German minority. The Germans complain that Poland is following a policy of nationalizing the economic life of the country, and of Polonizing cultural and educational institutions.[19] It is said that the members of the minority are practically excluded from the civil service; and that mining and foundry enterprises, which were in German hands and employed numerous German employees and workers, have been nationalized and brought under Polish control. The Germans contend that their workers are losing employment unless they consent to send their children to Polish schools. It is also claimed that the German teachers are being displaced by Poles whose mastery of German is faulty; and that the efficiency of the minority schools is being thus reduced below the level of Polish schools, so that they offer less attraction for children speaking both languages. The latest figures on the 1937 " school campaign " in Silesia show a decrease of about two thirds in the number of students attending the German minority schools during the last ten years.

While part of this decline may possibly be due to the superior quality of instruction in Polish schools, there is little doubt that Poland has done its utmost to reduce German influence in Upper Silesia and other former German provinces. Its attitude is inspired by the belief that the German minority is an advance guard of German imperialism. Un-

[19] J. C. Hesse: " The Germans in Poland," *Slavonic Review*, July 1937.

less the strength of the minority is reduced, Poland fears that Nazi Germany will use the racial argument to reopen the frontier question.

3. The Minorities Declaration of November 1937

Following the non-aggression pact of January 1934, Poland felt more free than ever to proceed with its Polandization policy. One of the chief advantages of this pact was that Poland could reduce German influence along its western frontier without protest from Hitler. Recurrent disputes, however, developed between the two governments over minority questions and, with the expiration of the Upper Silesian Convention in July 1937, new apprehensions arose.

The situation was envenomed by the tendency of newspapers in both countries to complain about the treatment of minorities, and attacks reminiscent of the period before 1934 occurred again. In order to remedy the situation, which threatened to nullify the effects of the Polish-German non-aggression treaty of 1934, a declaration promising protection of minorities was issued by the two governments on November 5, 1937. The Polish and German governments, says the declaration, " are convinced that the treatment of these [Polish and German] minorities is of the greatest significance for the further development of friendly relations and that in both countries the well-being of the respective minorities can better be guaranteed when it is assured that in the other country the same principles are being applied." For the first time the Polish minority in Germany outside of Upper Silesia was accorded protection of its rights by an international act. As for the Polish minority in German Upper Silesia and the German minority in Polish

Upper Silesia the rights guaranteed by the 1937 declaration are modest when compared with those of the 1922 Geneva Convention. The 1937 declaration repeats almost word for word the provisions of the minority treaty concerning the use of the minority language in personal and commercial relations, public assemblies, and the press. It guarantees the right of the minorities to create associations and educational institutions, and to profess their own religions. Moreover, "minority members shall not suffer any disadvantage in election or in the practice of an occupation, business, or profession. They will enjoy in economic matters the rights and privileges of all other members of the state, especially in matters pertaining to the ownership or purchase of property." On the other hand, the minorities owe complete loyalty to their state, which will not seek to bring about their forced assimilation. No effort is made to continue the elaborate machinery for protecting minority rights established in the 1922 convention.

Unlike the minority treaties of 1919, which guaranteed the individual rights of the minority, the interdiction of forced assimilation in the Polish-German declaration of 1937 seems to be based on an entirely different philosophy. "The mutual respect of the Polish and German nations [*Volkstum*] forbids every effort to bring about forced assimilation or endanger membership in or recognition of membership in a minority group in question," says the 1937 declaration. The assimilation of minorities thus becomes a problem of relations between nations — of the respect that one nation owes to the ethnic composition of another, instead of a violation of the personal rights.[20]

[20] For English text of the declaration, cf. *The Polish Information Bulletin*, November 15, 1937, Vol. VII, No. 148; for French text, cf. Rappaport: "Chronique Polonaise," *Le Monde Slave*, 1938, pp. 270 ff.

In spite of the solemn statements contained in the Pol-ish-German declaration of November 5, 1937, little was changed in the policies of those governments toward their minorities. The situation of the Polish minority in Ger-many, which except for Upper Silesia was heretofore bad, became even worse. According to Polish claims, there are nearly 1,500,000 Poles in Germany, two thirds of whom live in the frontier regions. In spite of their large number, the Poles in Germany have only ten elementary schools and two high schools. Together, all Polish public and private schools and nurseries have 6,500 pupils. A policy of Ger-manization is consistently followed by the government of the Reich. A documented memorandum of the Union of Poles in Germany, presented on June 6, 1938 to Dr. Frick, Reich Minister of the Interior, stated that since the Polish-German declaration of November 5, 1937 the situation of the Poles in Germany has "not improved; not only has the *status quo ante* remained, but the position of the Polish ra-cial group has, on the contrary, become notably worse." The memorandum charged that new restrictions have in-creased the discriminations with which the Polish minority meets in all fields — economic, political, and cultural.[21]

Unlike the Poles in Germany, the Germans in Poland are not grouped in one organization. The Berlin authorities are endeavouring to bring this about, on the model of the Henlein movement in Czechoslovakia. While these efforts have so far failed, a majority of the Germans are in full sympathy with National Socialism. The growth of Nazi influence among the German minority might have been checked by a more enlightened minority policy on the part of the Polish government, for many Germans in Poland

---

[21] *New York Times*, June 8 and 9, 1938; *The Times* (London), June 9, 1938.

originally opposed Nazi ideology. But owing to the severity of the Polish régime, many are moving into the Nazi camp. As a result of the new electoral law of 1935, the Germans no longer have any representatives in the Sejm. Moreover, the two Germans named to the Polish Senate by the President are both Hitler sympathizers.

The growth of Nazi influence among Polish Germans was [22] increased by the *Anschluss* and the Munich accord. Many Germans in Poland now profess to believe that they are the next to be reclaimed. The minority issue arising out of the Polish-German frontier, including Danzig, seems destined to prevent any real understanding between Berlin and Warsaw.

[22] Hesse, op. cit.

CHAPTER X

✧

THE MINORITIES: THE
UKRAINIANS

1. A Disinherited People

WHAT the Polish problem was in the nineteenth century, the Ukrainian problem may become in the twentieth. Considerably more numerous than the Poles, the Ukrainians are the largest national group in Europe to whom the doctrine of self-determination has not yet been applied. Before the World War the Ukrainians were ruled by Russia and Austria-Hungary. After the war and Peace Conference they were divided up among four powers — Soviet Russia, Poland, Rumania, and Czechoslovakia. Only in Rumania can the Ukrainians be regarded as a minority; in the other three countries they constitute a compact majority in the areas they occupy. Owing to their division, the Ukrainians are not likely to win their independence and unity without the aid of some great power. The indifference of the Western democracies to Ukrainian claims has given Hitler an opportunity to revive a policy which Germany endeavoured to apply during the World War. Nazi Germany, which wants to weaken Russia and obtain the raw materials of the Soviet Ukraine, may seek to achieve these objectives by sponsoring Ukrainian independence. It would be a mistake, however, to believe that the Ukrainian movement is due only to Nazi machinations. The Ukrainian people existed long before modern Germany was created; and their problems antedated Hitler.

The territory inhabited today by the Ukrainian peoples is larger than that of modern Germany. Extending from the northern shore of the Black Sea to the Carpathian Mountains, it occupies the basin of the Dnieper and a large part of that of the Dniester. Within this area live approximately 40,000,000 Ukrainians. Although they constitute the majority of the population in this region, they live side by side with important minorities, particularly in the towns — Russians, Poles, Jews, and Tatars. In addition to the Ukrainians living in Eastern Europe, Ukrainian colonies are scattered throughout Siberia, the principal of which is in the "Green Ukraine" near Vladivostok,[1] with about a million inhabitants; there are about 750,000 Ukrainians in the United States, and half a million in Canada. The Ukrainian groups in the Western Hemisphere stimulate the independence movement by intellectual leadership, propaganda, and financial aid.

From the ethnic point of view, the Ukrainians belong to the eastern branch of the Slavonic peoples, in contrast to the Poles and Czechs, who belong to the western branch. Known as the Little Russians, they are much closer to the Russians proper than to the western or southern Slavs. The

[1] Basile Paneyko: "Le Problème Ukrainien," *L'Esprit International*, January 1939.

Ukrainians have a single language, varied only by local dialect, and a distinct culture represented by folk-poetry — the " duma " or semi-epic poem — and folk-music. The great writer Gogol, who wrote in Russian but whom the Ukrainians claim as one of themselves, said: " Everything is filled with song, everywhere breathes from them the great freedom of Cossack life." [2]

The history of Ukrainian literature begins in 1798 with the publication of Kotlyarevsky's *The Æneid Turned Inside Out*, and during the nineteenth century the work of the leading Ukrainian poets, Shevchenko and Franko, became well known. The President of the first Ukrainian *Rada*, or Assembly, in 1917, Professor Hrushevsky, was a distinguished historian, author of an eight-volume work on the history of the Ukraine.[3] Today the Ukrainians have important educational and scientific institutions, and have published a Ukrainian encyclopædia.

Although the Ukrainians have a common culture and history, they have been politically divided for many centuries. About 30,000,000 live in Soviet Russia at present and between 5,000,000 and 7,000,000 in Poland.[4] Though at the end of the eighteenth century Tsarist Russia tolerated the development of Ukrainian culture, subsequently it adopted a sternly repressive policy, forbidding the use of the Ukrainian language. As a result, the cultural leadership

[2] Quoted in D. Snowyd: *Spirit of Ukraine* (New York: United Ukrainian Organizations of the United States; 1935), p. 75.

[3] I have relied on an abridged *History of the Ukraine* by Michael Hrushevsky, translated into English by Wasil Halich and to be published shortly.

[4] The Polish census of 1931 made a distinction between the Ukrainian and Ruthenian mother tongues: 3,202,000 gave Ukrainian as their mother tongue, while 1,219,000 gave Ruthenian. *Petit Annuaire*, p. 22. About half a million Ukrainians live in Hungary, and about as many in Rumania. Cf. p. 274.

passed to Lwów, the capital of Eastern Galicia. The Austrian régime, for political reasons, encouraged Ukrainian nationalism as a check against both the Russians and the Poles. Consequently, the Ukrainians of Eastern Galicia are more advanced today than their compatriots in Russia.

The two branches are also divided along religious and political lines,[5] the former being Uniat, the latter Orthodox.

This division between Galicia and the Ukraine may have been accentuated since the World War. At first Soviet Russia encouraged a policy of cultural autonomy in the Ukraine, and Ukrainians of Eastern Galicia at that time looked to Russia for aid. But following the Kiev trials of 1930, which revealed the existence of an independence movement, Moscow returned to the policy of the Tsars. The liquidation of Ukrainian intellectuals by the Bolsheviks has well-nigh destroyed nationalist leadership in the Soviet Ukraine and disillusioned the Eastern Galicians as to Soviet support.

2. The Cossack Tradition

Ukrainian historians, such as Professor Hrushevsky, deny the Russian thesis that the eastern Slavs were an established unity in prehistoric times. They contend that the southern group of eastern Slavs were independent of the Russians proper. In the opinion of the Ukrainians, the Kingdom of Kiev, which flourished during the ninth and tenth centuries, was Ukrainian rather than Russian.[6] During this period the

[5] Cf. p. 33.
[6] Professor Clarence A. Manning, of the Department of East European Languages of Columbia University, writes me that " prior to 1500 there are few clear indications of a difference between Great Russian and Ukrainian in language, and it is almost impossible to separate the two

Kiev kings were known as Ruthenians, and the term *Russ*, which Russia subsequently adopted, was first applied to Kiev and the surrounding country. Although the Kingdom was divided among a number of princes, the first of whom was King of Kiev, a body of common law called "Ruthenian Truth" generally prevailed and, with the acceptance of Christianity, a common church was established subject to the Metropolitan of Kiev.[7]

During the thirteenth century the Kiev Kingdom fell apart, owing to internal conflict and attack from the Tatars. As the "Song about Igor's Regiment" expressed it:

"Sorrow filled the Ukraine
While the princes quarrelled with each other
And the heathen brought affliction."

Although the princes fled the eastern part of the Kingdom, the western part, called Galicia, continued to develop. Its ruler, King Daniel, became a vassal of the Tatar Khan about 1245. Despite the decline of the Tatars, the princes of Kiev failed to restore their former Kingdom; and in 1339 Poland and Hungary made a secret treaty agreeing to divide up Galicia — prophetic of the policy followed by these two powers at the expense of Czechoslovakia in 1938. About 1340 King Casimir, after persuading the Tatars not to interfere, succeeded in conquering Galicia with the aid of Hungarian troops,[8] creating a division between the eastern

groups in essential elements of culture. But it is unqualifiedly false to state that Kiev in the tenth century was as distinct from the rest of Russia as are the Ukrainians from the Czechs. The Tatar invasions and the rise of Poland-Lithuania broke a unity that was slowly developing. When Moscow freed itself from the Tatars, it resumed a development which it had always regarded as an outgrowth of Kiev."

[7] Hrushevsky, op. cit., sec. 32.
[8] Cf. Stanisław Zakrzewski: *Zagadnienia Historyczne* (*Historical Problems*) (Lwów, 1936), Vol. II, pp. 245 ff.

and western Ukraine which has continued to the present day. Under Polish domination the breach widened between Russian proper and the Ukrainian (south Russian) language. The latter acquired a number of Polish words, originally of German origin.[9]

When the Kingdom of Lithuania was at its zenith, between the thirteenth and fifteenth centuries, it seized most of White Russia, drove the Tatar horde out of Kiev, and tried to deprive Poland of Galicia as well. But this struggle came to an end with the union of Poland and Lithuania on Jadwiga's marriage; and by 1569 the whole of the Ukraine had become part of the Polish Kingdom. Poland then endeavoured to drive out the Orthodox Church in favour of Catholicism. The people of the Ukraine put up such resistance that Poland agreed that the Bishop might be named by the Metropolitan in Kiev, although in Galicia they finally accepted the Uniat Church.

During the 15th and 16th centuries the Ukraine was subject to repeated invasions from the Mongolian tribes which raided this part of Europe for slaves. Nevertheless, the eastern Ukraine, because of its natural wealth and estates abandoned by the Kiev nobility, soon attracted emigrants from Polesie, Volhynia, and White Russia — poor people who entered the country, organized bands, and spent the winter on the steppes or in vacant castles on the Dnieper. The people who adopted this way of living became known as Cossacks.[10] About the middle of the sixteenth century these bands developed a military organization to resist attacks from the Tatars. This organization

[9] "The Two Ukrainias" (by a Correspondent), *The Economist*, February 4, 1939. For the Uniat Church cf. p. 33.
[10] William Penn Cresson: *The Cossacks* (New York: Brentano's; 1919).

soon attained a reputation for prowess and daring. They built forts known as *seeches*, and constituted a democratic society, in which a *Rada*, or Assembly, delegated the powers of government to an elected *Hetman*. The Cossacks themselves were marauders, attacking the caravans of Turks and Armenians, raiding the Tatars, and making life miserable for the Poles who endeavoured to govern the country. Farmers moved in behind the Cossack forts and colonized the steppes; and a struggle ensued between these farmers, organized on a democratic and carefree basis — using as a base the Zaporog Cossack Republic — and the Polish authorities who wished to impose their feudal institutions and make their rule effective. While the existence of the Cossack army was finally recognized, the Polish kings insisted that its members be registered to prevent it from harbouring runaway serfs.

Although the Cossacks kept alive the sentiment of Ukrainian unity, Professor Hrushevsky writes of this period: "Under the Polish-Lithuanian rule of the fifteenth and sixteenth centuries, Ukrainian cultural life suffered a set-back. We know it was closely connected with the church and that the church with all her Orthodox officials was accustomed to be under the care and protection of the government." But, as the Poles "hated the Orthodox Church, it fell into decline and with it went the old culture. Fewer priests gained a higher education, the old schools passed away, and literature and art were debilitated. . . . The Orthodox Church was the only national organization. . . . Ukrainian culture could not stand the competition of Polish culture, which was upheld by force. Polish culture in the fourteenth and fifteenth centuries was a very poor copy of contemporary German and Italian culture. It gained ascendancy over the Ukrainian not because of its superiority but because it had the power of the government behind it."

If the ancient Kingdom of Kiev represented the first period of Ukrainian independence, a second and briefer epoch came with the successful revolt against Poland by the Cromwell of Eastern Europe, Bohdan Khmielnicky, in 1648. This revolt, which nearly destroyed Poland, was caused by the efforts of Polish nobles to expropriate Cossack lands, and of the Jesuits to carry on propaganda against the Orthodox Church. Although Khmielnicky was originally inspired by a desire to gain special rights for the Cossacks, the Ukrainian people took advantage of his military successes to join in plundering the Polish nobility and Jews, and to show " the existence of a separate Ruthene or Little Russian national consciousness." [11] Influenced by this movement, Khmielnicky said: " Prior to this time I fought because of the wrong done unto me personally; now I shall fight for our Orthodox faith. . . . I am a small and insignificant man, but by the will of God I become the independent ruler of the Ukraine." [12] Poland ended the war by the Treaty of Zboriz, in which it agreed that the Cossack army might be increased to 40,000 and that their families might occupy the land claimed by the nobles. For a year and a half Khmielnicky ruled the Ukraine as an independent prince.

When Póland again attacked, Khmielnicky realized that he must find outside support or be overwhelmed. Consequently he called a general assembly of his followers and told them they must choose between four protectors: the ruler of Turkey, the Khan of the Crimea, the King of Poland, and the Tsar of Russia. The first two were dis-

[11] Phillips: *Poland*, p. 41.   [12] Hrushevsky, op. cit., p. 327.

carded because they were Moslems; Poland was hated because it was Catholic; but the protection of the Tsar was
accepted by acclaim because he was Orthodox. On January 8, 1654 the *Hetman*, with his council and army, took an
oath of allegiance to the Tsar. Delegates thereupon proceeded to Moscow and asked for recognition of the laws
and freedom of the Zaporog army and people. The Tsar
agreed to respect the right of the army to its own courts
of justice. The size of the army was fixed at 60,000 men,
headed by a *Hetman* elected by the Cossacks; the nobles
living in Ruthenia were to keep their privileges, and the
Cossacks were to keep their lands. Local administration
would be in the hands of the mayors, who would collect
the taxes; the salaries of all officials were fixed in the treaty
and were to be paid by the Tsar. The Tsar promised to
support the Cossacks against Poland, and the *Hetman*
agreed not to establish any relations with the Sultan of Turkey or the King of Poland without the consent of the Tsar,
although he could receive ambassadors from foreign countries. These provisions were embodied in the Treaty of
Pereiaslav of March 14, 1654.[13]

Following Khmielnicky's death in 1657, the Cossacks began quarrelling among themselves; and Russia and Poland,
after a long war, purchased peace by dividing up the
Ukraine in the Peace of Andrussova of 1667. Polish rule
now extended not only over Galicia, but over the Ukraine
up to the Dnieper River proper; while Russia took everything on the left bank of the river, in addition to the city
of Kiev. Although the Cossack government disappeared
in the area ceded to Poland, it continued to exist in the Rus-

[13] For the report of the Russian delegates at Pereiaslav, and other
documents, cf. *Traité de Pereiaslav* (Lausanne: Rédaction de l'Ukraine;
1916).

sian Ukraine. Here, however, the Eastern powers intrigued in the election of the *Hetman*, much as the Western powers interfered in the election of the Polish King.

The last great rising of the Ukraine against Russia was led by the *Hetman* Ivan Mazeppa, who formed an alliance with King Charles II of Sweden in order to win complete freedom. But the two allies were defeated by Peter the Great at Poltava in 1709, a battle which served notice that Russia had become a strong power. Following this battle, Russia began to encroach on the liberties of the *Hetmanshina*, as the Ukrainian government had been called. So long as the Ukrainian Church had been under the Patriarch of Constantinople, it had been virtually self-governing — a centre of Ukrainian culture. But in 1685 the Metropolitan of Kiev submitted himself to the Patriarch of Moscow, and thereafter the Church became a Russifying influence. In 1720 Moscow issued an order forbidding all publications in the Ukrainian language, except religious books copied from the Russian; and in 1762 Catherine suppressed the institution of the *Hetman* and the entire Ukrainian government, breaking up the country into Russian provinces. The grandchildren of the Cossacks who had fought for independence now desired only to keep their land. To maintain a superior social position, they accepted Russian culture. Similarly, in Galicia the upper classes became Polonized. "The Ukrainian masses," according to Professor Hrushevsky, "did not have wide political knowledge; national feeling was weak, and the national sentiment in their culture was negligible." [14]

When Poland was partitioned at the end of the eighteenth century, Austria-Hungary received Galicia, making its eastern frontier the river Zbrucz; while Russia added to

[14] Hrushevsky, op. cit., p. 479.

its territory the remaining part of the Ukraine held by Poland under the agreement of 1667. Ever since the time of King Daniel a cleavage has existed between Galicia, where most of the Ukrainian population clings to the Uniat Church, and the Russian Ukraine, the inhabitants of which have been Orthodox. This difference in geography and culture is much deeper than the political differences between the three parts of Poland which developed during the nineteenth century. And it is a difference which still handicaps the development of Ukrainian unity.

The rise of Ukrainian nationalism during the nineteenth century was the work largely of intellectuals, who revived interest in the folk-stories of the past, perfected the Ukrainian language, and developed its literature. Although the upper classes in Galicia for the most part came to regard themselves as Poles, occasionally the scion of a distinguished family would feel the force of his ancient heritage and proclaim himself a Ukrainian. Today an outstanding example of this tendency is Count Szeptycki, Metropolitan of the Uniat Church at Lwów, who regards himself as a Ukrainian, although his brother is a Polish general. Until recently, however, the masses of the Ukrainians were little affected by the nationalist movement. Largely illiterate, the Ukrainian peasant, like the Polish peasant, was chiefly preoccupied by the bare struggle for existence. But just as the Polish peasant became conscious of nationality during the nineteenth century, so now Ukrainian nationalism seems on the point of becoming a mass movement.

3. The Ukraine and the Balance of Power

Long before the World War the Ukraine question received international recognition. With its absorption of the

Ukraine, Russia rose to the position of a great power which threatened to dominate not only the Crimea, but the Balkans and even Constantinople. From the days of Louis XIV, France hoped to maintain its supremacy in Europe by forming an alliance with an independent Ukraine. Napoleon thought that the Ukraine would obstruct Russian domination of the Black Sea and provide France with markets and raw materials.[15] At the end of the World War, France again returned to these ideas. Thus General Anselme, commander-in-chief of the Allied forces in southern Russia, wished to make use of the Ukrainians in the fight against the Bolsheviks, and a French colonel proposed that the railroads and finance of Ukraine be submitted to French control.[16] But France decided to cast its lot with the Tsarist Russians who opposed the independence movement.

During the nineteenth century Germany and Austria were disturbed by Russia's claim to hegemony over all the Slavs, and feared that Russian imperialism might dominate Central Europe. Following the Polish insurrection of 1863 the Tsar adopted stern measures against the Ukrainian language and schools, fearing autonomy movements among all Slavic nationalities. He had reason to be afraid that Austria, backed by Germany, would try to weaken, and indeed break up, Russia.[17] In 1888 a friend of Bismarck, Eduard Hartman, published an inspired article in the *Gegenwart*, saying that the peace of Europe could be secured only by a partition of Russia, following which the Ukraine was to

[15] Cf. R. Martel: "Le Problème de l'Ukraine," *Politique étrangère*, December 1938.

[16] Élie Borschak: *L'Ukraine à la Conférence de la Paix (1919–1923)*, extrait du *Monde Slave* 1937–8, p. 57; Walter R. Batsell: *Soviet Rule in Russia* (New York: The Macmillan Company; 1929), p. 200.

[17] A great plan against Russia was devised by the Polish Prince, Adam Czartoryski. M. Handelsman: *La Politique ukrainienne du Prince A. Czartoryski avant la Guerre de Crimée* (Warsaw, 1937).

be placed under Austrian guarantee.[18] German settlers also colonized sections of the Ukraine before the war.

Austria made use of the Ruthenians not only against Russia but also against the Poles. In 1891, as a result of a new election law, a group of Ukrainophile deputies appeared for the first time in the Reichsrat, where they announced their support of a policy to develop a Ukrainian state within the Habsburg monarchy. Although the Poles continued to dominate the local government of Galicia, the Ruthenian language was officially recognized, and Ruthenian schools multiplied.[19] Alarmed by these developments, the Poles in Galicia contended that the Ukrainian national movement was revolutionary and should be repressed. This assertion was not without truth, as the peasant uprising of 1902 demonstrated. Moreover, part of the Ukrainians who called themselves the " Old Ruthenes " did not believe in a united and independent Ukraine, but favoured association with Russia. The Poles allied themselves with this group in order to prevent the development of a Ukrainian national movement in Galicia. The Poles, therefore, endeavoured to divide the Ukrainian forces in two, and with some success; for in the 1907 elections five Russophile Ukrainians were elected to the Reichsrat.

Austria then shifted its policy and appointed a new viceroy, Count Andrew Potocki. Under his influence the conservative Poles, in alliance with the "Russian National Party," won a majority in the Galician Diet of 1908. Russia and Austria engaged in a struggle to win the support of the Ukrainian elements against the others. Following Count Potocki's assassination in 1908 by a Ukrainian student, the Austrian authorities appointed as viceroy of

---

[18] Phillips, op. cit., p. 219.
[19] Aulneau: *Histoire de l'Europe Centrale*, p. 362.

Galicia a non-noble, Dr. Bobrzynski, who denounced the whole Russophile movement. He recognized the Ukrainians as a separate nationality, and again endeavoured to win their loyalty to the Habsburgs. In the following years the situation in Galicia was critical, many Poles being murdered by Ruthenians. In 1913 the Poles decided that if Germany became involved in war with Russia arising out of the Balkan conflict, they would side with Moscow; for if Germany conquered Russia, it would establish an independent Ukraine state at the expense of Poland. The suspicions of the Poles were increased by the publication in 1914 of a series of documents showing that the Ukrainophile movement was financed by Germany.[20] It was also reported that Kaiser Wilhelm II had promised the new Ukrainian state to the children of the Archduke Ferdinand by a morganatic marriage. Although the Poles in Galicia had prospered, many now turned against Austria, because they believed it had become an instrument of Pan-Germanism.

4. German and Polish Designs

As a result of the Russian Revolution of 1917 Germany found itself in a position to carry out its traditional ambitions. In June 1917 a *Rada* at Kiev had demanded recognition of Ukrainian autonomy by Moscow, including the restoration of the liberties recognized by the Treaty of Pereiaslav of 1654. The provisional government declined to grant these demands, fearing they would mean eventual independence and the loss of indispensable grain. Following the Bolshevik uprising, the *Rada* on November 20, 1917 proclaimed the " People's Ukrainian Republic," while hold-

[20] Phillips, op. cit., p. 226.

ing the door open to co-operation with Russia. Despite its professed belief in self-determination, the Soviet government charged that the *Rada* was bourgeois and sent an ultimatum threatening war if the Ukrainian troops were withdrawn from the front.[21] Following an invasion by Russian troops, the *Rada* issued a *Universale* on January 22, 1918 proclaiming its sovereignty to the whole world.

Meanwhile Germany was endeavouring, without success, to negotiate peace with the Bolsheviks at Brest-Litovsk. The Central Powers, hoping to bring pressure on the Russians and desperately in need of Ukrainian grain, signed a treaty with the Ukraine on February 8, 1918, over Trotsky's violent protests. In effect, Austria ceded to the *Rada* the district of Cholm, which the Poles regarded as an integral part of their territory, and promised that the Ruthenian districts of Galicia and Bukovina would became a Ukrainian province within the Austro-Hungarian Empire. For its part, the Ukraine undertook to deliver to the Central Powers agricultural produce estimated at about a million tons annually. Such was the "Bread Peace" which Austria-Hungary particularly needed.[22]

In the Treaty of Brest-Litovsk, of March 1918, Russia agreed to conclude peace at once with the Ukrainian People's Republic and to recognize the peace treaty made by it with the Central Powers. This treaty saved the Ukrainian government from complete overthrow by Soviet troops. Although about half a million German troops now occupied the Ukraine, they were bitterly resisted by the Ukrainian peasants. The latter, having divided up the large estates,

---

[21] Batsell, op. cit., p. 211.
[22] Cf. J. W. Wheeler-Bennett: *The Forgotten Peace: Brest-Litovsk, March 1918* (New York: William Morrow & Co.; 1939), p. 154.

refused to cultivate grain for shipment to the Central Powers. As a result of passive resistance and the exaggerated estimates of the *Rada,* only 42,000 truck-loads of grain were exported to the Central Powers during the entire period of occupation.[23]

The situation having become desperate, Marshal Eichhorn, commander of the German army of occupation and uncrowned king of the Ukraine, issued a decree on April 6, 1918, without the knowledge of the *Rada,* stating that a peasant who acquired more land than he could cultivate was liable to punishment.[24] When the *Rada* indignantly declared the order to be illegal, Eichhorn drove it out of office and installed as *Hetman* a pro-German puppet, General Pavlo Skoropadsky, former Tsarist officer of Ukrainian descent. Although Skoropadsky gained the support of the conservative landowners by promising to restore the large estates, the peasants rose in rebellion. The more Skoropadsky depended on the Germans, the more the Ukrainian peasants sympathized with Communism. Following the withdrawal of German troops in the summer of 1918 and the conclusion of an armistice in the autumn, Skoropadsky was overthrown by a directory headed by Petlura.

Meanwhile, similar developments were taking place in the western Ukraine, or Galicia. As the Austro-Hungarian Empire began to disintegrate, Ukrainians from Galicia, Bukovina, and sub-Carpathia held a constitutional convention on October 18, 1918 and proclaimed an independent Western Ukrainian Republic. Ukrainian volunteers and soldiers from the Austrian army seized Lwów on November 1 in the name of the new Republic. On January 22,

[23] Ibid., p. 318.
[24] James Bunyan: *Intervention, Civil War and Communism in Russia, 1918* (Baltimore: Johns Hopkins Press; 1936), pp. 3, 6.

1919, representatives of the two republics met at Kiev and proclaimed a federation (which proved more symbolic than real), vesting supreme authority in a directory headed by Petlura.

Attacked fiercely by Poles and Russians, the Ukrainians strove in vain for recognition at the Paris Peace Conference. The Allies might have been successful in their anti-Russian policy had they supported these claims. But they listened to the Tsarist Russians, who demanded the maintenance of the old Empire; they listened also to the Poles, who contended that the Ukrainians were under the domination of both the Bolsheviks and the Germans, and that Galicia had formed part of the old Polish Kingdom and could not possibly maintain an independent government. When the Polish troops began to move against the Ukrainians, the Peace Conference endeavoured to arrange an armistice, but Poland declined to accept it unless its territorial demands were recognized.[25]

Meanwhile the Supreme Council of the Allies discussed various solutions for the problem of Eastern Galicia: independence; autonomy under control of the League; or division between Poland and the Soviet Ukraine. The Polish commission of the Conference reported against any proposal which would extend the frontiers of Russia to the Carpathians, asking that for the sake of European peace a common frontier should be established between Poland and Rumania, on condition that Eastern Galicia receive autonomy within a Polish state. On April 4 the Polish Diet passed a resolution asking that the Polish government make every effort to prevent whatever danger threatened the integrity of Galicia, which had continuously belonged to Poland since the fifteenth century. It added that the Ukrainian

[25] Borschak, op. cit., p. 29.

population should be given a measure of autonomy, without prejudice to Polish unity. Meanwhile, despite the pleas of the Peace Conference, Polish troops continued to fight the Ukrainians, and M. Dmowski, one of the Polish delegates, demanded the right to occupy the whole of Eastern Galicia up to the Rumanian frontier, claiming that the Ukrainians were commanded by Austrian and German officers.[26] When, on May 27, the Supreme Council again appealed to Poland to accept an armistice, Piłsudski replied that Poland had launched a new offensive against the Ukraine. On June 18 the British proposed to the Peace Conference that a High Commissioner responsible to the League of Nations be named for Eastern Galicia, to control the Polish troops ostensibly fighting to defend the country against Bolshevism. The Italians demanded autonomy for the disputed area, under Polish sovereignty. The Poles, however, continued to fight, and the Council of Four on June 25 reluctantly notified the Polish government that, in order to guarantee the lives and property of Eastern Galicia against the danger from Bolshevik bands, Polish forces would be authorized to pursue their operations to the Zbrucz River. This decision, however, was not to affect the political status of the country. Thus fortified, the Polish troops under General Haller, who had returned from France, drove the Ukrainian forces across the Zbrucz into the Russian Ukraine, where the People's Republic was also struggling against the Bolsheviks. By July 1919 the Poles had occupied Eastern Galicia.

Finally, on November 20, over the protest of Poland, the Supreme Council adopted a statute for Eastern Galicia, pro-

[26] The Ukrainians replied that they had a few officers who had originally served in the Austrian army, but that they would gladly exchange them for French or Allied officers.

viding that Poland should administer the area for twenty-five years under the control of the Council of the League of Nations, which might extend the mandate at its expiration. A Diet of Eastern Galicia, elected by secret and proportional suffrage, was to have large legislative powers, including the right to enact agrarian reforms (at the expense of Polish landlords); the Polish Cabinet was to include a Ukrainian Minister for Eastern Galician Affairs; and each Ministry was to have a special bureau for the same purpose. Eastern Galicia was to have a special budget; its officials were to be recruited among the local inhabitants; while Ukrainian army units were to garrison Eastern Galicia, and to be employed by Poland in time of war for the defence of national territory.[27] As the Allied powers were not prepared to send troops to Eastern Galicia, they could do nothing to impose a solution which Poland believed would involve the loss of Eastern Galicia after twenty-five years.

Meanwhile, the Allies decided to supply arms not to the Ukrainians, but to Admiral Kolchak, who insisted on being recognized as the head of the whole of pre-war Russia except ethnic Poland. Crushed between the Poles, the Bolsheviks, the Tsarist Russians, and the Allies, the Ukrainian governments gave way, not only in Eastern Galicia but in Russia as well, and the peasants in the Soviet Ukraine grudgingly accepted Communism.

Discouraged by the situation, the Galician army went over to Denikin, a Tsarist general, who was soon defeated. Petlura, also threatened with defeat, believed that his only hope lay in enlisting Polish aid, and fled to Warsaw. Here he concluded a secret alliance on April 24, 1920 with Piłsudski, who was about to launch an offensive against Russia on behalf of his " federal ideas." Petlura now accepted

[27] For text of this statute, cf. Borschak, op. cit., p. 130.

the Polish occupation of Eastern Galicia; in return, Poland recognized the government of the Ukrainian People's Republic with Petlura as its head, and concluded with it a military convention.[28] This desertion of Eastern Galicia by Petlura caused him to be regarded as a traitor by many Ukrainians; and he received nothing for this sacrifice because Piłsudski's offensive against Kiev proved a failure. By the Treaty of Riga of March 1921, Poland recognized the Ukraine as part of Soviet Russia. Meanwhile, Petlura managed to reach Paris, where he was assassinated in 1927. The attempt of the Spa Conference in 1920 to induce Poland to accept the Allied decision as to Eastern Galicia in return for military aid against the Bolsheviks failed. [29]

Following the defeat of the East-Galician Ukrainian army, all political parties united in the Ukrainian National Council which, under the leadership of Dr. Eugene Petruszewycz in Vienna, claimed to be the government of the Western Ukrainian People's Republic. Practically all Ukrainians obeyed the instructions of this body, and Dr. Petruszewycz became the virtual dictator of the Ukrainians in Eastern Galicia — although the country was under Polish occupation. On February 14, 1920 a convention of all Ukrainian political parties, held in Stanislawów, proclaimed absolute opposition to Poland, and the determination to fight for the independence of the Ukrainians of Eastern Galicia. In January 1922 a second convention reaffirmed the resolution of 1920 and pledged support to the Petruszewycz régime. In August 1922, the fate of Eastern Galicia not having been yet definitely decided by the Conference of Ambassadors, the Ukrainian National Council proclaimed a boycott of the Polish Parliamentary elections,

[28] Paweł Shandruk: "The Polish-Ukrainian Treaty of April 1920," Wchód-Orient, Nr. 1-2, 1935. Borschak, op. cit., p. 176.
[29] Cf. p. 77.

refusing to recognize the province as part of the Polish state.

In an apparent effort to conciliate the Allied Powers as well as the Ukrainians, the Polish Parliament passed the law of September 26, 1922 which, in addition to accepting the principle of autonomy for the Polish provinces generally, established a detailed, autonomous régime for the three provinces inhabited by Ukrainian majorities — Lwów, Tarnopol, and Stanisławów. In each of these three provinces a Diet was to be established, containing two chambers — one of Ukrainian deputies and the other presumably Polish. These Diets were to deal with questions relating to religion; public instruction; welfare and health, except sanitary inspection; construction of highways and local railways; agrarian questions, except agrarian reform; protection of industry and commerce; and the local budget. The two chambers of the Diet could deliberate separately on ethnic matters; and the schools maintained by each chamber were to employ the language decided on. The state was prohibited from colonizing the territory of these three provinces; and the law promised the establishment of a Ukrainian university, supported by state funds and organized on a basis of autonomy. The laws of the province were to be published in both languages, and the autonomy provisions were to be carried out within two years.[30]

On March 14, 1923 the Conference of Ambassadors — after pointing out that Poland had recognized " that as concerns Eastern Galicia the ethnographical conditions made a régime of autonomy necessary," and had accepted the minorities treaty of 1919 — decided to recognize the frontiers of Poland as embracing Eastern Galicia. As a result

[30] For the French text of this law, cf. Mirkine-Guetzevitch: *La Pologne*, p. 93.

of the Treaty of Riga of 1921 and the 1923 decision, Polish
sovereignty was recognized not only over Eastern Galicia
but over the north-western Ukraine, including Chełm,
Polesie, and Volhynia and covering about thirty-five per
cent of its present territory. Poland thus obtained title to
this territory without having to give anything more than a
moral pledge in favour of autonomy.[31] No steps have been
taken to carry out the unilateral promises made in the autonomy law of September 1922, and Eastern Galicia is still
governed from Warsaw.

5. Polish Policy

The Ukrainians form the majority of the population in
Eastern Galicia and Volhynia. About 3,500,000 are found
in Eastern Galicia proper; and about 1,500,000 in the areas
ceded by the Treaty of Riga. In the cities, however, the
population of this area is predominantly Polish and Jewish;
and the land has been owned largely by a Polish minority.
During past centuries the Uniat Church in Eastern Galicia
has gradually eliminated the Orthodox Church; and today
less than 0.5 per cent of the entire Ukrainian population is
Orthodox.[32] In contrast, the Ukrainians in the Russian territory ceded to Poland by the Treaty of Riga of 1921, except for the Polonized Catholic gentry, are Orthodox. Although the Uniat Church was originally created to win
over the Ukrainians to Poland, it now serves as a national

[31] Czechoslovakia, on the other hand, was directly obligated to grant
an autonomous régime to the sub-Carpathian Ruthenes, a pledge not completely carried out until after the Munich accord of 1938. Cf. R. L. Buell:
International Relations (New York: Henry Holt & Company; revised
edition, 1929), p. 227.
[32] *Petit Annuaire*, p. 25; also Adolf Krysiński: *Ludność Ukraińska w
Polsce w świetle spisu 1931 (The Ukrainian Population in Poland according to the 1931 Census)*. The Ukrainians claim 7,000,000.

church, playing a role not unlike that played by the Catholic Church with respect to Polish nationalism during the nineteenth century.

The Ukrainian peasants, moreover, have developed advanced co-operatives, despite the lack of government aid and credit such as are extended to Polish co-operatives. The number of Ukrainian co-operatives increased from 926 in 1924 to 3,272 by 1936, while the membership rose from 148,000 to 598,000.[33] These co-operatives are of great economic value — thus, they largely dominate the dairy industry in Eastern Galicia — and they serve as centres of political education and national activities. Unable to find employment in government or education, the growing Ukrainian intelligentsia has assumed the leadership of the co-operative movement and, like the Uniat priests, keeps in close touch with the Ukrainian masses.

Politically the Ukrainians are better organized than any other minority in Poland. The leading party, U.N.D.O. (Ukrainian National Democratic Union), originally believed in fighting for complete independence; but an even more radical group, composed largely of landless workers and poorer peasants, favoured union with Soviet Russia. Many of these, particularly the younger people, resorted to terroristic activities, so as to prevent the masses from becoming reconciled to Polish rule. Some joined the Ukrainian Military Organization,[34] a revolutionary group directed from abroad by Colonel Konowalec and apparently supported by German, Lithuanian, or Czechoslovak funds.[35]

---

[33] Rappaport: " Chronique Polonaise," *Le Monde Slave*, 1938, Vol. II, p. 254; *Petit Annuaire*, p. 106.

[34] M. Feliński: *The Ukrainians in Poland* (London, 1931).

[35] In May 1938 Colonel Konowalec was assassinated in Amsterdam, apparently by Soviet agents. The *Schlesische Zeitung* reported that the Carpatho-Ruthenian Guards have taken the name of Konowalec Guards.

Following the military occupation of Eastern Galicia in 1919, Poland did its best to disrupt the Ukrainian national movement, and Polish colonists were settled on lands which the Ukrainians regarded as their own property. A Ukrainian leader declares that Poland applied to Eastern Galicia and Volhynia, a "colonial policy," utilizing such well-known imperial methods as military, industrial, and agrarian colonization. He charges that Poles monopolized all public employment, undermined instruction in the Ukrainian language, imposed *numerus clausus* in higher education, took measures against the co-operatives, and prosecuted all sorts of Ukrainian associations, going so far as to dissolve the Ukrainian Boy Scouts, and imposing prison sentences totalling not only hundreds but thousands of years.[36] The Polish government seemed to believe that by such measures it could assimilate the Ukrainians, while repressing any agitation for independence. Even today the Polish nationalist believes that the assimilation of the Ukrainian and other Slavic minorities in Poland is feasible. The program of the Nara party expressly states: "We shall win the Slavic minority through assimilation of the masses and fight against hostile individuals." [37]

As a result of Polish policy and Ukrainian agitation, terrorist activities in Eastern Galicia reached fever-pitch in 1930. Hundreds of buildings and estates belonging to Poles were burned, several post offices were robbed, and a leading Polish advocate of rapprochement with the Ukrainians, M. Tadeusz Hołówko, was assassinated in 1932. Although the Ukrainian political parties denied any connection with these acts, Ukrainian villages sheltered the terrorists, pre-

[36] B. Paneyko: "Autour du Problème Ukrainien," *L'Esprit International,* January 1939.
[37] *Zasady programu Narodowo-Radykalnego (Principles of the National Radical Program)* (Warsaw, 1937).

venting their arrest by Polish authorities. In 1930 the government, using the army, embarked on a policy of "pacification," punishing entire villages in which terroristic acts had occurred. The punishment not only fell on innocent and guilty alike, but in numerous instances took a particularly brutal form,[38] although few if any Ukrainians were killed. Not only the Ukrainian leaders, but liberal opinion in Poland and elsewhere protested against this application of the primitive principle of collective responsibility, regarding it as one of the blackest pages in Polish history.

Eventually, in January 1932, the League Council, to which an appeal had been made, reported that while Poland did not persecute its Ukrainian minority, it had been badly served by the excessive zeal of some officials. The report called attention to the conciliatory attitude taken by the new Minister of the Interior, M. Pieracki, and expressed the hope that the government would persist in this attitude.[39]

Although M. Pieracki was subsequently assassinated by a Ukrainian revolutionist, peace gradually was restored. The Ukrainian leaders reached a compromise with the government before the 1935 elections — called the "normalization" policy. In return for being guaranteed eighteen seats in Parliament — a proportionate increase in representation over the old Parliament — the Ukrainians agreed to participate in the elections, which many Poles proper boycotted. In return for a promise of Ukrainian co-operation, which

[38] *Polish Atrocities in Ukraine*, published by the United Ukrainian Organizations of the United States, 1931. This volume summarizes the debate in Parliament, newspaper articles, and other material from the Ukrainian point of view.

[39] Minutes, League Council, January 30, 1932, sixty-sixth session, seventh meeting, p. 18.

included support of the army, the government also undertook to employ more Ukrainian teachers, to instruct its
officials to treat its Ukrainian subjects with more consideration, and to employ the term Ukrainian rather than
Ruthenian. It also promised to establish a chair of Ukrainian Literature at the University of Lwów.[40]

Between 1935 and the autumn of 1938 a truce existed on
the question of Eastern Galicia. Postponing its demands for
independence, the U.N.D.O. agreed to give the 1935 compromise a chance and meanwhile to work for the autonomy
promised by Poland in the 1922 law. The international
situation also worked against the movement for Ukrainian
independence. It is reported that the non-aggression pact
made in 1932 between Poland and Russia contained secret
clauses stipulating that both governments would follow
parallel policies directed against Ukrainian nationalism in
their respective countries.[41] Moreover, the Polish-German
non-aggression pact of 1934 removed another source of outside support for the Ukrainian independence movement.

Poland, however, failed to take advantage of this truce
to remove basic Ukrainian grievances. The Ukrainians continue to insist that agrarian reform has injured the landless
Ukrainian peasant, because the estates which have given
him employment are being broken up and given to Polish colonists. They complain that there are few, if any,
Ukrainians occupying the several thousand administrative
positions in Eastern Galicia and Volhynia, and that no
Ukrainian ranks above a non-commissioned officer in the
army. They assert that Poland is endeavouring to break up
the unity of the Ukrainians by making a distinction be-

[40] For the Ukrainian reaction to the 1935 election, cf. *Questions Minorities*, No. 3, 1935.
[41] Paneyko, op. cit. Cf. p. 324.

tween Ukrainians proper and Ruthenians, and point out that no Ukrainian university has yet been established, and very few Ukrainians are admitted to the University of Lwów.

Out of a total of between 120 and 140 students in the Lwów medical school, only two Ukrainians were admitted in 1931, nine in 1932, six in 1933, and ten in the two following years. As a result of this *numerus clausus* many Ukrainians have studied abroad — for example, at the Ukrainian university at Kharkov in the Soviet Ukraine, the Ukrainian University in Prague, in Berlin, and elsewhere. Before the World War twelve subjects were taught in the Ukrainian language at the University of Lwów, but today all courses are taught in Polish. An equally serious complaint relates to the primary-school situation. Under Austrian rule there were two school systems, Polish and Ukrainian, existing side by side in Eastern Galicia. This régime was changed when the 1924 school law introduced the mixed Polish-Ukrainian school. Ukrainians regard these schools as instruments of assimilation, for, although there are certain Ukrainian courses, the teacher is invariably Polish. The Ukrainians point to the fact that since 1924 the number of purely Ukrainian schools has declined from 2,417 to 457, while the mixed schools established since that year have increased to 2,230.[42]

[42] According to the *Ukrainian Encyclopædia*, Vol. III, p. 870, there were only 134 Ukrainian schools in 1930. None of the Ukrainian secondary schools outside of Lwów receive state support. In the summer of 1938 the Polish government, following a convention of June 20, 1938 with the Vatican, destroyed 112 Orthodox churches belonging to Ukrainians in Volhynia. It took the view that these churches had originally belonged to the Uniat faith but had been confiscated by the Tsar. It was also aroused by the fact that the priests in the area continued to be Russians. Previously Polish policy had been to use the religious differences between the Ukrainians of Eastern Galicia and Volhynia to break up the unity of

Although the " normalization " agreement of 1935 was maintained during the recent elections to the Polish Parliament — the Ukrainians obtaining the same representation as before — the truce established in 1935 was severely strained in 1938. The agitation of the Sudeten Germans for autonomy in Czechoslovakia found a response in Eastern Galicia. In January 1938 a Congress of the U.N.D.O., meeting at Lwów, demanded territorial autonomy — by which it meant a Ukrainian Diet, government and territorial army. On May 7 the U.N.D.O. issued a manifesto protesting against the " forced " conversion of Ukrainians to the Catholic faith, condemning the Polish policy which denies the Ukrainians the right to acquire land and refuses to grant them educational opportunities or government employment, and demanding autonomy.

The Ukrainian question reached its crisis after the Munich accord of September 1938. Following this accord Czechoslovakia granted autonomy to sub-Carpatho-Ukraine, thus extending self-government to a branch of the Ukrainian people. The success achieved by sub-Carpatho-Ukraine had an electric effect in Eastern Galicia, where the Ukrainians clamoured more than ever for their rights. Poland's effort to establish a common frontier with Hungary was inspired largely by a desire to turn over to Hungary the sub-Carpatho-Ukraine in the belief that Budapest would quickly terminate these newly won liberties. To the Ukrainians of Eastern Galicia the pro-Hungarian policy of Poland was really an anti-Ukrainian policy. New tensions consequently arose as a result of which the Polish authorities felt obliged to resort to measures of repression.

As a result of these developments, the Polish policy of

these peoples; but in this instance the Polish authorities antagonized the Orthodox as well as the Uniats.

repressive assimilation seems to have been strengthened. Poland believes that there is danger of revolt in the Ukraine, and that any concession in the way of self-government now would be interpreted as a sign of weakness. This policy is satisfactory to the Polish nationalists, who contend it will result in the assimilation of the Ukrainians. They claim the latter are not really different from Poles, except that they have an inferior culture. The nationalist makes the conventional argument that the Ukrainian movement is purely artificial — the work of " agitators " supported by unfriendly powers. He argues that the Ukrainian language in Eastern Galicia is only a local dialect, and that Ukrainian children, if they are sent to Polish schools, will soon become Polonized. He asserts that large masses of the Ukrainian people care nothing about the nationalistic movement.[43]

Piłsudski, however, never accepted such arguments. He dreamed of a Poland federated with Lithuania and the Ukraine, forming a great Slavic power which would hold the balance between Russia and Germany. The expedition to Kiev in 1920 and the agreement with Petlura was to serve as the beginning of a Polish-Ukrainian federation. True, he did not propose to include Eastern Galicia in the future Ukrainian state, but he apparently believed that this state could serve as a bridge between Ukrainian and Polish culture. Although Piłsudski's ideas in this respect have not been carried out, they live on in one form or another. Many Poles realize that citizenship cannot be imposed by brute

[43] The opinion that no real independence movement exists so far as the Russian Ukraine is concerned was given support by Mr. Wheeler-Bennett, who said, with reference to the 1918 Ukrainian Republic: " The separatist movement had no roots in the country, and the people as a whole were completely indifferent to national self-determination; this had been thrust on them by a group of political dreamers whose power derived from the presence of German bayonets." Wheeler-Bennett, op. cit., p. 316.

force. Thus the late Tadeusz Hołówko declared in the Sejm on February 9, 1931: "We do not care for any national assimilation, we do not want to Polonize by force, we desire only to educate them [the Ukrainians] to become good Polish citizens."[44]

This policy of co-operation with the Ukrainians, which has always been advocated by the Socialists and Democrats, has in recent years won the support of intellectuals and political writers of the "Promethean" group. Their magazine, *Polityka*, is the most outspoken supporter of Polish-Ukrainian understanding. This school points out that for centuries Eastern Galicia has been inhabited by both Poles and Ukrainians. Eastern Galicia is essentially a bi-national province, and peace and order can be maintained only if both nations enjoy equality of treatment. Consequently, the Ukrainians in Eastern Galicia should be granted a large share in the administration of the province; Ukrainian state and municipal employees should be appointed; Ukrainian co-operatives and economic institutions should be supported by the state in the same measure as are the Polish institutions. Poland should abandon the illusion of assimilation and frankly recognize the existence of a separate Ukrainian culture. The system of mixed schools should be given up and a Ukrainian school system similar to the one that existed before the World War established. Complete freedom of development should be given to the Ukrainian cultural institutions, and a Ukrainian university created in Lwów, the capital of Eastern Galicia.

The adherents of the "Promethean" group believe that if such a liberal policy toward the Ukrainians is adopted by

---

[44] Cited by Piotr Włodarski: *Zagadnienia narodowościowe w Polsce odrodzonej* (*Nationality Problems in the Reborn Poland*) (Warsaw, 1936).

Poland the loyalty of the Ukrainians toward the Polish state would be secured. While their "Promethean" dream of dismemberment of the U.S.S.R. and establishment of a United Ukraine under Polish leaders might be a menace to European peace, their advocacy of fair treatment of the Ukrainians in Poland is sound, since it would strengthen the country internally by increasing the loyalty of Ukrainians toward the state.[45]

6. Autonomy or Collaboration?

With the capitulation of France and Britain to Germany at Munich in the fall of 1938, and the subsequent division of Czechoslovakia into three parts, the danger to Poland in Eastern Galicia has obviously increased. Should Germany succeed in controlling the resources of the Soviet Ukraine and Eastern Galicia, it might become the predominant power in Europe, if not in a large part of the whole world.[46]

For the moment, Hitler appears to have postponed a decision with respect to the Ukraine until the Mediterranean question is settled. The problem, however, is bound to grow in importance, not only because of Germany, but because of the Ukrainians themselves. While the Ukrainian movement in the nineteenth century was largely the work of a handful of intellectuals, the spirit of nationalism is now

[45] Aleksander Bocheński: *Problem Ukraiński w Rusi Czerwonej* (*The Ukrainian Problem in Red Ruthenia*) (Warsaw, 1937); Włodzimierz Bączkowski: *Grunwald, Czy Piławce?* (Warsaw: Myśl Polska; 1937).

[46] An editorial in the *Schlesische Zeitung* (Breslau) declared that, with the establishment of the Carpatho-Ukraine, "the Ukrainians become a nation, bearing part of the burden of a state. . . . Now, more than in the last twenty years, the problem of Ukrainian nationality has become the centre of European interest. This problem must be solved now! The interests of European peace and civilization demand . . . the creation of an independent Ukrainian state." For text of this editorial, cf. *New York Herald Tribune*, January 15, 1938.

taking hold of the Ukrainian masses, already resentful because of their intense poverty, which Poland has done nothing to remedy. It is only natural that the Ukrainian nationalist movement, like the American Revolution, should accept foreign support for whatever motive it may be offered.[47]

The history of the 1918 Republic, however, shows how difficult,[48] if not impossible, it would be for Germany or any other power to rule the Ukraine through a puppet government, or compel the peasants to deliver grain. While the Ukrainians might accept German aid, once they secure independence they will not willingly become an instrument of German policy.

Had Poland actually granted autonomy to Eastern Galicia in 1923, a rapprochement between these two Slavic peoples might already have been effected. But there are obvious dangers today in extending to the Ukraine a régime which should have been established sixteen years ago. Confronted by the example of the Sudetens in Czechoslovakia, Poland has some basis for fearing that the granting of Ukrainian autonomy would serve merely as a prelude to foreign intervention and eventual loss of territory. The more the Ukrainians demand complete independence, the more difficult it will be for Poland to grant them even a degree of self-government.

Yet the task of bringing about an understanding with the Ukrainians, even at this late date, should not prove insuperable. Although the Ukrainians in Eastern Galicia today are not as well off as under Austria, they have not been

[47] An eyewitness writes that when Hitler entered Vienna in March 1938, a Ukrainian group from Eastern Galicia presented him with a bowl of roses with this inscription: " *Dem Grössten Führer, dem befreier unterdrückter Völker: Die Ukrainer.*"

[48] Cf. p. 268.

treated as severely as the Ukrainians in Soviet Russia. They
are still free to use their own language, church, and co-
operatives, and have their own newspapers and political
parties. Poland probably exploits Eastern Galicia less brutally, if less successfully, than would either Soviet Russia
or Nazi Germany. For its part, Soviet Russia will not willingly give up the Ukraine, which is probably the richest
area in the U.S.S.R. Until Russia disintegrates as a result of
either internal causes or a general war, the unification and
independence of the Ukrainians is not likely to be realized.[49]
Even then the Ukrainians in Russia have been separated so
many centuries from the Ukrainians in Eastern Galicia that
their unity may prove difficult to achieve. Germany might
conceivably assist in the establishment of an independent
Eastern Galicia, perhaps joined to the Slovak protectorate,
at the expense of Poland; but such a state would lack economic foundations, because of its relatively small size, and
could not hope to be really independent of Germany. Poland, meanwhile, insists that it will forcibly resist any German invasion.

Under these circumstances, some Poles believe that they
can afford to ignore the complaints of the Ukrainians and

[49] Although most of the Russian émigrés follow General Denikin in
opposing the idea of reducing Russian territory, General Y. G. Val, one
of Denikin's associates, has written a book which declares: "We may be
certain that in the future other nationalities in Russia will realize their
independence. . . . Non-Muscovite people have not succumbed to Communism. . . . Either these various nationalities will save central Muscovy
from Bolshevism and realize their own independence, or the Communist
régime, which unites all these nationalities by force, will remain. We
must choose either Muscovy with the hope that the newly created states
will be in alliance with her, or the strengthening of the Communist International and its spread outside the boundaries of the Russian Empire. . . .
Only through the Ukraine will it be possible to return to Russia." For a
translation of a chapter from this book, the English title of which is *The
Importance of the Ukraine in the Problem of Liberating Russia from
Bolshevism*, cf. *Ukrainian Weekly*, October 22, 1938.

simply apply a repressive policy. But the Poles have merely to read their own history to realize the danger of such a course. In the long run, genuine national movements cannot be repressed by force; and the only way that Poland can escape the danger of a developing Ukrainian nationalism cutting across four countries is by coming to terms with the Ukrainians in Eastern Galicia.

This does not necessarily mean the establishment of an autonomous régime, under which the Ukrainians would become a self-contained unit, subject to shadowy controls from Warsaw. It does mean a policy of collaboration, in which Ukrainians would be given opportunities more nearly equal to those enjoyed by Poles somewhat along the lines suggested by the Promethean movement. If it is not possible to create a Ukrainian university, then the universities of Eastern Galicia and other provinces should give instruction in Ukrainian language and history and find room for as many Ukrainian students as are qualified. The government should also make an effort to improve the economic and social situation of the Ukrainian as well as the Pole. No rapprochement is possible so long as the Polish government ignores the claims of the Ukrainian peasant for agrarian reform. Finally, a political solution is necessary. It is not enough to guarantee the Ukrainians a certain number of seats in the Sejm. They should be given the same opportunity to advance in the civil service and the army as Poles. Although, on account of the strong independence movement, Ukrainians cannot now be allowed to take over all the administrative positions in the Ukrainian districts in Eastern Poland, they could certainly be scattered through these districts, and promoted on a basis of efficiency and loyalty to the state. Poland, in short, might well apply to Eastern Galicia much the same policy followed by pre-war

Austria, and for the same reason — to win the loyalty of the Ukrainians so they will not conspire with unfriendly foreign powers.

The eventual result of such a policy of collaboration — in contrast to autonomy — might well lead to Piłsudski's dream of a federation of Slavic peoples, starting with Poland, Lithuania, and Eastern Galicia. The establishment of such a state, by the voluntary consent of its participating peoples, would markedly contribute to the stabilization of European peace. But so far none of the other Slavic peoples has been attracted to this idea, largely because Poland has consistently sought to dominate these other peoples with its own culture and force, rather than to co-operate with them on a basis of equality. Poland has not wished to share any of its glory with other branches of the Slavic race — witness its systematic efforts to destroy the position of Czechoslovakia.[50] Unless this type of imperialism is curbed, the Ukrainian problem may yet prove to be Poland's undoing.

[50] Cf. p. 336.

CHAPTER XI

THE MINORITIES: THE JEWISH QUESTION

NEXT to the Ukrainians, the Jews are the largest minority in Poland. Today there are about 3,300,000 Jews (3,113,-900 of Jewish faith according to the 1931 census), constituting about 10 per cent of the population. Except for the United States, Poland has the largest Jewish population in the world. The proportion of Jews in Poland to the total population, however, is much higher than in the United States, where they constitute only 4 per cent.

1. The Jewish Tradition

The Jews in Poland have a tradition of more than a thousand years. In the early Middle Ages a powerful state, inhabited by the Khazars, existed on the coast of the Black Sea; and early in the eighth century Buland, ruler of the

Khazars, formally adopted the Jewish religion. Subsequently this country, like so many other areas of Eastern Europe, was absorbed by the growing power of the Kingdom of Kiev. To the present day the Mongoloid features noticeable among the Polish Jews would indicate that, after the downfall of this Eastern European Jewish state, some, probably the ruling classes, migrated to Poland. Some anthropologists, however, attribute such features to the Mongol invasions.

Even before Poland accepted Christianity at the end of the tenth century, Jewish travellers and merchants crossed Poland from west to east. Between the tenth and twelfth centuries such travellers came to know Poland well and furnished the first geographical descriptions of that country. Many of the Jews, in this early period, settled on the land, especially in Silesia. From the beginning of Polish history, foreign trade was in Jewish hands. Their numbers were increased when Casimir the Great invited the Jews to the country for the purpose of carrying on commerce and industry. In the Middle Ages the situation of the Jews in Poland was better than in any other country. Except for a few outbreaks instigated by city competitors, such as the guilds, the Jews enjoyed in Poland a religious freedom unknown in many other countries. Poland became a place of refuge for the Jews.

Intermarriages between Poles and Jews were so frequent at that time that the authorities of the Church placed them under interdiction. "The influence of the Jew during the reign of the Piast dynasty" (the first Polish dynasty which ruled from the tenth to the fourteenth century), says one of the greatest Polish historians, "was great, greater than ever after. The Jew had greater culture and civilization, had money and larger connections than today; those connections gave him easy access to, and the confidence of, many courts." [1]

From the earliest times Jews in Poland were considered exclusively under the jurisdiction of the ruler, paying taxes only to him. In 1264 Boleslas the Pious, Prince of Great Poland, granted the Jews of his province a charter which formally recognized that they should be judged only by the ruler and not by the cities in which they lived. When the Polish provinces had become unified, this charter was accepted as defining the status of all Polish Jews.

Subsequently the Jews came to enjoy a considerable measure of self-government through their organized communities, called *Kahals*. Moreover, a national Jewish body called the " Congress of the Four Countries," consisting of representatives of the provinces of Great Poland (Poznań), Little Poland (Cracow), Red Ruthenia (Lwów) and Volhynia,[2] levied taxes on the Jewish communities for common purposes and represented all the Jews of Poland before the King and the authorities.

From the very beginning of the existence of a Polish state, and particularly following the reign of the most outstanding Polish King, Casimir the Great (1333–70), the Jews constituted the middle class. Unlike the West European countries, Poland did not develop a native bourgeoisie.[3] The *tiers état*, which in France was the King's main asset, was lacking in Poland. While despising them, both the King and the nobles supported the Jews since they constituted an important source of revenue and performed necessary

[1] Stanisław Zakrzewski: *Zagadnienia Historyczne* (*Historical Problems*) (Lwów, 1936), Vol. II, p. 23.
[2] Segal: *The New Poland and the Jews*, p. 178; also J. Ziemiński: *Problem emigracji żydowskiej* (*The Problem of Jewish Emigration*) (Warsaw, 1937).
[3] Cf. p. 36.

commercial tasks beneath the dignity and beyond the capacity of the gentry. The Jew served as an intermediary between the nobles and the peasants, being an instrument of exploitation. In pre-Partition Poland the Jew was one of the main elements in the social and economic structure of the country. Apart from Palestine the Jews have had a longer and more continuous tradition in Poland than in any other country. For a time during the Middle Ages about four fifths of all the Jews in the world lived in Poland.

The only rivals of the Jews during this period were the Germans. Likewise engaging in commerce and industry, the Germans enjoyed even greater extraterritorial privileges than the Jews. Under the famous Magdeburg Law they were almost independent of the landowners, and had their own judiciary and police force. The local excesses against the Jews in the cities were usually stimulated by the Germanic elements, inspired more by economic than by religious motives. The monopoly of trade by Jew and German helps explain the gulf which arose between the towns and the countryside.

"The cities," says M. Kwiatkowski, now Vice-Premier and Minister of Finance, "were founded on the basis of foreign law, and were populated by a population alien to the national and social organism of Poland. The cities did not seek this exclusive position; it was established and maintained by the law itself, as one of the fundamental principles of internal policy. In 1505, 1538, and 1550, laws were adopted forbidding the gentry, under penalty of losing gentry rights, from engaging in commercial or industrial occupations. Thus a Chinese wall was gradually built up which kept the Polish nation producing grains, while the cities — those centres of commerce, wealth, culture, and international exchange — were transformed into foreign bodies, enjoying, however, the right to live off the Polish organism. What elsewhere was a foundation of strength and prosperity for the whole country, bringing progress and wealth and equalizing excessive social differences, became in Poland, on the contrary, an element of disorganization, the domain of foreign and sometimes hostile forces, rather a source of general poverty than a factor of growing economic strength in the country." [4]

At the time of the Partitions the Polish Jews, who formed ten per cent of the total population, suffered the fate of the Poles proper and even worse, because they became subject to the anti-Semitic discriminations imposed by the Partition powers during the nineteenth century.[5]

In the second half of this century, moreover, a movement arose to build up a native Polish middle class. Important industries were created in Congress Poland, which found their markets in Russia. Convinced after the failure of the 1863 insurrection that the independence of the country could not be won by revolution, Polish leaders called on the nation to strengthen itself economically and engage in " organic " rather than revolutionary work. " The enrichment of the individual for the benefit of the country," was the slogan of the so-called " positivist " school of thought.

2. The Rise of Anti-Semitism

Some Polish elements in the cities, especially after 1863, attempted to direct these realistic tendencies against the Jews, their economic competitors. In 1870 a pamphlet by

---

[4] Eugenjusz Kwiatkowski: *Dysproporcje* (*Disproportions*) (Warsaw, 1932), pp. 27, 28.

[5] S. Doubnov: *Histoire Moderne du Peuple Juif* (Paris: Payot; 1933), Vol. I, pp. 318 ff. Translated from the Russian by Dr. S. Jankelevitch.

Jan Jeleński was published, entitled *The Jews, the Germans and Ourselves,* in which " the nationalization of commerce and industry " was advocated. " We want to develop in our nation," says the pamphlet, " a drive to abolish the Jewish commercial monopoly created through the centuries." [6]

At that time the economic anti-Semitism of Jeleński found little echo among the Polish peasant and labouring masses, or the economists and publicists. A pamphlet published in 1875 by an editor of the *Commercial Gazette,* Bogumił Prawdzicki, describes the traditional position of the Jews in Poland. " Our Jews," says the author, " are a native city population, they are the *tiers état* in our country, similar to the *tiers état* existing in Germany, France, England, and elsewhere." This pamphlet protests against the claim that the Jews are not a productive element, and concludes that " the Jews are the basis of the national commerce, and even if they were only in this one branch of the national economy, they would be an indispensable and much needed element of our social and economic life." [7]

The drive toward the " nationalization of commerce and industry " assumed some importance only at the end of the nineteenth century. The National Democratic party, created in 1897 under the leadership of Roman Dmowski, included in its official program the fight against the Jews. It is interesting to note, especially in view of the present racial tendencies of that party, that the original program of the National Democrats made a distinction between (1) the Jews who have their own national aspirations, (2) neu-

[6] Cf. pamphlet of Jeleński: *Żydzi, Niemcy i My;* also S. Hirszhorn: *Historja Żydow w Polsce* (*History of the Jews in Poland*) (Warsaw, 1921), p. 219.

[7] Bogumił Prawdzicki: *Żydzi nasi wobec handlu i przemysłu krajowego* (*Our Jews and the National Commerce and Industry*) (Warsaw, 1875).

tral Jews, and (3) Jews who are a part of the Polish nation. The first should be fought as a hostile element; an economic crusade should be proclaimed against the second in order to destroy their commercial and industrial domination; but the last should be accepted within the Polish community on an equal basis with all other Poles.

The agitation against the Jews increased particularly in 1912–14. A Socialist candidate was elected from Warsaw to the Russian Duma in 1912 with the support of the Jews, defeating the candidate of the National Democrats. As a result a boycott against the Jews was organized by the National Democrats, in which Jewish stores were picketed, and Poles buying from Jews were terrorized. The boycott met with very little success and affected only the weakest economic Jewish elements, the small retail merchants and market-stall owners.[8] Whatever the immediate economic results of the anti-Jewish boycott, it showed a trend toward anti-Semitism among a section of the Polish city population, and a newly developing middle class organized in the National Democratic party.

Relations between Poles and Jews became worse during and after the World War. During the war the pro-Russian National Democratic party of Dmowski accused the Jews of supporting Germany. In the Ukraine, pogroms in Kiev and other cities were perpetrated by Ukrainians in 1919 and many Jews were killed.[9] At the same time the Jews of Eastern Galicia, who declared their neutrality in the Polish Ukrainian struggle over that province, were attacked by Poles on the pretext that they supported the Ukrainian movement for independence. Others charged that the Jews

[8] The history of the boycott of 1912 is found in the book of Dr. Ignacy Schiper: *Dzieje Handlu Żydowskiego na Ziemiach Polskich* (*History of Jewish Commerce in Poland*) (Warsaw, 1937), pp. 539 ff.

[9] Doubnov, op. cit., Vol. II, p. 844.

favoured the Bolsheviks. In Jewish history, the year 1919 was as terrible as 1648, 1768, 1881, and 1938.

In 1919 a mission under the leadership of Mr. Henry Morgenthau, Sr., was appointed by the American delegation at Versailles to investigate Jewish charges of anti-Semitism in Poland. This mission reported major excesses in eight cities, where about 280 Jews were killed and several hundred more were wounded. " It is believed," says the Morgenthau report, " that these excesses were the result of a widespread anti-Semitic prejudice aggravated by the belief that the Jewish inhabitants were politically hostile to the Polish State." [10]

The Polish government held the Jews responsible for the minorities treaty it was induced to accept at the Paris Peace Conference. In addition to providing general minority guarantees, this treaty contained special provisions protecting the Jews in Poland. According to Article 10, Education Committees appointed locally by the Jewish communities of Poland would, " subject to the general control of the State, provide for the distribution of the proportional share of public funds, allocated to Jewish schools " and for the organization and management of these schools. Moreover, according to Article 11, Jews could not be compelled to perform any act constituting a violation of their Sabbath, nor be placed under any disability by reason of their refusal to attend courts of law or perform any legal business on the Sabbath. This provision did not, however, exempt Jews from the obligation of citizenship such as military service. Poland undertook also to refrain from holding elections on a Saturday.

Nevertheless, the 1924 language laws, which granted the

[10] Full text, *New York Times*, January 19, 1920. The Jews in Poland generally resented the Morgenthau report.

minorities the right to use their own language in courts and public institutions, did not apply to the Jews, on the ground that, in view of the dispersion of the Jews throughout the whole country, all government functionaries would have to learn Yiddish — an impossible task.[11] Today the Jews constitute the only minority in Poland for which the state has made no financial provision as to minority schools. It does not appear, therefore, that Article 10 of the minorities treaty has been respected.

In June 1925, at the instance of Count Skrzyński, Polish Foreign Minister, who was soon to go to the United States, an "agreement" (ugoda) was concluded by the Grabski government with the Jewish Parliamentary Club. The agreement, which showed that the National Democrats did not hesitate to come to terms with the Jews when in power, consisted of two declarations unilaterally made by each party. The Jews declared their loyalty to the Republic and recognized their duties as citizens, while reserving to themselves the right to defend Jewish interests within the limits of the constitution. Premier Ladislas Grabski, on behalf of the government, expressed his satisfaction with the Jewish declaration and promised that, " on its side, the government will give greater attention to the needs of the Jewish people in the domain of instruction, culture, and economic life."

As a result of this agreement a few ordinances were issued to satisfy the most pressing demands of the Jews. The Polish government also declared its sympathy with and support of the Jewish claims in Palestine. But nothing really basic was changed, no legislation was enacted to implement the agreement, or change the political and economic situation

[11] L. P. Mair: *The Protection of Minorities* (London: Christophers; 1928), p. 95.

of the Jews. Shortly after, the Grabski government resigned, and the agreement with the Jews seems to have been
forgotten.

With the advent in 1926 of the Piłsudski régime, the situation of the Jews altered considerably. Piłsudski himself
never indulged in Jew-baiting, and the government bloc
in the Sejm contained Jews as well as members of all other
nationalities living in Poland. But, on the other hand, cer
tain anti-Jewish laws inherited from the Partition period
continued to exist, and some Jewish elements, especially the
more enlightened and progressive ones, strongly resented
government interference in internal Jewish affairs and curtailment of the traditional autonomy of Jewish communities.

The Jewish community law of October 14, 1927 recognized the existence of the Polish Jews as a religious federation composed of individual communities, with a central
Religious Council of Jewish Communities, and with local
councils for each community. Nevertheless, the legislation
limited the rights of these communities largely to religious
and charitable matters, and gave the government large powers of supervision.[12] These included the right to veto the
choice of officers of the communities and even to replace
them under certain circumstances with government commissioners, as well as the right to control detailed items in
the community budgets, although these related largely to
the support of synagogues, supply of kosher meat, support
of Jewish philanthropic institutions, and religious education
of children.

In the opinion of many Jews who resented the control

[12] *Dziennik Ustaw*, R. P. No. 91, item 818. Cf. also the decrees of
October 1930 and December 1931. Ibid., 1930, No. 6, item 38; ibid., 1931,
No. 89, item 698.

reserved by the government over their communal affairs, this legislation did not respect the spirit of Article 10 of the minorities treaty between Poland and the Principal Allied and Associated Powers, which expressly recognized Jewish "communities." They also contended that only the repressive features of the law were enforced. The more progressive Jewish elements also criticized the right given to the communal election boards to deprive all those not practising their religion of the right to vote. They regarded such provisions as a reward paid to the Orthodox Jews for their support of the Piłsudski régime.[13]

In spite of repeated protests on the part of the Jews, it was only in March 1931 that the Polish Parliament finally

[13] The Jewish political parties in Poland can be divided into three blocs: the moderates, the Zionists, and the radicals. The moderates comprise the Orthodox group, " Agudas Israel," some industrial and economic groups, and the Jewish war veterans. For a time the Agudas was bitterly anti-Zionist, but within recent years has become pro-Palestinian. The moderate Jewish groups belonged to the non-party bloc and supported the Pilsudski régime. Since the New Camp of National Unity is anti-Semitic, the moderates have now joined the Zionists in the Jewish Parliamentary Club. The moderates participated in the 1935 and 1938 elections, and today have three out of the five Jewish deputies in the Sejm, two of them belonging to Agudas Israel and one being a war veteran. The moderates also have one of the two Jewish Senators nominated by the President, the other Jewish representatives being Zionists.

The Zionists are themselves divided. The Mizrachi, or Orthodox Zionist group, and one section of the General Zionists participated in the 1935 and 1938 elections. Another section of the General Zionists and the Zionist Labour party boycotted these elections.

Among the radicals will be found the Bund, which is the most important Jewish labour party. Affiliated with the Second International, it is somewhat more radical in its Socialism than the Polish Socialist party, with which it co-operates. Both Socialist parties boycotted the elections of 1935 and 1938 and opposed the Piłsudski régime. Although traditionally the Bund is strongly anti-Zionist, in recent years it has dropped its opposition to Palestine, although continuing to refuse to collaborate with other Jewish parties. In the recent municipal elections it scored a great victory over all other Jewish parties.

abolished the legislative discriminations against the Jews which had held over from pre-war days.[14]

3. *The Economic Boycott and the* Numerus Clausus

Since the death of Piłsudski and the endeavour to establish the Camp of National Unity, anti-Semitism has increased in Poland. Even the National Democratic party has been outdistanced in its anti-Semitism by other groups. The most visible form of anti-Semitism is an economic boycott applied by large sections of the public against Jewish enterprise, which has been approved by the courts, dignitaries of the Catholic Church, and the government. The head of the Catholic Church, Cardinal Hlond, in a pastoral letter issued in 1936, declared: " One does well to prefer his own kind in commercial dealings and to avoid Jewish stores and Jewish stalls in the market, but it is not permissible to demolish Jewish businesses." Official approval of the anti-Jewish boycott was given by the Prime Minister, General Składkowski, in the now famous statement of June 4, 1936. The Premier then said: " My government considers that nobody in Poland should be injured. An honest host does not allow anybody to be harmed in his house. Economic fight? All right! (*Owszem*)."

The purpose of the economic boycott is not only to assist Poles endeavouring to enter petty commerce, but to force the Polish Jew to emigrate. Polish opinion, particularly during the past five years, has become convinced that " migration " is the solution of the Jewish problem, although few

[14] For a history of these discriminations, cf. A. G. Duker: *The Situation of the Jews in Poland*, American Jewish Congress, April 1936.

Poles have any idea where the Jews should go. In addition, public opinion has agitated for the adoption of legislation similar to that adopted in Germany and Hungary, restricting the proportion of Jews in educational and professional life, or reducing them to second-class citizenship.

While so far the Polish government has declined to enact any avowedly anti-Semitic measures, the rising tide of agitation, no doubt encouraged by certain governmental influences, is impressive. During 1937 the Polish Union of Physicians and the Polish bar agitated for the adoption of an " Aryan " paragraph, reducing the number of Jews in these professions or excluding them altogether. A proclamation issued early in 1938 by the Union of Polish Catholic Lawyers, Union of Catholic Writers, Co-ordinating Committee of Academic Corporations, Union of Technicians and Engineers, and several other groups, reads as follows: " The simplest and most effective way of fighting the Jewish flood is the slogan: 'A Pole supports a Pole.' Depriving the Jews of earning money means that they will be forced to leave Poland. This is the only radical solution of the Jewish question. With the utmost forcefulness and with the deepest conviction of the necessity of self-defence, we urge all Christians not to sell to Jews any land or houses, nor to buy from Jewish stores, nor to employ Jewish lawyers, physicians, engineers, architects, artists, or any other professional men."

The Supreme Council of the Camp of National Unity, which reflects the attitude of many government leaders, declared in May 1938 that the Jews are an " element weakening the state "; that the best solution is emigration; that the percentage of Jews in certain professions should be lowered; and that it is necessary to defend the centres of Polish cultural and social life, such as the press, theatre, library, music, and radio, against their influence. The National Democratic party demands that Jews be prohibited from voting, holding any public office, or owning land. The program of the Naras, who left the National Democrats a few years ago, demands expulsion of the Jews from Poland and confiscation of their fortunes. "The Jews," says the Nara program, "should be deprived of their political rights, eliminated from all social associations, and denied the right to serve in the Polish army. They should be forbidden to participate in Polish enterprises, to employ Poles, or to work for Poles. The Polish schools should be free of Jews, and Polish cultural life should be closed to them. . . . A systematic and radical elimination of the Jews from Poland is the ultimate solution of the Jewish problem." [15]

The Polish universities have been a centre of anti-Semitism. National student organizations have staged, every year, anti-Semitic demonstrations and riots in favour of a *numerus clausus* for Jewish students in the universities. These manifestations, after 1926, when the Piłsudski régime came to power, were directed less against the Jews than against the government, which the Nationalists were trying to embarrass. Marshal Piłsudski understood the political significance of such student manifestations and did not permit them to assume undue proportions. A law limiting the autonomy of the universities, and allowing the police to intervene in case of disturbances, was passed in 1933. While this law was not frequently enforced, the nationalistic students, in Piłsudski's lifetime, did not dare to stage demonstrations of a very serious character. Following Piłsudski's death, the situation changed entirely. The Nationalists became bolder. As a result, the law of 1933 was altered to allow the intro-

[15] *Zasady Programu Narodowo-Radykalnego* (*The Principles of the National Radical Program*) (Warsaw, 1937), p. 10.

duction of " ghetto benches " as a " regulation of the rec-
torial authorities," without the need of direct intervention
by the government. Under such a provision, Jewish students could be compelled to sit in seats specially reserved
for them. Scores of Polish intellectuals and professors all
over the country protested against the ghetto benches, and
some refused to introduce them in their classrooms. Senator
Michałowicz, Professor at the University of Warsaw, who
saved the late Marshal Piłsudski from a Tsarist prison in
1901, refused to abide by the rector's instructions. Asked
by the Nationalist students to segregate the Jews, he declared: " The rector, being elected by the professors, has
a right to his own opinions. But may I also be granted the
right as a Senator of the Republic to abide by the laws of
the country? " M. Kulczycki, rector of the University of
Lwów, resigned, refusing to introduce ghetto benches. In
an open letter of January 11, 1938 explaining his resignation,
he said: " For the blackmail going on in the universities, not
only do those venerable institutions pay with their prestige,
but their autonomous régime is being destroyed, and their
ability to work is vanishing. It is easy to see that, under the
lofty slogans of national solidarity and defence of the Polish
character of our culture, the dignity of the autonomous authorities is being brutally challenged and the freedom of
science, without which science cannot exist, is being undermined. Science cannot develop under conditions of con-
straint — not because of the professors' fancy, but because science signifies free thinking. Thought that is not
free is not scientific. Without science it will be difficult to
live, not only for the professors but also for those who
are today destroying the Polish scientific institutions." In
spite of these protests and the manifestations of Jewish students, who remained standing throughout the lectures rather

than occupy the ghetto benches, the decision of the rectors establishing the ghetto benches in the universities was not modified.

The ghetto-bench restriction was applied even to the Wawelberg Engineering School in Warsaw. This school was founded before the World War by Jewish industrialists and bankers for the purpose of training much needed Polish technicians and engineers. In 1919 the owners of the school turned it over to the government under a contract which provided that no discrimination should ever be applied to any group of students. Nevertheless the authorities in 1938 insisted on introducing the ghetto bench and they actually expelled fifty Jewish students because they declined to accept such regulations. The son of the founder of the school has brought action in the courts against what is clearly a breach of contract as well as an ungracious act.

In addition to these ghetto-bench provisions, the Jewish young generation is injured by an unofficial *numerus clausus* which has existed in the Polish universities many years. As a result of increasing anti-Semitism, the percentage of Jewish students in the Polish universities declined from 20.4 per cent in 1928–9 to 11.8 in 1936–7 and 9.9 per cent in 1937–8.[16] It now appears that the proportion of Jews in the universities is lower than their proportion to the population as a whole. As far as the city population is concerned, the ratio is far less, as the Jews constitute about 27 per cent of the population of the Polish cities and, if permitted to do so, would go to the universities far more freely than the peasants.[17] Encouraged by their success in reducing the

[16] *Petit Annuaire*, p. 326. For the *numerous clausus* directed against the Ukrainian students, cf. p. 279.

[17] Of all the university students 37.8 per cent come from families of government officials or army officers, in contrast to 9.7 per cent who come from working-class families. *Concise Statistical Year-Book, 1937,*

number of Jewish students, the nationalist youth are now asking, not a *numerus clausus*, but a *numerus nullus* — that is, complete elimination of Jews from the universities.

Despite the fact that Poland has not officially enacted anti-Semitic legislation, the government has discriminated against the Jew by a number of administrative acts, and Parliament has enacted laws having a similar purpose, although not openly admitted. Thus it is reported that the Ministry of Commerce has deprived a number of Jewish importers at Gdynia of their licences. The Ministry of Finance has ordered many dealers in tobacco and liquor to keep their business open during the entire week, thus forcing the Jew to violate the Sabbath or lose his livelihood. Generally speaking, the government supplies liberal credits for non-Jewish activities, both to co-operatives and artisans, but refrains from helping the Jew. Moreover, the government radio spreads boycott propaganda. In this respect the very extent of *étatisme* may be used as an anti-Semitic weapon. So long as a competitive private economy prevails, the Jew's chance of survival in commerce and artisanship is greater than the Pole's. But when the government nationalizes industry, the situation is reversed. Invariably the government gives employment to the Pole at the expense of the Jew.

When the government, a number of years ago, decided to convert the tobacco business into a national monopoly, several thousand Jews were thrown out of business; but Jews were allowed to continue to sell the tobacco made by the government. In 1937, however, the government declined to renew their licences for this purpose and it is estimated that 30,000 Jews lost their livelihood. The appli-

p. 290. This social composition of the student body may explain the anti-Semitic trend in the universities.

cation, in January 1937, of the Shehitah law, restricting Jewish methods of slaughter on the ground that they are inhumane, also closed Jewish butcher shops, employing 20,000 people. These are probably the first two instances of wholesale elimination of Jews from industry as a result of government action.

Another instance of this tendency is provided by the law of May 4, 1938 reorganizing the bar and regulating the exercise of the legal profession. This law gives the Minister of Justice, on consultation with the Supreme Bar Council, the right to close the list of admission of lawyers and law clerks, or both, for a definite period of time in any district or locality. After the lists have been closed, the Ministry may make any exceptions he wishes. As a result, admission to the bar is being denied young Jewish lawyers, while Poles are admitted through the power to make exceptions. The official Polish news agency frankly declared that the object of the new law was to reduce the " disproportionate number of lawyers belonging to minority nationalities. . . . The present situation, where the Jews constitute 53 per cent of the lawyers, and in some judicial districts even 73 per cent, can no longer be tolerated."

Curiously enough, while the Jews have constituted 53 per cent of the Polish bar, Jewish students are only a minority in the law schools.[18] The explanation for this situation is that they are virtually excluded from government judicial and administrative positions requiring legal training. It is estimated that there are about 12,000 positions in the Polish civil service requiring legal training, of which only about 5,000 are held by qualified lawyers. The re-

[18] In 1936-7 the Jewish law students were only 9.4 per cent of the total; and even in 1928-9 the most prosperous year in Poland, they constituted only 27.7 per cent of the total. *Petit Annuaire*, p. 326.

maining positions are held by comparatively untrained Poles, while Jewish lawyers are denied public employment. Since the Jewish graduates of the law faculties cannot become judges, notary publics, or government employees, they crowd the legal profession engaging in private practice.

Although the Camp of National Unity and the government have repeatedly decried the use of violence against the Jews, and the government has arrested offenders in this respect, it is not unnatural that in this heated atmosphere many anti-Semitic outbreaks should have occurred during the past few years. Since 1935 there have been several hundred cases of violence done to Jews, the most serious of which was the pogrom at Brest-Litovsk in May 1937. Following the murder of a Polish policeman by a Jew, fierce rioting broke out in which sixty Jews were injured, two subsequently dying; Jewish property to·the value of three million zlotys was destroyed. These measures of violence, accompanied by the boycott generally, have injured the economic position of the Polish Jew. Largely as a result of the boycott, the number of Jewish shops in Łódź decreased by 500 during 1936, while non-Jewish shops increased by 2,000. Whenever a pogrom occurs, Jewish capital is lost and cannot be entirely replaced. During 1938, however, the intensity of anti-Semitism in Poland on the surface seemed to decline. This development was due to both internal and external causes. Anti-Semitism reached its height when the Camp of National Unity made an effort to come to terms with the Right. With the failure of this effort,[19] government forces seem to have imposed a curb on anti-Jewish excesses. Externally, the triumph of Hitler at Munich, the German and Hungarian partition of Czecho-

[19] Cf. p. 111.

slovakia into three parts, and the controversy over the deportation of about 15,000 Polish Jews living in Germany [20] worked to weaken the Polish elements favouring a pro-German, anti-Semitic policy.

Nevertheless, on December 21, 1938 General Skwarczyński, head of the Camp of National Unity, which had just won the elections, introduced into the Sejm an interpellation on the Jewish question, which reiterated previous declarations that the Jews were an obstacle to the development of the Polish nation, and asked the government to take energetic measures to reduce the number of Jews in the country. Poland should benefit from any international plan worked out on behalf of German Jews; appropriate territories for Polish Jews should be secured and Polish emigration financed by international means. Colonel Wenda, Chief of Staff of the Camp of National Unity, declared that the departure of the Polish Jews was a necessity on account of national defence. The economic structure of the country should be placed in the hands of patriotic elements which in case of crisis would support the national cause.

While a number of intellectuals,[21] Socialists, and Trade Unionists have protested against this policy of anti-Semitism, there seems little doubt that overwhelming opinion in Poland today favours the elimination of the Jew from economic life and the " Polonization " of commerce. The first

[20] Cf. p. 347.
[21] A considerable amount of literature opposing anti-Semitism has developed in Poland in recent years. University professors, writers, social workers, and others have opposed the anti-Jewish excesses and the methods of the nationalists. A large section of the press has refused to follow the anti-Semitic trend. Cf., for instance, a series of articles published in a pamphlet called: *Polacy a Żydach* (*Poles about the Jews*) (Warsaw, 1937); also, Antoni Gronowicz: *Antysemityzm rujnuje moją ojczynnę* (*Anti-Semitism is Ruining My Fatherland*) (Lwów, 1938).

step in this direction is the economic boycott, the second emigration. The third step of out-and-out Nazi legislation depends on whether Poland becomes totalitarian.

4. Causes of Anti-Semitism

There are many reasons for this movement against the Jews. Already unpopular, the government does not want to risk the loss of further support by enforcing the constitution on behalf of the Jews or any other minority. The opposition, for its part, is tempted to resort to anti-Semitism as a means of embarrassing the government. No doubt, too, the conservative landholding classes hope to divert the peasant's attention from agrarian reform by rousing him against the Jew and urging him to enter businesses in the city hitherto occupied by Jews. Moreover, the rise of Nazi Germany has undoubtedly quickened the racial idea in Poland. Throughout Eastern Europe Hitler is using anti-Semitism as an instrument of policy.

The two most important causes of anti-Semitism in Poland are religious and economic. Among the Polish Jews leaders may be found who are thoroughly assimilated; but to a far greater extent than in Hungary or Rumania, Polish Jewry as a whole is unassimilated. The ordinary Jew speaks Yiddish, a combination of Hebrew and German, and is influenced by a particularly formidable type of orthodoxy, or *rabbinism*, of the *Tsadika* or *Wunderrabi* variety. While some Jews contend that the government obstructs assimilation, there is little doubt that the most powerful factor which keeps the Jew separate from the Pole is the type of orthodoxy which dominates a large part of the Jewish population. The American visitor unaccustomed to the Polish tradition wonders why more interracial disputes have

not occurred when, on visiting a typical village, he sees
the Orthodox Jew, wearing his skullcap, black boots, long
double-breasted coat, curls and beard, mingling with the
Poles proper. The government may think it to its interest to support the Orthodox Jews against their more assimilated brethren, but the foreign observer is nevertheless
struck by the readiness of the ordinary Poles to accept the
assimilated or baptized Jew as an equal. In government
departments, in the army, in the banks, and in newspapers,
one finds baptized Jews occupying important positions.
This class, which in Nazi Germany is subjected to bitter
persecution, has been freely accepted in Poland. With the
growth of nationalist spirit among both Jews and Poles,
the trend toward assimilation seems to have been arrested.
It remains true, however, that the Polish attitude toward the
Jew is governed by racial considerations to a lesser degree
than the attitude of other peoples.

The Poles, nevertheless, advance many criticisms against
the Jews. In a recent pastoral letter the Primate of Poland,
while condemning acts of violence against the Jews, said:
" It is a fact that the Jews fight against the Catholic Church
and give themselves up to free thought, constituting the
advance guard of a godless life, of the Bolshevik movement,
and of subversive action. It is a fact that the Jewish influence on morals is destructive and that the Jewish printers
propagate pornography. It is a fact that the Jews are em-
bezzlers and usurers and that they engage in the white-slave
traffic." [22]
In the country one is told that the peasant is miserably

[22] He added: "Let us be just. All the Jews are not so. A number are
pious, honest, just, charitable, and well-doing." The criminal statistics
do not entirely support the Primate's charges. They show that more
than five times as many Catholics as Jews are convicted of engaging in
the white-slave traffic. *Petit Annuaire*, p. 352.

exploited by the Jewish trader. It is also said that the Jew was not patriotic during the World War and the struggle against Soviet Russia, and that Jewish employers are the most flagrant violators of labour legislation. No doubt these charges are false or exaggerated; but when even a small minority is guilty, the whole Jewish people is blamed.

The strongest argument against the Jew is that he occupies a predominant position in commerce, in crafts, and in many other branches of economic life. Such a position was justified when Poland was a feudal domain; but the Poles argue that just as none of the great liberal democracies can tolerate this form of racial monopoly, so Poland must reduce the influence of the Jew and " Polonize " commerce and industry. This feeling is intensified with the suffering produced by economic depression.

While the Jews constitute less than 10 per cent of the population, they control nearly half the commercial enterprises of Poland; 47 per cent of the artisans, half the lawyers, and a large percentage of the doctors are Jews.[23]

More than half the textile industry in Łódź is Jewish; and some estimate that half the real property in Warsaw and other cities is also Jewish. An authoritative Jewish source states that " at the present time nearly 25 per cent of the economic activities of the cities is found in Jewish hands. . . . What is particularly important is that at the period in question (1921) the Jew constituted 51.6 per cent of the employers. Even admitting that this percentage has decreased a little since then, it is nevertheless true that, up to the present time, nearly half the enterprises in the cities are directed and administered by Jews." [24]

[23] The districts of Poznań, Pomorze, and Silesia are excluded from these estimates since these areas have a very small Jewish population.
[24] *La Situation économique des Juifs dans le Monde*, p. 196.

Although the Jews dominate many branches of economic life, the gradual processes of economic and social development are tending to reduce this predominance and orient Jewish activities in new directions. Moreover, the proportion of Jews to the non-Jewish population has shown a steady decline. Thus between 1900 and 1936 the non-Jewish population in Poland increased nearly 40 per cent, but the Jewish population only 6.6 per cent.[25] The natural rate of increase of the Jewish population during 1937 was only 8.7 per thousand, as compared with 11 for the Roman Catholics. For the period of 1931–5 the Jewish increase was 9.5, as compared with 13.1 for the Poles proper.[26] In contrast, a far greater percentage of the Jews than of the Poles migrated from Poland before the World War.[27] Although in recent years the Polish population has continued to increase more rapidly than the Jews, the proportion of the latter who have been able to emigrate has declined. Instead of being more than twice the annual increase of 30,000, the rate of Jewish emigration within recent years has been only about 60 per cent of such increase.[28] Jewish emigration has, however, averaged about 26.6 per cent of the total emigration, or more than twice the proportion which the Jews

[25] Ibid., p. 209.
[26] *Petit Annuaire*, p. 46. In view of the inaccuracy of Jewish vital statistics, these figures should be taken with reservations.
[27] Between 1895 and 1933 general emigration was 133,400, or 48.9 of the total annual increase; but average Jewish emigration was 65,500, or 216 per cent of the annual Jewish increase. Jan Ziemiński: *Problem Emigracji Żydowskiej* (1937), p. 72.
[28] General emigration increased from 54,600 in 1936 to 102,400 in 1937. Jewish emigration averaged about 17,000 annually in the five years between 1931 and 1935, while declining from 16,900 in 1936 to 8,900 in 1937. *Petit Annuaire*, p. 55. Apparently this decline was due to the temporary curtailment of emigration to Palestine. Thus, although the annual average of Jewish migration to Palestine between 1927 and 1937 was 7,100, in 1937 only 2,900 went to this destination.

bear to the Polish population as a whole. As a result of disproportionate emigration and a slower rate of natural increase, the Jewish population is not holding its own in comparison with the Poles.

Moreover, a change in the economic and social structure of the Jewish population seems to be slowly taking place. Thus their position in the cities has declined more rapidly than in the country as a whole. Out of twelve cities which had Jewish majorities in 1921, only one still did in 1931. There has also been a decline in the proportion of Jews in commerce and certain branches of artisanship. Between 1921 and 1931 the number of non-Jews engaged in commerce increased 3 per cent, in contrast to the Jews, who decreased 8 per cent. Out of one hundred merchants in Warsaw working on their own acccount in 1921, 73 per cent were Jews, but in 1931 only 65.9 per cent were Jews. These declines were registered before the present anti-Semitic movement in Poland developed, and seem to be largely the result of natural economic development. For example, the progress of the Ukrainian co-operatives, which have not been assisted by government subsidies, has inevitably tended to eliminate many Jewish tradesmen.

Instead, the Jews have been turning to small industry. During the past few years Jews have entered a number of branches of industry working for export. Unlike the artisan who sells directly to a client, the industrialist sells to an anonymous market, and hence is not so subject to anti-Semitic attacks. Jews have played a fundamental part in the industrialization of Poland, which is slowly taking place; and they would doubtless have done more had the field been competitive — and the state neutral. In any event, the role of Jews in Polish life, wholly apart from the boycott, has been slowly changing from commerce to industry.

If the Jew dominates certain branches of economic life, he plays a very subordinate role elsewhere. As to the general standard of living, it is estimated that at least a million of the 3,300,000 Jews are living on the verge of starvation. If anything, they are worse off than the submerged Polish peasant since they cannot grow their food. In Warsaw nearly a third of the population receives Passover relief, and the percentage in other cities is even higher.

Moreover, Jews probably do not constitute more than 1 per cent of the total farm workers, while Jewish farm-owners are apparently even fewer in number. Administrative authorities seldom permit a Jewish purchase of land, and Jews do not profit from agrarian reform. Few Jews, moreover, are found in government service. Of the 64,500 government employees in Warsaw in 1931, less than 2 per cent were Jewish, although among municipal employees, it is larger — 7.6 per cent.[29] Even in city districts having an overwhelmingly Jewish population the public officials are usually non-Jewish. If those supporting the program to Polonize commerce were animated by considerations of justice, they would also advocate an increase in the proportion of Jews in agriculture and government employment.

5. Polish Misgivings as to Anti-Semitism

Some thoughtful Poles have misgivings about the recent anti-Semitic trend. First, the fear is expressed that the violence which inevitably seems to be the accompaniment of any anti-Semitic movement will not be confined to the Jews but, unless checked, will eventually be extended to non-Jewish opponents of extreme nationalism. This tendency means an increase in anti-liberalism in Poland or, what

[29] La Situation économique des Juifs, p. 322.

is more likely, deepening chaos which would eventually threaten public order. Second, it is feared that the present methods aiming to eliminate the Jews from economic life will react disastrously on the Polish economic situation. The Jews perform an economic service to Poland more cheaply than such service can now be supplied by Poles proper. The Jew is making a contribution to the industrialization of the country, particularly in the field of export, which is of paramount importance owing to the need for foreign exchange. Already experience has demonstrated that Christian merchants sent to replace the Jews in distant villages have great difficulty in keeping alive; while Poles may eventually develop into tradesmen, it is clear that any abrupt repression of Jewish economic life means a setback for the industrialization movement on which the welfare of the Polish people depends. Desirable as a certain amount of emigration may be, the departure of 30,000 Jews in 1934 and 1935 cost the Bank of Poland nearly 50,000,000 zlotys.[30] Even if Jewish migration on a large scale were possible, Poland could hardly allow the unlimited export of capital.

Finally, those Poles who question the validity of the present anti-Semitic movement realize that the country may have to choose between the course followed by Germany and the more liberal course followed by the Western democracies. They do not want anti-Semitism to be the bond leading Poland into the German camp.

To the foreign observer two things would seem to be clear. First, that Jewish emigration from Poland on any large scale does not represent a realistic program. Particularly in view of the prior claims of the German refugees, the Polish Jew is likely to meet increasing difficulties in finding opportunities abroad — more difficulties than the

[30] Rose, op. cit., in *Politique étrangère*.

Polish emigrant proper.[31] The Jewish population in Poland is so large that probably the most the Poles can expect is that the proportion of Jew to non-Jew should not increase. Any attempt to expel this large mass from Poland would be as impossible as an attempt to compel the American Negroes, also constituting ten per cent of the population in the United States, to emigrate from this country. The circumstances of history oblige Jew and non-Jew to live side by side in Poland. The problem of statesmenship is to see to it that they live peacefully.

Secondly, the demand for the "Polonization" of commerce is natural if this demand means a gradual reduction of Jewish predominance in certain branches of economic activity in favour of readjustments elsewhere. Such readjustments are already taking place as a result of normal economic developments. But if they are hastened by repressive means, the general economic life of the country is bound to suffer. For example, today only 5 per cent of the Polish population is engaged in commerce and insurance, as compared with more than 12 per cent in Britain and the United States. If commerce as a whole remains at its present low level, its "Polonization" will injure the Jew and increase the cost of living to the consumer generally. On the other hand, if commerce is increased as a result of industrialization, new jobs for Poles and Jews alike will be created. Under an industrialized economy, bringing about an increasing flow of wealth, the opportunity for both will be increased. To take another example, the number of physicians in Poland today is only 3.7 per 10,000 of population as compared with 12.4 in the United States, 7.3 in Germany, and 5.0 in the U.S.S.R. The enactment of legislation reducing the number of Jewish doctors in Poland would in-

[31] Cf. p. 228.

jure not only the Jew but the population as a whole, which already does not receive adequate medical care. An increase in national income, however, would permit the employment of more Polish doctors without displacing a single Jew.[32]

The number of engineers is also quite inadequate to meet the industrialization program. While it is estimated that about 2,000 Jewish engineers are without work, the country has only 10,000 Polish engineers, when it needs about 30,000 for the industrialization of the country. Legislation still further reducing Jewish opportunities under such circumstances undoubtedly injures Poland as well as every minority.

The Jew feels that he is a citizen of Poland as much as the Pole; and, naturally, he suffers from the humiliation created by any anti-Semitic policy. His rights have been guaranteed by the Polish constitution and by the minorities treaty of 1919.

Poland cannot perhaps be expected to be over-scrupulous as to its international obligations at a time when greater powers have shown themselves indifferent about maintaining the principles of international law. And in some ways it is rather remarkable that Poland has not yielded to the temptation to adopt Nuremberg legislation. One reason may be that racialism is ill-adapted to a Catholic country and that a number of leading families have Jewish blood.

If this problem is examined from the point of view of Polish self-interest, the conclusion is hard to avoid that the present forms of anti-Semitism are working toward disruption of the country's economic foundations. A policy of migration, applying to Jews and non-Jews alike, is desirable,

[32] Army leaders have recently requested a more liberal policy in the medical schools in view of the needs of national defence.

provided impossible hopes are not created. A policy of increasing productivity, both agricultural and industrial, will do much more to hasten readjustments in the Jewish structure of Poland and create opportunities for every group in the population.

Poland's Jewish problem is altogether different from that of Germany. The number of Jews in the latter country is so comparatively limited and the government is so strong, both internally and internationally, that Germany can adopt a policy of expulsion at much less cost than Poland. Although the latter country has less than half the population of Germany, it has nearly five times as many Jews. It cannot possibly hope to get rid of them. Poland's solution is not deportation but readaptation. This can be done by increasing the productivity of the country, by extending educational facilities to the Jews as well as to the non-Jews, and particularly by retraining the Jewish traders or their sons, to fit them to earn a living in other occupations.

Jewish leaders in Poland could do their part toward diminishing the causes of inter-racial friction by endeavouring to remove admitted abuses, expressing deep concern with the efforts of Poland to solve its truly difficult problems, and pledging the loyalty of Jewish citizens to the Polish state.[33] In particular, it should be recognized that

[33] On November 11, 1938, the twentieth anniversary of Poland's independence, the Central Committee of the Zionist Organization in Poland, one of the political divisions among the Jews, issued a declaration expressing "joy and pride" at the progress of the past twenty years. The declaration stated that the Jewish minority would always be mindful of its obligation to the state, asking in return an equal opportunity with all other citizens to enjoy the rights which the state provided. It added that "it is natural that those of Polish nationality should occupy a special position in the State," but that "the interests of the Polish State demand that these non-Polish nationalities feel free and happy in Poland, united by a strong tie of civil attachment and common responsibility for the fate, security and the development of the Republic." The Jewish national minority, according to this statement, rejects "the theory of Jewish mass

many of the activities of the Jewish middleman who lives off peasant trade may have been economically justified and socially tolerated under more primitive forms of economy, but that the sooner these forms of distribution can be replaced by more modern methods, the better off the Jew as well as the peasant will be. If the Jews are given adequate educational and economic opportunities, they will gradually rid themselves of a form of life which now marks them apart.

For many years foreign philanthropic organizations, such as the Joint Distribution Committee, the Jewish Colonization Association, and ORT, supported largely by Jewish funds from America and Britain, have sent large sums to Poland for the aid of Polish Jewry. Thus in 1937 the Joint Distribution Committee and its affiliated agencies granted $945,000 for aid in Poland. Nearly all of this went to loan societies of one kind or another, child care, and other forms of economic and welfare assistance.[34] The relief thus extended has served to mitigate Jewish suffering; and perhaps for this reason some extreme Polish nationalists have demanded that the Free Loan Kassas be repressed since in their opinion they merely strengthen Jewish influence.

While this relief work has been extremely beneficial from the humanitarian standpoint, the funds thus expended have not materially contributed to the retraining of the Jewish population. Nevertheless, a number of Jewish training centres are already preparing Jewish agriculturists and artisans, and one plan provides for the expenditure of

assimilation, but leaves to every individual the right to determine his own nationality. . . . Our postulate of national-cultural autonomy for the Jewish community in Poland flows out of the consciousness of the positive value of the peculiar, centuries-old Jewish culture. . . . This right to a free national-cultural development we advocate in opposition to unnatural assimilation on the one hand, and the forced ghetto on the other."

[34] *Aid to Jews Overseas, Report of the Activities of the American Jewish Joint Distribution Committee for 1937,* p. 27.

$9,000,000 over four years, raised largely from foreign philanthropic sources, upon the extension of such training centres, the development of new Jewish industries by means of loans, the improvement of Jewish agriculture, and the promotion of Jewish emigration. Funds expended along these lines would, in the long run, be more productive for Poland and of more real assistance to Jews than purely relief contributions.

6. A New Minority Policy?

Thus it is evident that Poland has a serious minority problem affecting the relationship of the dominant group to more than a third of the whole population. Speaking in Parliament on June 24, 1938, Prime Minister Składkowski said that the people of Poland should realize that " the destinies of the Republic depended in large part upon the attitude it adopted toward its minorities." The minority deputies were quick to point out, however, that the Prime Minister offered to make no changes in existing minority policy.

It is possible that so long as a general war does not break out, Poland can remain indifferent to its minorities problem. Nevertheless, should war come without Poland having made a greater effort to ensure the loyalty of its nationals, the country may suffer severely. If the Prime Minister meant to be taken literally, one may expect Poland to reconsider its minority policy in the future.

CHAPTER XII

✸

FOREIGN POLICY

POLAND'S foreign policy, to a greater extent than that of most countries, is governed by history and geography. The country lies between two great totalitarian powers, and is in danger of being crushed by their conflicting ambitions. Nor has lack of natural frontiers improved Poland's position. Despite its control of the Free City of Danzig and the port of Gdynia, Poland has no secure access to the Baltic Sea or a fleet worthy of the name. The German navy, which dominates the Baltic, and German military forces — particularly air power — operating from Germany and East Prussia, would not find it difficult, in a localized war, to close the Vistula and cut the rail routes joining Poland to the Baltic.

Apart from the Carpathians and the Polesie marshes, Poland has only flat land frontiers. It is doubtful whether fortifications on such a terrain could long hold back an invader of overwhelming force. No matter how bravely Poland might fight, it could hardly hope to win a localized war against either Russia or Germany. It must rely not only on its own military force,[1] but also on diplomacy, to protect its security. Poland's greatest danger is isolation. If it cannot depend on allies or a collective system of security, its position will be extremely precarious.

1. The Policy of Balance

Polish foreign policy is based on the principle of "balance." This principle is applied with two objectives in mind: to obtain outside assistance in case of attack by either Russia or Germany; and to keep Russia and Germany apart.[2] For should these two powers either clash or form an alliance, Polish independence would be jeopardized.

To achieve the first aim, Poland, until the advent of Hitler, made a sincere effort at collaboration with the League of Nations.[3] It was a leading supporter of the ill-fated Geneva

[1] The Polish army actually numbers 266,000 men, of which about 18,000 are officers; the air force has about 8,000 men, and the navy 6,000. In addition, a Frontier Protection Corps guards the country's borders. About 300,000 recruits are yearly called to the colours for a period of obligatory service of two years. It is estimated that Poland has about 3,000,000 trained reserves. The chief strength of the army is its infantry, the endurance and devotion of which is historical. Today Poland makes its infantry and cavalry weapons, and even artillery up to the larger calibres and the necessary ammunition. "Our foot and horse equipment can stand beside the best in Europe. Only our supplies of automatic rifles are still unsatisfactory." General W. Sikorski: "Poland's Defenses," *Slavonic Review*, January 1939. The 1938–9 budget appropriated 800,-000,000 zlotys for national defence; 27,400,000 for the soldiers' billeting fund; 37,000,000 for frontier surveillance corps; 17,900,000 for frontier guards; 45,900,000 for military pensions; and 105,400,000 for war pensions. Together with the sums being spent on public investment largely for military purposes and military appropriations found in other chapters, the total appropriations for national defence constitute about fifty per cent of the budget.

[2] Cf. three articles by C. Smogorzewski: "Poland's Foreign Relations," *Slavonic Review*, 1937, 1938.

[3] Alexandre Bregman: *La Pologne et la Société des Nations* (University of Geneva, 1932, Thesis No. 7).

protocol of 1924 and the principle of sanctions generally, and it applied sanctions against Italy in the Ethiopian war. Its efforts at that time were inspired by a desire to create a general European system which would underwrite Poland's frontiers.

To meet the menace of non-League states, notably Germany and Russia, Poland also adopted a policy of alliances. On January 19, 1921 it concluded an alliance with France.[4] A few months later, on March 3, 1921, Poland and Rumania concluded a much more precise alliance, in which they promised to give each other armed assistance.[5]

An effort to effect a rapprochement between Poland and the Little Entente was made in November 1921, when Foreign Minister Skirmunt of Poland and Foreign Minister Beneš of Czechoslovakia signed a treaty of friendship at Prague. The agreement provided for benevolent neutrality in the event of an attack on either by a third state, permitted free passage of war materials, and prohibited propaganda directed against the other. Poland was to disinterest itself in the Slovakian question, while Czechoslovakia did the same with respect to Eastern Galicia.[6] Had this agreement been ratified, a basis might have been laid for solid opposition to German expansion. Poland was still bitter, however, over the attitude of Czechoslovakia toward the Polish-Russian war of 1920 and the Teschen question. Moreover, it feared Russia, not Germany, and failed to ratify the agreement.

By 1923, having secured international title to Eastern

[4] League of Nations, *Treaty Series*, Vol. XVIII, p. 12. While this treaty did not commit either party to more than consultation in the event of attack, it was followed by the military convention of June 27, 1922, the terms of which were not published.

[5] Ibid., Vol. VII, p. 78.

[6] F. J. Vondracek: *The Foreign Policy of Czechoslovakia, 1918–1935* (New York: Columbia University Press; 1937), p. 180.

Galicia, Poland realized the importance of coming to terms with the Little Entente; and in a speech in the Polish Parliament of July 25, 1923, Foreign Minister Seyda proposed that the Little Entente be organized into a four-power pact, mutually guaranteeing the frontiers of the four states concerned.[7] Following the Locarno agreements, which pleased Czechoslovakia no more than Poland, Foreign Minister Skrzyński went to Prague in April 1926 and again proposed an alliance. But, according to Polish sources,[8] Czechoslovakia declined on the ground that Poland might soon go to war with Germany over the so-called Corridor, with Lithuania over Vilna, and with Russia over the eastern frontier. An alliance with Poland would have strengthened Prague's strategic position with respect to Germany. This lack of unity among the Slavic states of Central Europe in 1938 contributed to the dismemberment of Czechoslovakia.

Poland's hopes of guaranteeing its frontiers against Germany by means of its French alliance suffered a setback with the conclusion of the Locarno agreements in 1925. These agreements guaranteed Germany's western frontier with France but not the Polish frontier with Germany. When Poland raised objections regarding the grant of a permanent seat on the League Council to Germany, the League gave it a semi-permanent seat in 1926. Germany's reoccupation of the Rhineland in 1935, which made it more difficult than ever for France to march to Poland's aid, further impaired the French alliance and the value of the League so far as Poland was concerned. With the construction by Germany of the new Siegfried line of fortifications, France lost what lever it could still use against the Reich.

[7] Casimir Smogorzewski: "Poland and Czechoslovakia," *Gazeta Polska* (Warsaw), June 8, 1938.
[8] Smogorzewski: "Poland's Foreign Relations."

2. Poland and Russia

Having unsuccessfully attempted to build up an alliance system to check its two powerful neighbours, Poland endeavoured to separate Russia and Germany by making friends with one at the expense of the other. In the early post-war years Poland was alarmed by the possibility of a Russo-German combination, when these two powers concluded the agreement of Rapallo in 1922. During the French occupation of the Ruhr in the following year, Russia threatened to mobilize if Poland attempted to take advantage of the crisis to seize East Prussia.[9] This apprehension was decreased when Poland concluded a non-aggression pact with Soviet Russia on July 28, 1932. But the hopes aroused by this pact were not realized, partly because fear of Communism is probably as great in Poland as in Hungary.

To this fear of Communism was added the historical fear of Pan-Slavism. Since the war, Poland has continued to live in dread of Russia's return to Europe. When the French Foreign Minister Barthou proposed that Poland join France and Russia in the so-called Eastern Pact of 1934, Poland declined. Not only was it unwilling to guarantee the frontiers of Czechoslovakia and Lithuania, but Warsaw suspected that France was attempting to transfer to Moscow its obligations under the Polish alliance; and it realized that Russia would be in a far better position than France to send troops to Poland's aid in the event of German attack. But Poland does not want Russian troops on its soil because, remembering the history of the Partitions at the end of the eighteenth century, it fears they will not withdraw, and will

[9] Fischer: *The Soviets in World Affairs*, pp. 451, 831.

propagate Communist sentiment. Nor does Poland wish to serve as the spearhead of a Red Army attack on Germany.

The situation was made worse, as far as Poland was concerned, when Russia joined the League of Nations in 1934, and France and Czechoslovakia concluded their alliances with Russia in 1935. Geographically, Russia could go to the aid of Czechoslovakia only by crossing the territory of Poland or Rumania. But Poland does not admit this right of passage to Russian troops.[10] Consequently, any effort by Russia to extend military assistance to Czechoslovakia involved the risk of war with Poland.

Rivalry with Russia has also arisen in the Baltic area. At the end of the World War these states had reason to fear Russian imperialism. And Poland, after the war, hoped to build up a Baltic bloc under its leadership which would come to terms with Russia as a unit. Russia, for its part, hoped to keep the Baltic states divided so as to increase its own influence, and showed its hostility to Poland by making an agreement with Lithuania in July 1920 recognizing Vilna as part of that country.[11] Russia's success in concluding this bilateral agreement marked the defeat of Poland's

[10] In a letter of June 26, 1936 Foreign Minister Beck made a declaration to the League Council emphasizing that sanctions against Italy under Article XVI had been taken by virtue of the " sovereign decision " of each government. League of Nations, *Official Journal*, Special Supplement 150, p. 339. On April 29, 1937 M. Spaak, Minister of Foreign Affairs of Belgium, declared in Parliament that the right of passage under Article XVI depended on (1) the consent of the Belgian government, and (2) the organization of a " common action " against the aggressor by the League Council. *Annales Parlementaires, Chambre des Représentants*, April 29, 1937, p. 1287. The French text, differing from the English text, says that League members " *prennent les dispositions nécessaires pour faciliter le passage à travers leur territoire des forces de tout Membre de la Société qui participe à une action commune pour faire respecter les engagements de la Société.*" The " *action commune* " envisaged by the French text apparently consists in those measures adopted by the League Council on which Poland would have a veto. Cf. p. 333.

[11] Fischer, op. cit., p. 717.

efforts to create a solid Baltic bloc. The Polish occupation of Vilna in October 1920 was partly intended to dislocate the frontier between Russia and Lithuania.

Although Russian aggression in the Baltic seems no longer an issue, Russia and the Baltic countries today live in fear of German aggression. The spearhead of a German movement would be Lithuania, not only because of the restoration of the German position in Memel in March 1939, but because Lithuania as a whole is the logical jumping-off place for a German move on Leningrad. Even if the rumour that the U.S.S.R. has a secret alliance with Lithuania is incorrect,[12] it would probably be to the interest of the Soviet Union to stop a German offensive by coming to the aid of Lithuania. But to do so, Russian troops would probably have to cross Polish territory. Thus the interests of Poland and Russia have seriously clashed over both the Lithuanian and the Czechoslovak questions.

Poland took advantage of *Anschluss* in March 1938 to settle its accounts with Lithuania and thereby weaken Russian influence in this area. Although Vilna was the capital of the mediæval duchy of Lithuania, the present Lithuanian minority in the city is less than one per cent of the total population, 66 per cent being Poles. Between the end of the fifteenth century and the Partition of 1772, the Lithuanian upper classes were Polonized; and subsequently Vilna became a centre of Polish culture. An awakening Lithuanian nationalism, however, began to claim the city at the end of the last century; and in 1918 it was made the capital of the Lithuanian Republic. After various armies had fought for its possession, Russia ceded the city to Lithuania by a peace

[12] The two governments are bound by a non-aggression pact of September 28, 1926.

treaty of July 12, 1920. Clashes subsequently took place with Polish troops, leading to the armistice at Suwałki in October 1920 and the drawing of the famous Curzon Line under League mediation, which allotted Vilna to Lithuania. But on October 9, 1920, the day before the agreement was to enter into force, the city was occupied by the Polish General, Żeligowski. Although Poland disavowed the General, he declined to evacuate the region so that the League might hold a plebiscite. After further League efforts had failed, the Diet of Vilna voted to unite with Poland, a decision ratified by the Polish Parliament on March 24, 1922. On March 15, 1923 the Conference of Ambassadors confirmed a frontier which left Vilna with Poland. Lithuania declined to recognize it, and in its constitution subsequently proclaimed Vilna as the capital. It also declined to have any diplomatic or economic relations with Poland, even refusing to allow railroad connections or to accord any rights to the Polish minority. This " dead frontier," three hundred miles long, lasted for eighteen years, preventing the establishment of peaceful relations.

When on March 11, 1938, during the Austrian crisis, a frontier incident involving the death of a Polish soldier on Lithuanian territory took place, the Polish government addressed an ultimatum to Kovno on March 17, demanding unconditional restoration of diplomatic relations within forty-eight hours as the only means of guaranteeing security. At the same time, it mobilized troops along the Lithuanian frontier. The ultimatum was far less drastic than the demand of the Polish nationalists, who (despite a run on the Warsaw banks) clamoured for a Polish naval base in Lithuania, a tariff union between the two countries, and the suppression of those articles in the Lithuanian constitution designating Vilna as the capital. Some even demanded complete annexation, as before 1772.[13] The moderation of the Polish ultimatum may have been due to the pressure of France, Britain, Russia, and possibly Germany, which has its own plans for Lithuania. Having failed to obtain support from the U.S.S.R., the Kovno government accepted the Polish ultimatum, promising to restore diplomatic relations before April 13 and to open railway and postal traffic. While the Lithuanian constitution still contains the article proclaiming Vilna to be its capital, the settlement of March 1938 undoubtedly increased Polish influence in Lithuania and constituted a setback for the Soviet Union. Poland will always strive to exclude the influence of both Russia and Germany from Lithuania and to induce the latter country to follow the Polish policy of "balance."

In recent years the anti-Russian school, carrying on the Piłsudski tradition, has been strong. It believes that Poland can best escape being crushed by its two powerful neighbours if it forms an alliance with Germany to dismember Russia and drive Soviet influence out of Central Europe and Lithuania.[14] The Promethean movement, perhaps the most active if least influential branch of this school, believes that Russia is the "sick man" of the twentieth century, fated for partition, and that Poland should get its share.[15] Supporters of this view believe that if Poland joined Russia against Germany, it would suffer serious injury, because Germany would then be tempted to come to terms with Moscow rather than face a hostile Russo-Polish alli-

[13] For a summary of these events, cf. Rappaport: "Chronique Polonaise," p. 250.

[14] Cf. E. Studnicki: *Polen im politischen System Europas* (Berlin, 1936).

[15] Adolf Bocheński: *Między Niemcami a Rosją* (*Between Germany and Russia*) (Warsaw: Polityka; 1937).

ance. The Promethean movement proposes, therefore, that Poland " liberate " the subject nationalities of Soviet Russia, thus restoring Poland to the position it had in Europe under the Jagellon dynasty. The creation, at Soviet expense, of an independent Ukraine and Georgia bound to Poland would, it is alleged, remove the constant pressure against Poland from the east. Thus one writer states: " The disintegration of Russia into its former component parts is to the fundamental interest of the Republic of Poland. . . . This is the only means of extracting Poland from the constant danger of being crushed between the two present-day powers represented by its eastern and western neighbours." [16] The Promethean movement even envisages the " liberation " of Siberia from the " yoke " of Russian oppression.[17]

Should Russia become involved in war with Japan, it is not impossible that the Polish government would endeavour to put some of these ideas into effect. It is doubtful, however, whether Poland, even with Japan's assistance, could dismember Russia along the periphery unless the U.S.S.R. went to pieces at the centre. Even then it is not likely that Germany would allow Poland alone to devour the remains. Germany itself would like to " liberate " the Ukraine, at the expense of both Soviet Russia and Poland.

The weakening of Russia may serve as a temptation to Poland; but the more Russia is weakened, the greater becomes the danger that Germany will dominate not only south-western Russia but Poland itself. Meanwhile strained

[16] J. Dąbrowski: " Poland and the Future War," quoted by T. Radwański: "The Geopolitical Situation of Poland and the Promethean Movement," *Wschód-Orient*, No. 4 (1935). The same view is advanced by T. Radwański: "The Promethean Movement and the Potential War Strength of the U.S.S.R.," ibid., No. 4 (1936).

[17] W. Pelc: "The Siberian Question and the Promethean Movement," *Wschód-Orient*, No. 1-2 (1937).

relations between Poland and Russia have worked against Polish economic interests. It is a question whether Poland can solve its serious over-population problem without developing an extensive trade with Russia. Some Poles believe that Russia might even absorb, economically speaking, a number of Polish immigrants. In 1938 Poland's trade with Russia was only one per cent of its total foreign trade, although the Russian market was of vital importance to Congress Poland before the World War. An exclusive understanding between Poland and Russia remains unlikely for ideological as well as historical reasons. Yet Poland has more to gain, economically and politically, than any other country from a general movement to bring Russia into some orderly and peaceful relationship with the rest of Europe.[18]

3. Poland and Germany

Owing to the heated controversy over Danzig, the so-called Corridor, and Upper Silesia, Poland's relations with Germany until 1933 were worse than with any other power. Leaders of the German Republic could not believe that Poland was more than a " temporary " state (*saison Staat*); and the policy adopted at Rapallo was undoubtedly inspired by a desire to destroy Poland. Republican Germany engaged in a series of controversies with Poland over frontier and other questions, and carried on world-wide propaganda to convince neutral opinion that the Polish frontier was one of the major injustices of the Versailles settlement. Stresemann, in his letter to the Crown Prince of September 7, 1925, wrote that " the third great task of Germany is the

[18] This line of reasoning finally prevailed in Warsaw following Hitler's success at Munich. On November 26, 1938 Warsaw and Moscow made an important agreement. Cf. p. 349.

readjustment of our Eastern frontiers, the recovery of
Danzig, the Polish Corridor and a correction of the frontier
in Upper Silesia." [19] In 1931 Chancellor Brüning sounded
out the leading European capitals to see to what extent they
would accept territorial revision at the expense of Poland. [20]

As the fear of Germany increased and Polish alliances
weakened, [21] Poland began a searching reconsideration of
its foreign policy. Piłsudski was the first statesman to fore-
cast the rising power of the new Germany and the significance of the Nazi movement. His intuition also indicated
that neither France nor Britain could be counted on to
maintain the treaty structure of Europe by force. On January 26, 1934, without consulting Poland's ally, France,
Piłsudski concluded the famous non-aggression agreement
with Hitler. The two countries expressed their determination to " base their mutual relations on the principles contained in the Pact of Paris of August 27, 1928. . . . Both
governments declare that it is their intention to reach direct understanding on problems concerning their mutual
relations. . . . In no case, however, shall they have re-
course to force in order to settle such questions under dispute." The declaration was to remain in force during a
period of ten years, but if neither government gave notice
of its termination six months before or after this period of
time, it was to continue in effect. [22] That Hitler could so
suddenly abandon the revisionist campaign of the German
Republic represented one of the most surprising *volte-faces*

[19] Gustav Stresemann: *His Diaries, Letters, and Papers* (London:
Macmillan & Co.; 1935–7; 2 vols.), Vol. II, p. 503.

[20] Casimir Smogorzewski: " Poland: Free, Peaceful, Strong," *Foreign
Affairs*, July 1935.

[21] Cf. p. 323.

[22] For an English translation, cf. *Documents on International Affairs*,
edited by J. W. Wheeler-Bennett (New York: Oxford University Press;
1934), p. 424.

in modern history. By this move Germany made the first dent in the French alliance system, removed the danger of an attack from Poland, secured a shield against Russian attack, and was able to concentrate its forces against Austria. The German-Polish non-aggression pact ended the isolation into which Nazi Germany had been plunged.

Poland, through this agreement, cast off its semi-colonial status and was recognized as a great power. Having thus demonstrated its complete independence of France, it now became an object of solicitation on the part of all Europe. The agreement also dispelled the bitterness which had existed between Poland and the German Republic. The German campaign for revision of the Polish frontier, the Polish-German tariff war, and the support hitherto given by Germany to the minorities within Poland came to an end or were moderated. Poland, without fear of attack, could now consolidate its position in the former German provinces, which it thought it could do since its population increases more rapidly than that of Germany. Momentarily Poland had diverted German expansion toward other parts of Europe and gained time for rearmament. In view of the unwillingness of France and Britain to prevent treaty violations by Germany, and continued uncertainty regarding France's internal situation, the Polish-German agreement undoubtedly served the immediate interests of Poland. For the time being at least, it prevented Poland from becoming engaged with Germany in the type of controversy in which Czechoslovakia soon found itself involved. Poland, however, paid a price for this settlement. Thus it was obliged to acquiesce in the Nazification of the Free City of Danzig, subject to the retention of certain economic rights,[23] and

[23] Cf. M. S. Wertheimer: "The Nazification of Danzig," *Foreign Policy Reports*, June 1, 1936.

it contributed to the enormous strengthening of Germany. Poland now ceased being a *status quo* power and moved into the revisionist camp.

The actual text of the non-aggression pact of 1934 expressly exempted from its provisions the prior obligations of Poland, such as those arising out of the French and Rumanian alliances and the League Covenant. Technically there was nothing to prevent Poland from continuing its former policy. But in fact Poland proceeded to go considerably beyond the published provisions of the non-aggression pact. It now showed its hostility to the whole thesis of " collective security " as compared with the German thesis of " bilateral pacts." This attitude may have been due to a secret agreement. A more plausible explanation for Poland's policy, however, was its belief that the League had become an ideological alliance inspired by Russia and directed against the Fascist states — a belief reinforced by the withdrawal of Germany, Italy, and Japan. In an address to the foreign affairs commission of the Polish Sejm in January 1938, Foreign Minister Beck expressed the fear that " the meetings at Geneva had become doctrinaire conferences, to the detriment of world politics." It was impossible for Poland, he said, " to ally itself with doctrinaire blocs or to allow our country to become the instrument of a policy which it has not itself fixed." [24] In the autumn of 1938 Poland declined to stand for re-election to the League Council, in marked contrast with the eagerness it had hitherto shown to obtain such honours.[25]

[24] Rappaport, op. cit.
[25] On September 16, 1938 M. Komarnicki, Polish delegate, informed the League Assembly that his government agreed that " it has the sovereign right to determine the attitude which it must adopt in each international situation regarding the application of Article XVI of the Covenant." He reiterated the view he had expressed before the Committee of Twenty-Eight dealing with the amendment of the Covenant. *Verbatim*

Despite the 1934 understanding with Germany, Poland had no intention of breaking off its alliance with France. Warsaw could safely make friends with Berlin only if it retained certain bargaining counters and remained strong. Colonel Beck now proceeded to strengthen the Polish-Rumanian alliance, facilitated by the resignation of Foreign Minister Titulescu who had favoured a pro-Russian policy. When Germany reoccupied the Rhineland in March 1936, Poland offered to mobilize if France did likewise. But France declined, thus confirming Poland's diagnosis of the European situation.

In an effort to repair the balance of power damaged by the Rhineland reoccupation, Marshal Rydz-Śmigły went to Paris in the fall of 1936, returning the visit of General Gamelin, French Chief of Staff, to Warsaw. Here the Franco-Polish alliance was strengthened by an agreement of September of that year,[26] and the Marshal was reported to have promised that Poland would fulfil its obligations under the League Covenant if Czechoslovakia was the object of unprovoked aggression — a promise subsequently denied.[27] In return, France agreed to make a loan of $63,-000,000 to Poland, partly for the purpose of developing the central industrial district to be capable of producing munitions.[28]

When Germany struck an even more serious blow at

Record of the Nineteenth Ordinary Session of the Assembly, Fifth Plenary Meeting, September 16, 1938; also Official Journal, Special Supplement No. 180, p. 15.

[26] Foreign Minister Delbos, in Journal Officiel, Débats parlementaires, Chambre des Députés, Session Extraordinaire 1936, première Séance du 29 Décembre 1936.

[27] The Polish Embassy in Washington on December 31, 1936 denied that this obligation was undertaken. New York Herald Tribune, January 1, 1937.

[28] Cf. p. 160.

European equilibrium by annexing Austria in March 1938, Warsaw did nothing to correct the balance, the official view being that the Danubian area was of secondary interest to Poland. In the midst of the subsequent Czechoslovak crisis, Poland even took what amounted to a pro-German attitude. The official press openly attacked the Prague government, while paying marked attention to the complaints of the Slovaks although they had been considerably better treated than the minorities in Poland.

Now France was allied with both Poland and Czechoslovakia. The former, in the agreement of 1921, had promised to consult with France on all questions of foreign policy. Despite the new loan from Paris, Warsaw actually demonstrated its hostility toward France's ally, Czechoslovakia. Such a situation would be difficult to duplicate in modern diplomatic history. During the spring and summer of 1938 the British and French Ambassadors in Warsaw pleaded with the Polish government not to weaken Czechoslovakia in this crisis, nor to join Germany in an attack for the purpose of dismemberment. In May, and again in June, the Polish government gave rather lukewarm assurances. Polish methods changed when Britain and France proposed that Czechoslovakia cede the Sudeten area to Germany.[29]

It was clear to most observers that if Czechoslovakia became a satellite of Germany, Nazi pressure on Poland would greatly increase. Once in control of the Prague government, Germany would be in a position to carry on intrigues in Polish Ukraine and build a corridor in the direction of Kiev. It may be argued that, in assisting German efforts to dismember Czechoslovakia, Poland thus injured its own interests. To understand Polish policy in this ques-

[29] Cf. p. 340.

tion, it is necessary to review the relations between Poland and Czechoslovakia, as well as the policies of France and Britain.

4. Poland and Czechoslovakia

Although both Poland and Czechoslovakia belonged to the Slav race, they had a long history of mutual jealousy. For a time in the fourteenth century a Czech King occupied the Polish throne, while during the sixteenth century the Polish monarchy of the Jagellons also occupied the thrones of Bohemia and Hungary. Czechs and Poles, however, intermittently struggled for possession of the same territory in Central Europe.

Following the battle of the White Mountain in 1620, Bohemia lost its independence and thereafter the Czechs became wards of the Habsburgs. In the nineteenth-century struggle to recover their independence, these Slavs looked to Russia for help. During the same period, however, some Poles, comparatively well treated in Galicia by the Habsburgs, developed an undying hatred of Russia, which they regarded as their greatest enemy. Although President Masaryk warned against "Pan-Slav and pro-Russian illusions," [30] the difference over the Russian question continued after the war. Czechoslovakia joined the Western powers in opposing the cession of Eastern Galicia to Poland. Poles

[30] T. G. Masaryk: *The Making of a State* (London: George Allen & Unwin; 1927), p. 143. A British Foreign Office memorandum of 1916 outlining a suggested basis of a European settlement, discussed the idea of adding Bohemia to Poland, as one alternative, stating that the Czechs "fully appreciate that they would benefit by the superior culture and civilization of the Poles." At the Paris Peace Conference, however, Lloyd George denounced Polish imperialism, while General Smuts said: "Poland was a historic failure, and always would be a failure, and in this Treaty we were trying to reverse the verdict of history." D. Lloyd George: *The Truth about the Peace Treaties* (London: Victor Gollancz; 1938), Vol. I, pp. 44, 692.

charge that during that period Czechoslovakia desired a common frontier with Russia at the expense of Poland, while Piłsudski wanted a common frontier with Rumania which would separate Russia from Prague.[31] When the Polish army was driven back to Warsaw by the Bolsheviks in 1920, the Czechoslovak government, influenced by the Communist attitude of local labour unions, prohibited for a time the transport of munitions across its territory and also objected to the passage of reinforcements from Hungary. While Germany adopted much the same attitude,[32] Poles continue to hold this incident against the Czechs. Professor Masaryk, toward the end of the war, wrote that " without a free Poland, there cannot be a free Bohemia ";[33] he warned General Weygand, however, when the latter passed through Prague as a member of the Anglo-French mission to Poland during the Polish-Bolshevik war, that it was useless to organize assistance for the Poles because the capture of Warsaw was inevitable, and such assistance would destroy the influence of the Western powers in the subsequent negotiations for peace. When Lord d'Abernon's book recording this conversation was published in 1931, it deepened Polish animosity against Prague.[34] Whatever its attitude toward Communism might be, Czechoslovakia was pro-Russian, Poland contended. In view of the wide gulf between the gentry outlook dominating Poland

[31] Wacław Łypacewicz: *Polish-Czech Relations* (Warsaw, 1936).

[32] Germany closed the Kiel canal to the shipment of munitions to Poland on the ground that such shipments violated its neutrality. This action was overruled by the Permanent Court of International Justice. Case of the S.S. *Wimbledon*, Series A, *Collection of Judgments*, No. 1, June 1923; R. L. Buell *International Relations*, p. 134.

[33] *L'Europe Nouvelle*, February 2, 1918, p. 179.

[34] Lord d'Abernon: *The Eighteenth Decisive Battle of the World* (London: Hodder & Stoughton; 1931). The author says that Paderewski was almost as gloomy at that time as President Masaryk.

and the staid bourgeois outlook of Czechoslovakia, it was not difficult for Poles to believe that Prague was a hotbed of Communism. The existence of a common frontier for nearly a thousand kilometres between Czechoslovakia and Poland increased the possibility that Prague might co-operate with Moscow in stirring up trouble among the White Russian and Ukrainian minorities. These fears were intensified when Russia and Czechoslovakia concluded their pact of mutual assistance in 1935. The fact that Czechoslovakia made greater political and social progress after the World War than other new countries also aroused Poland's jealousy.

The most concrete cause of controversy between these two states was the Teschen question. This district constitutes the south-east corner of the province of Silesia, and, after the fourteenth century, formed part of the " lands of the Bohemian Crown." [35] Although the Duchy of Teschen is small, it is important as a mining and railway centre. According to the Austrian census of 1910, nearly 55 per cent of the population of the district, totalling 426,000, was Polish-speaking, while 18.04 per cent spoke German, and 27.11 per cent spoke Czech.

On November 5, 1918 the two local councils, the Polish National Council and the Czech National Local Committee, agreed to a provisional frontier following ethnic lines. But the next month the Czechs became indignant when Poland announced that it would hold elections in the area. When Polish troops occupied almost all of the duchy,[36] Prague demanded the evacuation of eastern Silesia by Poland, and Czech troops seized the city of Bohumin, forcing the Polish

[35] H. W. V. Temperley, editor: *History of the Paris Peace Conference* (London: Oxford University Press; 1924), Vol. IV, p. 349.
[36] Kamil Krofta, *A Short History of Czechoslovakia* (New York, McBride, 1934), p. 148.

troops to withdraw. After vainly endeavouring to hold a plebiscite and then to arbitrate the question, the Conference of Ambassadors, in an agreement of July 28, 1920, divided up the duchy between the two countries. The award gave Poland the eastern part, including a large part of the town of Teschen; to Czechoslovakia it gave the town of Frystat, the whole of the Karvin mining area, and a considerable section of the railway. Czechoslovakia's share was considerably larger than that agreed upon in November 1918.[37] Although this division clearly subordinated the ethnic to the economic principle, opinion in Czechoslovakia was indignant that the government had accepted this compromise.

Nevertheless, for a time Poland attempted to improve its relations with Czechoslovakia and, although an alliance was not signed, on April 23, 1925 the two governments concluded an agreement providing for the arbitration and conciliation of all disputes except problems arising from territorial questions.[38]

As a result of this and other agreements, relations between the two Slavic countries improved. Finally realizing the German danger, Czech statements hinted in 1933 that it might be desirable for Poland to join the Little Entente.[39] But a new difference arose when the Little Entente accepted the Four-Power Pact in its final form, while Poland rejected it *in toto*. The conclusion of the Polish-German non-aggression pact of 1934 was a further blow at Slavic understanding; thereafter Poland's campaigns on behalf of the Polish minority in Teschen were intensified. In March 1934 tension reached its height over the arrest of three Poles

[37] Cf. Temperley, op. cit., map, Vol. IV, p. 348.
[38] League of Nations, *Treaty Series*, Vol. XLVIII, p. 383.
[39] Cf. Arnold J. Toynbee: *Survey of International Affairs, 1920–1936* (London: Oxford University Press; 1925–37), Vol. I, p. 287.

in Teschen who predicted a Polish invasion, and Poland in turn expelled twenty-one Czechoslovak citizens and prohibited the sale of three Czech newspapers. Warsaw declined the offer of Czechoslovakia to arbitrate the controversy under the terms of the 1925 convention or refer it to the League — an attitude which reinforced the suspicion that Poland had ulterior motives. Subsequently Poland charged that Czechoslovakia had granted asylum to Ukrainian refugees from Poland — a charge which Prague denied. The controversy continued until October 1935, when the Czech government withdrew the exequatur of the Polish Consul at Moravska-Ostrava, charging that he was intriguing with extremists in Carpathian Ruthenia and Slovakia and stimulating Polish propaganda in Teschen. Warsaw struck back by expelling two Czechoslovak consuls, and announcing the withdrawal of its Minister from Prague; once again it rejected the Czech offer of arbitration under the 1925 agreement. Subject to fluctuations, this tense atmosphere persisted until 1938.

In the spring of 1938 the Polish government again complained that Communist propaganda was emanating from Czechoslovakia against Poland.[40] Prague replied that it would repress any illegal activities on presentation of proof from the Polish government, but could not repress freedom of speech.

During the Czech crisis in September 1938, the Polish government remained vigilant, consistently demanding the same treatment for the Polish minority in Teschen as that extended to the Germans in Sudetenland. Following the Anglo-French proposals of September 18, 1938 with re-

---

[40] "The Czech Branch of the 'Komintern,'" *Gazeta Polska*, April 2, 1938. A second note was sent by Warsaw in July, complaining that the note of March 22 had not been given adequate consideration. *The Times*, July 28, 1938.

spect to Sudetenland, and Mussolini's speech of the same
day calling for "plebiscites for all nationalities that demand them," Poland became more precise in its demands.
In a note of September 21 the Polish government referred
to a declaration from Prague that the Polish minority would
not be discriminated against. Warsaw insisted, however,
that it would expect a settlement of the Polish minority
question "in the same manner as that of the territories of
the German population." At the same time it denounced
the Polish-Czech agreement of 1925.[41] The Polish government also protested to Britain and France that they had not
adequately considered its claims. A semi-official statement
added that if the Czech government accepted the Anglo-
French proposals, Poland would demand the annexation of
that part of Teschen-Silesia granted to it under the agreement of November 5, 1918.[42]

Troop movements now took place, a "volunteer corps"
was organized, and popular demonstrations were held in
favour of redeeming the "lands beyond the Olza."[43] The
Polish-Czech frontier was closed by the Prague government; Poles and Czechs were killed in clashes. Meanwhile,
the Polish and Hungarian authorities asked Hitler and Mussolini for help in advancing their claims. When the Soviet
government, in a note of September 23, warned that it
might denounce the non-aggression pact of 1932 if Polish
troops crossed the Czech frontier, Poland replied that this
affair did not concern Russia;[44] while Foreign Minister Beck

[41] *The Times*, September 22, 1938; *Le Temps*, September 23, 1938.
[42] Cf. the semi-official statement in *Illustrowany Kurjer Codzienny*,
quoted in *The Times*, September 22, 1938.
[43] Cf. M. W. Fodor dispatch, Prague, *New York Sun*, October 6,
1938.
[44] *Le Temps*, September 25, 1938. It was reported that in a radius of
200 miles along the Polish frontier between Kiev and White Russia 30
divisions of Russian infantry were concentrated, mostly on a war footing

proceeded to confer with the Japanese Ambassador. The determination of the Polish government to act was increased when the text of the Munich agreement became known. Poland had not been invited to the Munich conference, and could not consider itself bound by its decisions. At Munich Poland saw the ghost of the old Four-Power Pact.

On the day of the Munich communiqué the Polish government sent an ultimatum — its third note since September 21 — demanding the evacuation of Teschen and the sections west from Ropice to Darkov by the next noon, and surrender by October 10 of the districts of Bohumin, Frystat, and Jablunkov; and suggesting a plebiscite in the districts of Frydek and Slezska Ostrava.[45] Despite an appeal from Secretary Hull not to use force, and an offer for mediation from the British and French Ambassadors, the Polish government indicated that the return of Teschen-Silesia could be realized only by Poland itself. On October 1 Prague yielded, and during the next ten days the Polish troops took over the stipulated areas.

This settlement apparently gives Poland the area allotted in the provisional agreement of November 5, 1918 and, in addition, the district of Bohumin. Poland feared that Bohumin, an important strategic and railway centre, might fall under German domination. To avert this danger, it occupied the town three days ahead of schedule. In 1918 a majority of the people in these districts, except Bohumin, may have been Poles, but, as a result of immigration from

— a stronger force than the whole peace-time Polish army. The Russian divisions numbered nearly 350,000 men and were supported by 3,000 planes, 2,000 tanks, and five cavalry corps. According to this observer, Russia could very easily create a Sudeten problem within Poland by endeavouring to liberate " the Ukrainians and White Russians there." Riga dispatch, *The Times*, September 26, 1938.

    [45] *Prager Press,* October 4, 1938.

Czechoslovakia proper and other causes, the population in all four districts except Jablunkov, according to the Prague census of 1930, was predominantly Czech, as follows: [46]

	Frystat	Bohumin	Teschen	Jablunkov	Totals
Total	91,054	51,011	53,976	31,358	227,399
Czechs ...	52,285	35,714	23,204	9,436	120,639
Poles	29,790	4,755	21,424	20,261	76,230

Poles justified the annexation of 120,000 Czechs and 18,000 Germans in order to " liberate " 80,000 Poles, on the ground of restoring the situation existing in 1918 Poland also claimed that the Czech census was inaccurate.

In securing Teschen, Poland improved its strategic position against Germany and annexed rich coal and coke resources. This abundance of riches led Poland to seek out new foreign markets. The annexation of Teschen was a factor leading to the new trade agreement with Russia.

Opinion in the democratic countries condemned Polish policy toward Czechoslovakia during this period, and particularly its seizure of Teschen, but the Western world could not reasonably expect Poland to go further than France and Britain in supporting Czechoslovakia against German threats. It was inevitable that with the German

[46] Figures taken from Czechoslovakia Statistical Office, *Statisticky Lexicon obci v Republice Ceskoslovenska* (Prague, 1935), Vol. II. In 1918 Poland demanded the districts of Bilsko, Teschen, and Frystat, as well as the community called Hrusov in the district of Frydek. All these districts went to Poland in 1938 except Hrusov, which remains in Czechoslovakia. In the Trencin district in Slovakia, Poland demanded the city of Cadca and thirteen villages in 1918. In 1938 it received in this area only two communities, called Skalite and Cierne. The city of Cadca remains in Czechoslovakia. Likewise in 1938 Poland realized a part of the demands made in 1918 in respect to the districts of Orava and Spis. The section in Spis ceded to Poland contains a valuable part of the Tatra Mountains, including a well-kept natural park.

acquisition of the Sudetenland Poland should try to recover Teschen, to which it had a better historic title.

The Polish public hailed the return of Teschen, and the press stated the hope that a firm basis had now been laid for co-operation between Warsaw and Prague. The Polish government, however, took the initiative in supporting Hungarian claims against Czechoslovakia, one government newspaper, *Kurjer Polski*, even advocating Slovak independence under joint Polish-Hungarian guarantee. For many years Poland had talked of establishing a common frontier with Hungary at the expense of Czechoslovakia, thus erecting a new barrier to German expansion. It had never ratified the Treaty of Trianon, which had deprived Hungary of Slovakia and Carpatho-Ruthenia (Ukraine), and now asked that these territories — or at least Ruthenia — be returned to Budapest, although neither had a majority of Hungarians. Poland wished to prevent Germany from making use of the Carpatho-Ukraine as a base for Greater Ukraine propaganda.

Warsaw and Budapest hoped to secure the support of the great powers and Rumania for a common frontier. In Poland popular demonstrations in favour of this idea took place. The Youth Group of the Party of National Unity declared: " The century-old wishes of the two sister nations must be fulfilled. We fight for the Poland of the Jagellos." A meeting of representatives of the seventeen leading conservative papers in Warsaw said that this vital problem must be solved even if the price was mobilization.[47] On October 19 Foreign Minister Beck paid a visit to King Carol, to win him over to the Polish-Hungarian project by offering Rumania the south-east corner of Carpathian Ru-

[47] N. Udardy: "Poland's Effort to Obtain a Common Frontier with Hungary," *Danubian Review* (Budapest), November 1938.

thenia, containing 40,000 Rumanians.[48] For obvious reasons, neither France nor Britain took any interest in these Polish designs; and Soviet Russia, which had more at stake than any other power in blocking further German expansion, could not be expected to support the Poles in view of past conflicts. Although Italy originally supported Hungarian ambitions,[49] it soon became evident that Mussolini could not pursue a policy in Central Europe independent of Hitler. The Munich agreement of September 30 had provided that if the question of the Polish and Hungarian minorities in Czechoslovakia was not settled within three months, it should be referred to a further meeting of the four great powers. On October 31, however, it was announced that Czechoslovakia and Hungary had agreed that their differences should be arbitrated jointly by Germany and Italy.[50] The desire of Hungary to have Poland act as one of the arbiters over the Ruthenian question was set aside. Although the Vienna award of November 2 gave Hungary a part of Ruthenia, it did not establish a common Polish-Hungarian frontier.[51] Thus despite the return of Teschen, Poland suffered a major diplomatic defeat.

For a number of years before the Munich crisis Poland had considered the possibility of establishing a great bloc of states stretching from the Baltic to the Black Sea — the New Europe. Foreign Minister Beck made many visits to the capitals of the countries concerned, with a view to promoting the project. It might have had a chance of success had Poland been willing to bury its differences with Czechoslovakia and Lithuania and to accept commitments linking up the Baltic, Little, and Balkan En-

[48] Warsaw dispatch, *New York Times*, October 19, 1938.
[49] Rome dispatch, ibid., October 3, 1938.
[50] *New York Times*, November 1, 1938.
[51] Ibid., November 26, 1938.

tentes. But Poland chose to cast its lot with Germany in 1934 and follow bilateral policies. In particular, the Baltic countries were suspicious of Poland, believing that Foreign Minister Beck was co-operating with Hitler to establish German supremacy in this area.[52] Poland's efforts to form close relations with Hungary, and even Bulgaria, also aroused apprehension among states which might otherwise have joined in a real Central European bloc.[53] It became evident after Munich that Poland lacked the strength to erect a firm barrier against Germany from the Baltic to the Black Sea, once Hitler had established his control over Vienna and Prague.

For the moment, the Munich conference and its aftermath severely strained relations between Warsaw and Berlin. The two countries had seemed to move together when they made an agreement on July 1, 1938 diverting German coal purchases from Czechoslovakia to Poland, and the more important arrangement of October 17, 1938, by which Germany agreed to grant Poland a $23,000,000 credit.[54] But Poland's seizure of Bohumin, together with its attempt to liquidate Carpatho-Ukraine, angered the Nazis. They showed their displeasure by expelling from Germany about 15,000 Polish Jews, ostensibly to protect Germany against the application of a Polish decree that might have deprived some Jews living in Germany of Polish citizenship.[55]

[52] M. Pernot: "Les Rélations entre la Lithuania et la Pologne," *Politique étrangère*, June 1938.

[53] For one such proposal, made before the Munich crisis by a Rumanian authority, cf. Michel Antonesco: "Une Nouvelle Formule de sécurité en Europe Orientale," *Affaires Danubiennes* (Bucharest), July 1938.

[54] Cf. p. 198.

[55] *New York Herald Tribune*, October 31, 1938. The law of March 25, 1938 authorized the Minister of the Interior, on recommendation of the Foreign Ministry, to deprive of Polish citizenship a person (1) who has spent five years of continuous residence abroad, (2) who has acted against the interest of the Polish state while abroad, or (3) who did not

While Poland's independent foreign policy, which reached its climax with the Teschen ultimatum, alienated the west, Warsaw believed more strongly than ever that, if Czechoslovakia could not depend on help from France, its own alliance with Paris had become of little importance. France had acquiesced in the Polish Partitions at the end of the eighteenth century and, despite its alliance, could do so again. The situation as seen by a leading conservative paper in Poland, *Czas*, just before the Munich agreement was as follows: " We are informed that certain French circles have threatened us with a denunciation of the alliance with Poland. . . . From whatever circles these threats come, it is unfortunately not difficult to say that the manner in which France has treated its alliance with Czechoslovakia has well demonstrated what this alliance was actually worth. This example is rightly or wrongly a warning for the other allies of France. Under such conditions all threats to denounce the treaty lose much of their importance."

5. *Poland after Munich*

Notwithstanding the reduction of Czechoslovakia as a result of the Munich conference, some Poles professed to believe that they could count on the unilateral promises of Hitler not to menace their own country. Others believed that German expansion would continue in the direction of the south-east, rather than turn toward the Baltic or the Ukraine.[56] In his Sportspalast speech of September 25, 1938, Hitler declared he had informed Chamberlain that Germany had no further territorial ambitions in Europe; he also

---

return within a definite period when called on by a Polish consular authority to do so.

[56] Cf. p. 267.

declared that the non-aggression pact with Poland of January 1934 would " bring about lasting and continuous pacification " — a view reiterated in his speech to the Reichstag of January 30, 1939. Some Poles clung to the hope that the new Germany wants to have only Germans within its own borders, in accordance with the doctrine of *Volkstum*,[57] and they pointed out that there is no district in Poland where Germans now constitute more than ten per cent of the total.

For a people like the Poles, who pride themselves on realism, Poland's independence must seem to rest on a very fragile basis if it depends merely on Hitler's self-restraint. The Third Reich may have postponed the effort to realize its ambitions, but there are few indications that the Nazi régime has abandoned any of Germany's traditional designs; and, as we have seen, these ambitions conflict with vital Polish interests both in the Baltic and in the Ukraine. From the economic point of view, Poland's position in respect to Danzig is relatively strong. Should Germany annex the Free City, Poland could divert trade to Gdynia, to Danzig's great injury. Nevertheless, Hitler's racialism has frequently overridden economic considerations in the past; and should he decide to seize Danzig, Poland would suffer pressure on two frontiers, since Memel has been regained. Whether it could long hold Gdynia and the Corridor under such circumstances is problematical.

Realizing these dangers, Poland after the Munich conference not only tried to establish a frontier with Hungary but attempted to improve its relations with Russia and Lithuania — an effort which produced a considerable degree of success.

In what proved a futile effort to protect Memel, the

[57] Cf. p. 4.

Prime Minister of Lithuania, the Reverend Vladas Mironas, declared in Parliament on December 1, 1938 that his government had decided "radically to change the attitude adopted for many years toward our southern neighbour [Poland] and to eliminate all factors contrary to the new situation." The government dissolved the League for the Liberation of Vilna, an anti-Polish organization; made a press agreement in which both Poland and Lithuania promised to forbid press attacks against the other; and concluded a trade agreement on December 22, 1938, containing the most-favoured-nation clause.

Of even more significance was a Soviet-Polish declaration of November 27, 1938 reaffirming the non-aggression pact which had been strained during the Munich crisis, and declaring that henceforth relations would be based on a neighbourly understanding. Negotiations led to the conclusion of a far-reaching trade agreement on February 19, 1939, the first between these two states based on the most-favoured-nation principle. As a result, Russia will export to Poland increased quantities of cotton, tobacco, manganese, asbestos, and graphite, while Poland will sell to Russia more coal, ferrous metals, cement, textile goods, textile machinery, leather goods, and artificial silk. Hereafter Russia will probably take six or seven per cent of Poland's trade instead of one per cent as in 1937.

Doubtless to avoid antagonizing Berlin, the Polish press minimized the Polish-Soviet declaration. Moreover, in January 1939 Foreign Minister Beck paid a sudden visit to Berchtesgaden, where he had a long interview with Hitler. Subsequently the differences over the Polish Jews were settled, while Foreign Minister Ribbentrop visited Warsaw at the end of the month.

At the same time Poland proceeded to resurrect its alliance with France and, according to one report, explored the possibility of creating a new Little Entente consisting of itself, Rumania, and Yugoslavia. Likewise it moved toward Italy, which is also interested in developing a new equilibrium in Central Europe. At Geneva Poland succeeded in inducing the League Council to keep its high commissioner, Professor Burkhardt, at Danzig. These various manœuvres indicated that Poland was continuing to follow the policy of "balance." In an interview of January 24, 1938, Foreign Minister Beck declared that " the foremost principle of Polish policy is the maintaining of good relations with our neighbours. This is why the Polish government attaches such great importance to its relations with Germany and Soviet Russia. The second principle of our policy is loyal observance of the alliances binding Poland to France and Rumania. The third is to oppose any decision made in matters concerning Poland without consulting her." He also said that Poland was interested in the colonial problem.[58]

Despite the efforts of both Germany and Italy to wean Poland away from France after Munich, Foreign Minister Beck declined to make any commitments. In fact relations between Poland and Germany became severely strained in February 1939 when great anti-German demonstrations, unknown since the conclusion of the 1934 non-aggression treaty, swept the country. The occasion was the mistreatment of Polish students in Danzig by German students, with the acquiescence of the Danzig police and authorities. Manifestations against Germany, lasting three days, and organized by nationalist and pro-Fascist students who otherwise are sympathetic to the Nazi régime, again confirmed the belief that the traditional opposition of interests between

[58] NANA dispatch, *New York Times*, January 25, 1939.

the Poles and the Germans continued to exist, notwithstanding the 1934 agreement.

Despite this deterioration Poland believed that Hitler had postponed a decision as to his future policy in Central Europe until after the Mediterranean crisis had been settled. But this respite was rudely broken when on March 14 Hitler brutally broke up Czechoslovakia into two German protectorates and allowed Hungarian troops to take over the Carpatho-Ukraine. Although a common frontier between Hungary and Poland was thus finally realized, this frontier adds little to the security of Poland, since Germany now dominates Slovakia more firmly than ever. The German pressure on Poland was increased when on March 23 Hitler forced Lithuania to cede Memel to Germany.

Confronted by Hitler's destruction of Czechoslovakia in patent violation of the Munich accord and these new demands on Danzig, Poland now realized that it would be the next object of the German offensive unless it showed a determination to fight, could strengthen existing alliances, and find new support. In the first week of March Foreign Minister Gafenco of Rumania paid a visit to Warsaw, as the result of which the Polish-Rumanian alliance was strengthened.

Meanwhile, British public opinion had been profoundly shocked and irritated at Hitler's violation of the Munich agreement and the destruction of Czechoslovakia. Belatedly realizing that unless resistance was offered, Nazi Germany would dominate Europe and a large part of the world, Prime Minister Chamberlain made a historic statement in the House of Commons on March 31, 1939. At that time he gave a temporary and unilateral assurance that " In the event of any action which clearly threatened Polish inde-

pendence and which the Polish Government accordingly
considered it vital to resist with their national forces, His
Majesty's Government would feel themselves bound at once
to lend the Polish Government all support in their power.
They have given the Polish Government an assurance to
this effect. I may add that the French Government have
authorized me to make it plain that they stand in the same
position as do His Majesty's Government."

When a London newspaper placed a restrictive interpretation upon the Chamberlain statement, a semi-official
source declared that this pledge covered Danzig and the
Corridor if Poland felt that its independence was threatened
there. By giving this pledge Britain formally abandoned its
refusal to accept obligations in Central Europe, and now in
effect proclaimed that its frontier was not only on the Rhine
but on the Vistula. Had Britain been willing to give this
guarantee five years earlier, Czechoslovakia probably would
still be in existence and Europe would not now be confronted with the imminence of war.

During the next week Foreign Minister Beck paid a visit
to London, as the result of which Britain and Poland agreed
to enter into a permanent and reciprocal undertaking to
replace the assurance given by Chamberlain on March 31.
Pending completion of the permanent agreement, Colonel
Beck declared that Poland would consider itself under obligation to render assistance to Britain under the same conditions as Britain would be obligated to render assistance to
Poland. This mutual-assistance pact applied to " any threat,
direct or indirect, to the independence of either." [58a] Al-

[58a] Statement of Prime Minister Chamberlain in the House of Commons April 6, 1939. At the same time an Anglo-Polish commercial agreement was discussed in which Poland would order British textile machinery
and increase its imports of tin and copper from India in return for British
credits. Britain subsequently relieved Poland of the necessity of formaliz-

though Poland still opposed any multilateral " peace front " against Germany and in this sense continued the policy of balance, it did accept bilateral obligations with Britain of a far-reaching nature.

The Nazis showed surprise and irritation at this shift in British policy. They warned Poland that Germany would never acquiesce in a policy of " encirclement," and the German press launched new campaigns threatening dire consequences to Warsaw if it proceeded to conclude the alliance with Britain.

Reports became numerous that Danzig would be annexed by Germany on Hitler's birthday, April 20, before the Polish-British guarantee had been implemented. A new factor suddenly disrupted these plans, if they existed, for on April 15 President Roosevelt addressed his dramatic appeal to Hitler and Mussolini asking a ten-year pledge of non-aggression toward thirty states, and proposing a peace conference. Although the message did not specifically mention Danzig, Roosevelt probably saved the Free City from German occupation and thereby averted, momentarily at least, a general war. Turning his attention from Danzig, Hitler devoted the next two weeks to preparing a reply to the Roosevelt plea. In a breathlessly awaited address to the Reichstag on April 28, the Führer not only rejected the President's offer for a multilateral agreement, but denounced the German-Polish non-aggression pact of January 1934. He added, contrary to previous professions, that the treaty provisions giving Poland a corridor to the sea prevented for " all time the establishment of an understanding between Poland and Germany."

---

ing the alliance, by stating that the provisional agreement would continue in effect. *New York Times*, April 25, 1939.

As a result of the abrogation of the 1934 pact,[58b] relations between Germany and Poland again became tense, and the Nazis reiterated, with the same vehemence as they had demanded the annexation of Austria and the Sudetenland, that Danzig must return to the Reich.

6. The Danzig Problem

Although about 95 per cent of the 406,000 inhabitants of Danzig are German, it has been an object of controversy between Poland and Prussia ever since the days of the Teutonic Knights. One of the original Hansa towns, Danzig remained outside the political limits of Germany until late in its history. From 1454 until the Partitions, Danzig was autonomous under the sovereignty of Poland. In 1793 it was annexed by Prussia, but by the Peace of Tilsit of 1807 it was again made a free city under the protection of France, Prussia, and Saxony. At the close of the Napoleonic wars it became an integral part of Prussia, where it remained until the Treaty of Versailles. In restoring the Free City of Danzig, the Paris Peace Conference merely followed historic precedent, except that the status of the Free City was now placed under guarantee of the League of Nations, represented by a High Commissioner. The Free City was tied to Poland by a customs union, and the railways and postal, telegraphic, and telephone service were placed under Polish control. The port was administered by a harbour board composed of five Poles and five Danzigers with a neutral president. Poland was to control the foreign relations of the City, but Danzig could not be used as a military base. In its internal affairs Danzig was made self-governing, the Danzigers electing every four years a legislative body, the

[58b] A German note of April 28, 1939 formally denounced the 1934 non-aggression pact.

Volkstag, of 120 members. The executive authority of the City was vested in a Senate elected by the Volkstag.

From the beginning a series of disputes took place between Poland and Danzig, many of which were referred to the League of Nations High Commissioner. In numerous instances the dissatisfied party carried a complaint to the League Council, and one dispute involving the right of Poland to maintain post offices in Danzig was referred to the Court of International Justice. German ill will was aroused by Poland's construction of the port of Gdynia, a few miles from Danzig on Polish territory, to which Poland diverted much of its transit trade. The Danzigers also became irritated by a decision of the League Council allowing Poland to use as a munitions dump the Westerplatte peninsula, which was a popular swimming resort. Following the Nazi advent in Germany, the situation in the Free City became momentarily tense when in March 1933 the Polish government increased the number of police beyond what it was entitled to maintain at Westerplatte, under the Polish-Danzig agreement of 1921 defining the relations with the Free City. Upon the intervention of the League Council, Colonel Beck agreed to withdraw these additional police, provided the Danzig authorities would safeguard Polish rights. In May the Nazis obtained a majority of the votes in the Volkstag election although not the two thirds needed to amend the constitution. Surprisingly enough, the new government of the City, headed by Dr. Rauschning, a native of German Poland, succeeded in improving relations with Warsaw. In August Poland and the Free City signed a harbour agreement in which Poland promised to prevent a further decrease in the amount of sea-borne traffic passing through Danzig, and to maintain Danzig and Gdynia in a position of parity. Subsequently it was agreed that all future differences over Danzig would be settled directly without appeal to the League of Nations. Thus, the Danzig issue was compromised even before the conclusion of the German-Polish non-aggression pact of January 1934.

Nevertheless, between 1933 and 1936 a struggle took place between the local Nazis, backed by Berlin, and the League High Commissioner, backed by Geneva, in which the Nazis insisted upon introducing a totalitarian régime into Danzig in violation of the democratic constitution,[58c] which the League had guaranteed. The Nazi terror was introduced and the Catholic and Socialist newspapers were suppressed and opposition parties liquidated. All civil servants were required to be Nazis, and a boycott against the Jews was inaugurated. At the request of the League Council the Permanent Court of International Justice gave an advisory opinion in December 1935, expressing the opinion that certain amendments made by Danzig to the Penal Code were in violation of the Danzig constitution since they gave judges power to punish individuals even for an act not prohibited by law. In January 1936 the League Council rebuked the Danzig representative, Herr Greiser, for not having carried out the Council's recommendations. Danzig did reform its penal code to conform with the World Court's opinion, but the Danzig Nazis again took courage as a result of the repeated blows suffered by the League elsewhere. Although the elections of April 1935 had shown that at least forty per cent of the Danzigers were opposed to the régime, the League powers finally gave way when they transferred Sean Lester, High Commissioner, from Danzig in September 1936. Curiously enough, Poland during this period made no effort to support the authority of

[58c] For details, see Mildred S. Wertheimer: "The Nazification of Danzig," *Foreign Policy Reports*, June 1, 1936.

the League and acquiesced in the violation of the Danzig constitution, on the understanding that Nazi-dominated Danzig would respect the economic and military rights of Poland in the City. The new League of Nations Commissioner, Professor C. J. Burckhardt, possessed little if any authority, and Danzig became a separate *Gau* in the Nazi party system and was ruled virtually by the *Gauleiter* appointed by Hitler. The Free City imposed legal discriminations against the Danzig Jews in November 1938, while many Danzig youths were required virtually to perform military service in Germany. In the midst of the Danzig unrest in the following spring, the Danzig Senate went so far as to prohibit the public commemoration by the Polish minority of the fourth anniversary of Piłsudski's death. Polish newspapers in Danzig are repeatedly suppressed.

It was inevitable after the achievement of Nazi ambitions in Austria and Czechoslovakia that Hitler should turn his attention to the Baltic. Although in his Reichstag speech of February 28, 1938 he agreed to respect Polish rights in Danzig, immediately after the Munich settlement of September the German government asked that Poland start conversations on the subject of changing the situation in Danzig and the so-called Corridor. On March 21, 1939 the German Foreign Minister stressed the importance of speed in the settlement of these matters. At this time Germany demanded the return of Danzig as a " free city in the framework of the German Reich " and the right to build a highway — reported to be fifteen miles in width — as well as a railroad across the so-called Corridor under German extraterritorial jurisdiction. In return Hitler would recognize Polish economic rights in Danzig, including the right to a free harbour, accept the present boundaries between the two countries, extend the non-aggression pact for twenty-five years, and allow Poland and Hungary to participate with Germany in guaranteeing the independence of the Slovak state, thus renouncing "any unilateral German hegemony in this territory." [58d]

Poland could not possibly accept these terms, because they would have placed the control of the Vistula and Poland's outlet on the Baltic at the complete mercy of Germany. Once Germany had fortified Danzig, it could easily dominate Gdynia and the Corridor. The position of Poland would be particularly vulnerable if Germany succeeded in building a fifteen-mile-wide road across Pomorze, policed by German soldiers. It would be only a matter of time before Germany, entrenched at the mouth of the Vistula, would dominate Poland proper and eventually the whole of Eastern Europe extending to the Black Sea. As Frederick II said in 1772, "He who holds Danzig holds Poland."

Hitler did not have the same case against Poland as he had against Czechoslovakia. The German Nazis were in complete control of all local affairs in Danzig, and Poland in the agreement of 1921 had authorized Germany to make use of nine railroad lines across Pomorze to East Prussia. Although Germany in fact used only two such lines, a million and a half passengers were carried in German trains across Pomorze, and four and a half million tons of freight, in 1938. The rates were identical with German rates, being paid in German currency to the Reich railroads, and passengers were not required to have Polish passports. The

[58d] Hitler's Reichstag speech of April 28, 1939. Colonel Beck declared in his address of May 5, 1939 that he heard of this proposal for a triple condominium in Slovakia for the first time in the Hitler speech of April 28, and he also declared that no formal proposal to extend the non-aggression pact for twenty-five years had been made.

trains were German except that they were hauled across the Corridor by Polish locomotives and crews. Consequently, there was little basis for the assertion that the Polish position in Pomorze — a territory now overwhelmingly Polish in character [58e] — is injurious to East Prussia or Danzig. Indeed it is only Polish commerce that keeps Danzig alive.

Although Poland could not, therefore, accept the German proposals, on March 26 it made a formal reply, proposing a common guarantee by Poland and Germany of the Free City which would apparently supplant the League guarantee. It expressed a willingness also to study with the German government the question of extending further the transit facilities across the so-called Corridor, subject only to the reservation that Poland could not surrender its sovereignty over any zones. Five days later Mr. Chamberlain extended to Poland the British guarantee. The only answer to the Polish counter-proposals was a German press campaign against Poland, and Hitler's speech of April 28 denouncing the German-Polish accord of 1934.

Carefully imitating Hitler's procedure, Foreign Minister Beck addressed the Polish Sejm on May 5 while at the same time submitting a formal memorandum to Germany. In a conciliating but firm statement, quite in contrast to Hitler's bellicosity, Beck declared that Poland could not possibly

[58e] The Prussian census of 1910 listed a total population of 964,704 in that part of West Prussia known as the Corridor, of which 411,621 were German-speaking, 433,281 Polish-speaking, and 104,602 Kashubs, who speak a Polish dialect. The eight districts forming the northern part of the "Corridor" never sent a single German deputy to the Imperial Reichstag before the World War. The Polish census of 1931 lists 1,086,-144 in the province of Pomorze, of whom 976,499 were Polish-speaking and 109,645 German. This shift represents the absorption of the Kashubs, the colonization of Poles from other parts of the country, and the departure of Germans.

accept Hitler's interpretation of the 1934 pact — namely, that Poland must isolate itself from all other countries. Poland could not surrender vital interests in return for the German recognition of rights which Poland already possessed and which Germany had accepted in 1934. Poland was willing to negotiate over Danzig, but it would not make one-sided concessions. At the same time Beck hinted that Germany had tried to tempt Poland with an offer to divide up a part of Russia.

The Polish memorandum presented the same day at Berlin declared that " The Polish government cannot accept an interpretation of the declaration of 1934 which would amount to a renunciation of the right (for it) to conclude political agreements with third parties, almost equivalent to renouncing independence of foreign policy." The Polish-British guarantee did not threaten the Reich any more than did the Polish-French alliance which the 1934 declaration had accepted. These guarantees would come into operation against Germany only in case it violated the Pact of Paris of August 1928, upon which the 1934 declaration rested. Germany had made far-reaching agreements with Italy and Slovakia since 1934, but it denied a similar right to Poland. Therefore, in the eyes of Poland, Germany had no ground for a one-sided denunciation of the 1934 agreement.

Confronted by the example of Czechoslovakia, Poland thus declined to yield to either the threats of the Nazis or the indirect pressure of its allies, Britain and France, which, if certain reports can be believed, were ready for a second " Munich " over Danzig if only Poland would agree. Early in the dispute Poland had mobilized 1,300,000 men; Polish crowds shouted that " East Prussia must be Polish "; the Polish Socialist workers remained at work in the munition factories on May Day; and the Ukrainian paper, *DILO*,

pledged the loyalty of the Ukrainians to the government.[58f]
On May 15 General Kasprzyki, Polish War Minister, ar-
rived in Paris to hold military conversations, the first since
Marshal Śmigły-Rydz's visit in 1936. Rumours of the movement of armed Germans in civilian clothes into Danzig, and
the announcement in May that Germany and Italy would
convert the axis into a military alliance, did not move Poland. Nor did the killing of a German butcher by a Pole
at Kalthof on May 21 lead to a serious crisis. Judgments are
still premature; but events may prove that the courage of
Poland, determined to fight for its vital interests regardless
of outside aid, has administered the first check to German
expansionism.

The Germans of Danzig did not wish to pay the price of
war for the sake of union with the Reich. Many valued the
economic advantages of Polish trade arising out of the Free
City status. Some also had been irritated by the fact that
Hitler in 1934 had sent as *Gauleiter* to Danzig a Bavarian,
Albert Forster, who soon forced the resignation of Dr.
Rauschning, who believed in a genuine Polish-German rec-
onciliation and opposed anti-Semitism. Moreover, Mussolini did not want to be drawn into a war over Danzig, for
he seemed to realize that in a general war Italy would be
the first and most vulnerable objective of an Anglo-French
offensive.

Although it is possible that Poland and Germany may
negotiate a compromise over Danzig the situation depends
upon Hitler's will alone. If he believes that France and
Britain will not fight over Danzig despite their promises, he
may order the Danzig Nazis to go ahead and declare the
union of the City with Germany, whether through plebi-

[58f] Americans of Polish descent in fifty-five cities had raised more than
$375,000 to aid the defence of Poland by May 4, after a three weeks' cam-
paign. *New York Times*, May 5, 1939.

scite or by decree of the Senate. Confronted by action which would probably be accompanied by attacks on the Polish minority, the seizure of the Polish munitions dump at Westerplatte, and the driving out of the Polish customs officials, Poland would undoubtedly exercise its right of armed intervention in Danzig, at the invitation of the League High Commissioner,[58g] to maintain order. In such a case Hitler would have a pretext to " rescue " Germans as he rescued them in Austria and the Sudetenland. In view of the Polish determination to fight, the risks of liquidating the Danzig question in this manner are far greater than any risks hitherto taken by Hitler. Consequently he may decide to bide his time and endeavour to wear Poland out by economic pressure and propaganda. How long Poland can stand the cost of maintaining an army of 1,300,000 on a war basis is a matter of opinion. In any case the epoch of history inaugurated by Piłsudski in 1934 has come to an end, and Poland once more has moved toward the west. The future may see a contest of nerves between Polish patriotism and Nazi fanaticism, the outcome of which no one can predict.

Whether the new British policy will succeed, and whether Hitler will refrain from assaulting Poland, thus remains uncertain. In view of Poland's pro-German orientation between 1934 and 1938 and its apparent delight at the partition of Czechoslovakia, public opinion in the Western democracies has lost much of its interest in Poland's future. Admittedly modern Poland has displayed some of the characteristics which brought about its destruction at the end of the eighteenth century; admittedly it has made mistakes. Nevertheless, the Western world today can be

[58g] League Council Resolution of June 22, 1921. Cf. C. Smogorzewski: *Poland's Access to the Sea*, p. 302.

too severe on Poland, do a grave injustice to that country, and injure the cause of world peace. Had Britain and France, not to mention the United States, shown any real determination to uphold the treaty structure of Europe or bring about world economic reconstruction, Poland undoubtedly would have remained attached to the League. In condemning Poland too uncritically, Western opinion overlooks the fundamental weaknesses in the past foreign policies of the great democracies.

If it were possible to localize a war between Poland and Germany, the Western world might conceivably be indifferent to Poland's fate. But it is difficult to see how such a war — or even any war between two great states — can be localized under modern conditions. Should Germany succeed in breaking up Poland and Russia, it would obtain resources capable of making it the world's strongest and most dangerous power. Strategic and political considerations may have justified France and Britain in throwing away the Czech forts and thirty-five Czech divisions, but if there is danger of a world war during the next few years, France and Britain cannot equally afford to throw away Poland's forty divisions. So long as these divisions are in the anti-German camp, the Nazis will have to fight on two fronts. This necessity has led to a German defeat in the past, and it may do so again in the future. Belated as the change may be, the British decision to guarantee Poland and other parts of Central and Eastern Europe against attack is justified on the ground of self-preservation.

7. Poland and the United States

The relations between Poland and America go back to our War of Independence. Two of the three most distin-

guished foreigners in the American Revolution were Poles
— Count Pułaski, who met his death on our behalf, and General Kościuszko. Another Polish soldier, General Krzyżanowski, fought on the Northern side in the American Civil
War. During the nineteenth century a number of American statesmen expressed sympathy with the Polish independence movement. In 1844 the New Hampshire legislature passed a resolution stating that the " cause of Poland
is the common cause of the friends of freedom throughout
the world." Several million Poles took up their residence
in the United States during the nineteenth and early twentieth centuries, largely to improve their standards of living. During the World War some of them returned to
fight on behalf of the Polish cause, while Polish propaganda found its most fertile soil in America. Woodrow
Wilson was the first world statesman to espouse Polish independence publicly, and the American experts at the Paris
Peace Conference were regarded by Lloyd George as " fa-
natical pro-Poles," [59] no doubt with some justification.

America's interest in Poland did not stop with the Peace
Conference. During the reconstruction period American
relief missions alleviated widespread misery in the country, and the United States extended post-war relief credits
amounting to about $160,000,000. In November 1924 the
two governments reached a debt agreement in fixing the
outstanding debt at $178,500,000. Poland agreed to repay
this debt within sixty-two years, at an average interest rate
of three per cent. After the Hoover moratorium of 1932
Poland, following the example of other governments, remained in default. Before the depression, American private
capital also interested itself in Poland, being largely responsible for the 1927 stabilization loan.

[59] Lloyd George, op. cit., p. 991.

Within recent years the relations between Poland and the United States have lacked the warmth which existed when Poland was fighting for its independence. In 1920 the State Department showed apprehension over Polish imperialism.[60] Since the World War many sections of American public opinion have become alienated from Poland. To a certain extent, the American picture of Poland has been distorted, as previous chapters have indicated; and it should be to the interest of the United States to improve its relations with this country because of the important role it may play in preserving peace in Europe — which means the world.

As the " fifth " power in Europe, Poland is making a determined effort to keep from being drawn into either the Communist or the Fascist camp. Lying between two great totalitarian imperialisms, its position is extremely difficult. But if it succeeds in keeping Russia and Germany apart, it may prevent either Fascism or Communism from dominating Europe. Poland is not a democracy in the American sense, but neither is it a totalitarian state. The Polish spirit is Catholic and individualistic. It will resist the ideology of the anti-Western powers provided the democracies give it proper support. If the United States wishes to strengthen Western civilization without becoming involved in political entanglements, and if it desires to advance its own economic interests, it should improve its relations with Poland.

A step in this direction was taken when the Export-Import Bank in Washington extended in January 1939 a nine-months credit of $6,000,000 at $3\frac{1}{2}$ per cent to the National Economic Bank of Poland to be used in the purchase of American cotton, in excess of normal Polish imports from this country. This credit enables Poland to increase its

[60] Cf. p. 78.

manufacture of textiles; and the hope is that it may similarly increase its textile exports, thus obtaining the exchange needed to repay the American credit. Until restoration of international confidence makes the resumption of private lending possible, such advances of the Export-Import Bank should aid the export of American goods, while rendering a service to Poland.[61] Thus even if trade between Poland and the United States does not directly increase, American credits may assist Poland in expanding exports to third countries. Poland has no assurance, however, that such exports will be large enough to cover the repayment of the American credits. From the immediate point of view this type of arrangement is not as attractive as the recent barter agreement between Berlin and Warsaw, in which Germany agreed to take a minimum quantity of Polish goods at a fixed price for a term of years.[62]

The relations between Poland and the United States may be improved also by the conclusion of a Hull trade agreement [63] and by settlement of the Polish default to the American government. Unlike the debts of many European governments, the Polish " war " debt was contracted not for belligerent but for relief purposes. There is no likelihood that Poland will be able to resume the annuities fixed in the agreement of November 1924. Nevertheless, these debts might be used to advance certain interests of the United States as well as alleviate Poland's desperate economic condition. Within recent years American public opinion has shown a deep interest in the problem of refugees, and it has done something to relieve the plight of the

[61] In its recent trade agreement with Russia, Poland undertakes to buy cotton from Russia. Such purchases are in addition to those made in the United States, and will be used in the manufacture of textiles which Russia will purchase.

[62] Cf. p. 199.

[63] See the note at end of chapter.

Jewish refugees from Germany and elsewhere. But it is equally important to *prevent* the creation of new refugee problems. Already many Poles are asking themselves whether they must resort to the brutalities committed by the German Nazis to call the attention of the outside world to Poland's over-population problem. To avert any such development, the United States could well afford to utilize the Polish debt so as to create a fund which would assist Poland in a development program. The United States would not appropriate any money to Poland, but it would offer to cancel the " war " debt if in return the Polish budget would appropriate say ten million dollars a year for twenty years toward an Industrialization and Migration Fund to be administered by the Polish government, subject to an advisory council, of which the American Ambassador might be a member. It would be understood that the Polish budget would be increased so as to provide such sums, rather than raise them merely by reallocating items from other chapters in the budget. The fund would be in zlotys and could therefore be raised without involving exchange problems. The establishment of such a fund would prove of importance to the internal development of Poland, while constituting the first step in an orderly program of assisted emigrations. Moreover, the settlement of the war debt question would remove the ban upon private loans to Poland under the Johnson Act. The removal of this ban at present may be only of academic importance. Nevertheless should European peace become more stabilized during the next few years, the resumption of private lending, subject to controls which did not exist in the boom period, may become possible. World economic recovery depends not only upon the resumption of trade but upon the restoration of the capital market.

Because of its great economic and financial strength the United States can exercise a powerful influence in favour of improved international relationships without accepting the risks involved in political alliances. In particular, America can contribute materially to a solution of Poland's extremely difficult economic and social problems. It can assist in keeping Poland out of the totalitarian camp.

NOTE

Polish-American Trade Possibilities

Before the depression Poland sent large numbers of immigrants to the United States, and it had liberal access to our capital market. Today, however, few Polish immigrants enter the country, and foreign lending has long since been suspended. At the same time, Poland enjoys the unique distinction of having expanded its exports fourfold to the United States since 1929. Its sales to America increased from $4,853,000 in 1929 to $19,568,000 in 1937,[1] although our exports to Poland fell off about $10,000,000 during the same period.

Nevertheless, Poland still has an adverse balance with the United States, which, because of the recent decline of American imports, jumped from about $9,000,000 in 1937 to more than $14,000,000 in 1938. This adverse balance means that Poland must use part of its much cherished free exchange to pay for a surplus of American goods. Confronted with the urgent need of husbanding every resource to industrialize as well as rearm itself, Poland must endeav-

[1] As a result of the new United States depression in 1937, they fell to $13,417,000 in 1938.

our to increase its sales to America and other countries or cut down purchases of non-essentials.

Recent increases of Poland's exports have been due largely to Polish ham, which has proved to be a delicacy to the American consumer. This ham has a different flavour from American ham, apparently because Polish hogs are fed on potatoes instead of corn; it also usually sells at a higher price.[2] Nevertheless, farm groups were influential enough to induce the House to pass a bill providing for a six-cent tax on such imports in March 1938. Fortunately for Polish-American relations, the Senate rejected the tax after representations from the administration. In 1937 Polish ham entering this country constituted less than one per cent of our total domestic production.

Poland is the " principal supplier " of imported hams to the United States; and in accordance with the Hull trade program, the United States could make a trade agreement with Poland which would lower or bind the existing duty on this commodity in return for concessions on behalf of American exports. It should be possible to grant a tariff quota on Polish ham, allowing a limited quantity to enter at the reduced duty. In the case of other articles shipped here, with a few exceptions such as alder plywood and

[2] Polish canned ham imports sharply increased in 1936 and 1937 largely because of the high prices of American hogs and pork in 1936 and 1937 caused by the drought. Imports rose from 3,600 pounds in 1935 to 18,700,000 pounds in 1936, and to 32,000,000 in 1937. Although in 1938 the ham imports declined only to 30,000,000, lower hog prices in America will probably make it difficult for Polish ham to maintain the 1937 peak, unless the tariff is lowered from the present level of 3.25 cents a pound. Largely as a result of the developing market, Polish plants equipped to make tinned hams increased from five in 1935 to twenty-nine in 1938. Poland keenly realizes the danger of overloading the American market, and is not subsidizing these exports. Even in the year 1937, when exports were depressed on account of the drought, the American farmer sold pork products abroad in considerable excess of the imports of pork products.

willow baskets, Poland is not the "principal supplier." Consequently it will be more difficult for the State Department to make concessions, out of fear of upsetting our commercial relationships with other countries sending us the same articles. Nevertheless, if Poland can liberalize its treatment of American imports, it should be possible for the United States to give something in return.

In this connection, Poland's position in the American market should improve as a result of the disappearance of Czechoslovakia. In April 1938 the United States made a trade agreement granting Czechoslovakia important concessions in our market, in respect to shoes, gloves, glassware, china, and other articles. Germany cannot claim to profit from the advantages of this treaty, particularly because it is on the American "black list." [3] Poland, however, is in the position to develop many of the specialty industries, such as gloves and glassware, which flourished in Czechoslovakia; and there is no reason why the United States should not encourage such a development by extending to Poland the same concessions which we originally made to Prague. Poland has the further advantage that its sales here are not subject to a boycott as are German goods because of Nazi anti-

[3] In 1936 the Treasury Department imposed countervailing duties on a number of German imports, under Section 303 of the 1930 Tariff Act, which authorizes such duties to offset the payment of export subsidies. Although many of these duties were subsequently removed as a result of Germany's promise to stop subsidies, German exports continued to be denied the benefit of the reduction of the trade-agreement duties, under a presidential order based on the Trade Agreement Act, because of Germany's "discriminatory treatment of American commerce." Germany has been on the U.S. "black list" since October 14, 1935. Cf. Paul B. Taylor: "Problems of German-American Relations," *Foreign Policy Reports*, July 15, 1938. On March 18, 1939 the Treasury again imposed countervailing duties of 25 per cent.

If Poland decides to meet German competition by subsidizing exports, it must be careful not to run afoul of Section 303 of our 1930 Tariff Act. Otherwise it may become liable to countervailing duties here. For a time

Semitism. Should Poland yield to the temptation to resort to totalitarian excesses, it of course would lose these advantages in the American market.

If a trade agreement is to be concluded, it will be necessary for Poland to give something to America in return for tariff concessions on our part. Poland, however, has been obliged to resort to an elaborate system of foreign trade permits and other devices, for the purpose of balancing exports against imports, in order to secure adequate exchange. If in accordance with this principle of bilateral balancing Poland asks the United States to increase its imports of Polish goods until they exactly equal Poland's purchases of our goods, the United States will have to say no. For it cannot undermine the principle of triangular trade, upon which the Hull trade program rests.

Although the United States does not demand that Poland abolish its quota system, it does ask that, in accordance with the most-favoured-nation principle, Poland grant this country a fair proportion of Poland's import quotas, based on some representative period in the past. In some trade agreements the United States has also asked that it receive a share of the available exchange allotted by the other government. Thus if Poland purchased four fifths of its autos in the United States in 1929, it should allocate four fifths of its exchange available for auto purchases to the American market today. Should Poland accept such a demand, it

Polish rye was subject to such a duty. Moreover under Section 201 of the Anti-Dumping Act of 1921 the Secretary of the Treasury is charged with the duty of determining if a commodity is being imported at less than its foreign market value; but he is obliged to impose an anti-dumping duty only when investigation establishes that "an industry in the United States is being or is likely to be injured." He thus has more discretion under the Anti-Dumping Act than under Section 303 of the 1930 Tariff Act. Cf. Ethel B. Dietrich: *World Trade* (New York: Henry Holt & Company; 1939), p. 69.

would have to rearrange its barter agreements with European countries, which would prove extremely difficult to accomplish. The United States might meet a practical situation by accepting a year more favourable to Poland than 1929 as the " representative period " upon which exchange quotas should be based.

Nevertheless it is not easy to reconcile the Polish economic system, which has established far-reaching controls over its entire economic life, and the American system, which in so far as the Hull trade program is concerned represents a modified form of economic liberalism. But just as Poland has reached trade agreements with Britain and France, it may yet find it possible to reach a similar agreement with the United States.

INDEX

Abernon, Lord d', 77, 78, 337
Act of 1815, 58
Act of Lublin, 28
Activists, 63
Agrarian conferences, 199
Agrarian reform, 112; capital needed, 210; criticisms, 211; national defense and, 212; status of, 209
Agricultural crisis, 190; exports, 148; prices, 123, 124, 127, 190, 192; production, 192; yield, 122, 203, 204
Agriculture, 19, 122, 145, 191
Airplanes, government ownership of, 158
Albert, Margrave of Brandenburg, 32
Alcohol monopoly, 165, 195
Alexander I, 56
Allenstein, 71
Anglo-American trade agreement, 123
Anschluss, 252, 326
Anti-Dumping Act of 1921, 371
Anti-German demonstrations of 1939, 351
Anti-Semitic discriminations, 292; student riots, 108
Anti-Semitism, 15, 157; causes of, 308; economic effects of, 316; history of, 292

Aristocracy, 156
Armament industry, government ownership of, 158
Army, 40, 118, 137; expenditures, 21
Article XVI, 325, 333
" Aryan " paragraph, 300
Assimilation of minorities, 276, 279, 281, 282
Augustus II, 43
Austria, 42, 66, 148; and Poles, 61; and Ukrainians, 265
Autarchy, 235; advocacy of, 187; drive, 135
" Authoritarian democracy," 101
Autonomy, Ukrainian, 278, 280; law of 1922, 273

Bacon, 133, 148; Export Corporation, 202; factories, 202
Balance, policy of, 321, 350
Balance of payments, 140, 147; and dumping, 180; frozen, 150
Balance of power, 41
Baltic, 12, 125, 320, 325; barons, 5, 7; bloc, 325, 346; countries, 6
Bank of Poland, 126, 132, 137, 158; reserves, 150
Bartel, Casimir, 90

i

A Note on the Type
IN WHICH THIS BOOK IS SET

This book was set on the Linotype in Janson, a recutting made direct from the type cast from matrices (now in possession of the Stempel foundry, Frankfurt am Main) made by Anton Janson some time between 1660 and 1687.

Of Janson's origin nothing is known. He may have been a relative of Justus Janson, a printer of Danish birth who practised in Leipzig from 1614 to 1635. Some time between 1657 and 1668 Anton Janson, a punch-cutter and type-founder, bought from the Leipzig printer Johann Erich Hahn the type-foundry which had formerly been a part of the printing house of M. Friedrich Lankisch. Janson's types were first shown in a specimen sheet issued at Leipzig about 1675. Janson's successor, and perhaps his son-in-law, Johann Karl Edling, issued a specimen sheet of Janson types in 1689. His heirs sold the Janson matrices in Holland to Wolffgang Dietrich Erhardt.

COMPOSED, PRINTED, AND BOUND BY *The Plimpton Press,* NORWOOD, MASS. PAPER MADE BY *S. D. Warren Co.,* BOSTON

F